NEW

Language LEADER

PRE-INTERMEDIATE

COURSEBOOK

IAN LEBEAU | GARETH REES

CONTENTS

Unit	Grammar	Vocabulary	Reading
1 Human Planet (p6–13)	Present simple and continuous: state and action verbs (1.1) Present simple / continuous questions (1.2) Adverbs of frequency (1.2)	Countries and regions: adjectives and nouns (1.1) Weather words; modifiers (1.2) Adventure holiday activities (1.3) Linking words: *but, and, also, when* (1.4)	My world, our world: a global online project (1.1) Understanding genre Surviving Siberia: climate versus lifestyle (1.2) A city guide (1.4)
2 People (p14–21)	Past simple: regular and irregular verbs (2.1) Use of the affirmative with time expressions (2.1) Past simple negatives and question forms (2.2)	Personality: adjectives and nouns (2.1) Weather words; modifiers (1.2) Character adjectives and *like, look like, be like,* etc (2.3) Linking words: *until, at first, then, at the moment, afterwards* (2.4)	Evaluation International Women's Day Awards (2.1) Increasing your understanding Biography of Osamu Tezuka and Frida Kahlo (2.2) A learning styles and strategies questionnaire (2.4) A reflective blog (2.4)
3 The Media (p22–29)	Past continuous (3.1) Defining relative pronouns: *who, which, where, that* (3.2)	The media (3.1) Nouns, e.g. *journalist / journalism* (3.2) TV programme genres, e.g. *comedy, politics* (3.3)	The story of the internet (3.1) Personal reflection News organisations around the world (3.2) A TV programme review (3.4)
4 Health (p30–37)	Present perfect (1) with time expressions (4.1) Articles (4.2) Giving advice with reasons (should + infinitive of purpose/in order to) (4.3)	Medical words (4.1) Reporting verbs, e.g. *states, claims, shows, thinks,* etc (4.2) Ailments, e.g. *backache* (4.3) Grammar of words; compound nouns; false friends (4.4)	Podcasts about different aspects of International Medi-Aid (IMA) exploring facts (4.1) Text about relationship between diet and mental health (4.2)
5 Natural World (p38–45)	Comparatives and superlatives; *as … as* (5.1) Expressions of quantity (5.2)	Landscapes: adjectives to describe place (5.1) Nouns and verbs (1), e.g. *damage* (n/vb) (5.2) Describing photos (5.3) Reference words: *it* and *its* (5.4)	Text about the island of Bora Bora collaboration (5.1) Animal invaders – how much danger are we in? Thinking beyond the text (5.2)
6 Society and Family (p46–53)	Predictions: *will, might* and *may* (*probably, definitely*) (6.1) First conditional (6.2)	Nouns and verbs (2), e.g. *consumer* vs *consume* (6.1) Family; negative adjectives: *un-* and *-less* (6.2) Expressing opinions (6.3) Linkers: *so, as, however* and *because of* (6.4)	Advert of future analysis (6.1) Article about low birth rate in Germany Understanding genre (6.2)

Listening	Speaking / Pronunciation	Scenario	Study Skills / Writing	Video
My world, our world entries (1.1) Conversation describing new holidays on offer (1.3) Discussing opinions about new holidays (1.3)	Long turn taking Describe favourite places (1.1) Discussion about different climates (1.2) Showing interest intonation for agreeing and disagreeing (1.3)	Key language: agreeing and disagreeing Task: making a choice Scenario: choosing holiday itinerary for tour operator	Write a short paragraph describing climate (1.2) Study skills: Dictionary skills: Understanding meaning Writing skills: Understanding text organisation descriptive writing: places	Meet the expert: an interview with James Moore, an expedition medical consultant about living in extreme places (1.2)
Stories of determination (2.1) Description of an inspirational person (2.2) Conversation discussing potential new flatmates (2.3)	Talk about stories of determination (2.1) Voiced and unvoiced consonants regular past endings (2.1) Collaboration Research and describe inspirational people (2.2) Word stress (2.3)	Key language: describing people Task: choosing a new flatmate Scenario: choosing most suitable flatmate	Write a short description of a determined person (2.1) Study skills: Learning styles and strategies Writing skills: Inferring a reflective blog	Meet the expert: an interview with Karen Rubins, a comic artist (2.2)
Stories about the early days of the internet analysing the topic (3.1) An introduction to a new TV programme, Fame and Fortune (3.3) TV programme development meeting (3.3)	was/were strong and weak forms (3.1) Interview about internet use (3.1) Word stress (3.2) Retell a recent news story (3.2) Intonation in short questions (3.3) Discussion about recent TV programmes or series (3.4)	Key language: making suggestions Task: designing a show Scenario: planning a TV programme	Write a short paragraph describing climate (1.2) Study skills: collaboration: working with others Writing skills: Summarising a TV programme review	Study skills video: collaboration: working with others (3.4)
Doctors expressing opinions (4.1) Student counsellor interviews (4.3)	Comparing life experiences (4.1) Justifying opinion Discussion about food and health (4.2) Interview about eating habits and diets (4.2) Phrase stress and rhythm (4.3)	Key language: giving advice and reasons Task: giving advice about health issues Scenario: giving advice to students	Write a summary about the eating habits and diets (4.2) Study skills: Guessing the meaning of un known words Writing skills: Inferring an informal email	Meet the expert: interview with Dr John Briffa, a doctor who specialises in nutrition, about brain food (4.2)
Nature programme about three islands (5.1) Conversation describing photos; choosing photos and reasons why (5.3)	Describe the islands; presentation to compare two places (5.1) Comparison of personal lives (5.2) Strong and weak forms (schwa) (5.3)	Key language: justifying choices Task: giving reasons and making choices Scenario: describing photos to partner and selecting which ones to use	Write a short paragraph describing climate (1.2) Study skills: developing self-awareness Correcting your writing Writing skills: Understanding text organisation writing comparative paragraphs	Meet the expert: interview with Gareth Philips, a professional photographer about the selection of photos (5.3)
Meeting between futurologist and a business investor; evaluating and predicting (6.1) Conversation about specific problems and possible solutions (6.2) Television talk show about family matters (6.3)	Making future predictions (6.1) Discuss Q about family; Discussion about family dilemmas; contractions: 'll (6.2) Word linking (6.3)	Key language: expressing opinions Task: having a discussion Scenario: discussion about family matters in a talk show	Write paragraph(s) about predictions for a specific society and country (6.1) Study skills: Critical Thinking: judging reliability, considering evidence, developing self-awareness Writing skills: Understanding text organisation a short article	Study skills video: a short lecture on critical thinking (6.4)

CONTENTS

Unit	Grammar	Vocabulary	Reading
7 Science (p54–61)	Obligation: *should, must* and *have to* (7.1) *had to* and *could* (7.2)	Science and crime (7.1) Nouns, adjectives and verbs with prepositions (7.2) Developing an argument (*This means that ... etc*) (7.3) Scientific fields and inventions/discoveries (7.4)	TV programme reviews: a documentary and a crime drama (7.1) Webpage about Stephen Hawking; justifying selections (7.2)
8 The night (p62–69)	Verb patterns (8.1) Future intentions: *going to, hoping to, I'm going to, I'd like to* (8.2)	Expressions with sleep, e.g. *sleep badly, have a sleepless night*, etc (8.1) Jobs; *-ing/-ed* adjectives (8.2) Expressing preferences; Night out entertainment, e.g. *go out for dinner* (8.3)	Email exchange about a talk on sleep (8.1) Ordering ideas Article about night workers (8.2) Sydney festival events listing (8.3) A short mysterious story (8.4)
9 Work and industry (p70–77)	*Used to* (9.1) Present simple passive (9.2)	Work and working conditions, e.g. *colleague, employee, good pay, opportunities to travel*, etc (9.1) Compound nouns (9.2) Negotiating; Price/Quantity, Delivery, Payment negotiation phrases (9.3) Linkers: sequencing phrases, e.g. *to begin with ...*, etc (9.4)	Email from HR asking for employee opinion about the company (9.1) Making informed guesses Use of gold in industry (9.2) The early stages of making chocolate (9.4)
10 Global affairs (p78–85)	Present continuous for future arrangements (10.1) Past simple passive (10.2)	People and organisations (10.1) Global companies (10.2) Adding emphasis using adverbs; Adjectives to describe experiences, e.g. *magical, memorable* with *just* and *only* (10.3) Importance markers Linkers: *although, on the other hand, therefore* (10.4)	Encyclopaedia entry about the United Nations ; evaluating opinions (10.1) History of Apple; identifying key dates (10.2) Background info on the bid cities (10.3) The advantages and disadvantages of phone-tapping (10.4)
11 The environment (p86–93)	Present perfect (2): *for/since* (11.1) Phrasal verbs (11.2) Question tags (11.2)	Noun phrases: noun + *of* + noun, e.g. the consequence of change (11.1) Containers and materials (11.2) Regeneration needs (11.3)	Extreme weather web search (11.1) A discussion in the press about packaging (11.2) A funding proposal Regeneration project information (11.3) Action group newsletter; A report; Plans for a new airport terminal (11.4)
12 Sport (p94–101)	Second conditional (12.1) *too* and *enough* (12.2)	types of sports to collocate with *do/go/play* (12.1) linking words (12.2) Sports personalities (12.3)	Open letter to the Minister of Sport; evaluating effective language (12.1) Magazine article about female football fans (12.2) an English course advert a formal email (12.4)

Language reference (p101-125) | Meet the Expert (p126-130) | Communication Activities (p131-148)

Listening	Speaking / Pronunciation	Scenario	Study Skills / Writing	Video
Interview with a crime documentary researcher; making personal connections (7.1)	Discussion about crime and science; Discussion about rules and regulations in students' own lives (7.1)	Key language: developing an argument	Research and write a short description of a famous person's life and work (7.1)	Meet the Expert: an interview with Huw James, a scientist who specializes in astronomy, about black holes and astrophysics (7.2)
Radio programme for intellectual discussion about important inventions and scientific discoveries (7.3)	Discussion about famous scientists and their discoveries; Discussion about attitudes to science (7.2)	Task: making your case	Study skills: making notes Writing skills: analysing data Describing charts	
	Word stress and the schwa (7.3)	Scenario: discussion about the top inventions/ discoveries		
	Discuss type of notes and ways to make notes (7.4)			
Presentation about sleep; Evaluating performance (8.1)	Discussion about sleep Quiz about sleep patterns (8.1)	Key language: discussing preferences	Write a short paragraph describing climate (1.2)	Meet the Expert: an interview with Karen Fowler, a communications manager, about working in the dark in Antarctica (8.2)
Conversation planning a night out at festival (8.3)	Contractions Discussing future plans, hopes and dreams (8.2)	Task: making a future plan	Study skills: remembering vocabulary; evaluating methods	
	Sentence stress: key words and clarity (8.3)	Scenario: planning a night out	Writing skills: prediction A narrative	
Interview with two employees exploring the topic (9.1)	study vs working discussion Comparison of the way people used to live and work today with the past 's' in used to (9.1)	Key language: making offers and proposals	Write a paragraph comparing life in past to now (9.2)	Study skills video: a short talk about the history of chocolate (9.4)
Business people negotiating a deal (9.3)	Talk about industries/well-known business (9.2)	Task: having a negotiation	Study skills: Giving a short talk; analysing performance	
Discussing opinions about new holidays (1.3)	Numbers (9.3)	Scenario: negotiating a deal	Writing skills: Describing a process	
A meeting to discuss a trip schedule (10.1)	General discussion about the United Nations; Interviews to check social arrangements (10.1)	Key language: giving examples	Write a paragraph summarising next week's social arrangements (10.2)	Meet the Expert: an interview with Nick Cooper, a brands specialist, about what makes a global brand (10.2)
The history of Apple (10.2)	Exchanging knowledge about global companies; exploring the topic talking about big businesses and globalisation (10.2)	Task: giving a presentation	Study skills: improving your listening: predicting content, predicting vocabulary, importance markers	
An Olympic bid presentation (10.3)		Scenario: making an Olympic bid		
A talk about INTERPOL (10.4)	Pausing and emphatic stress (10.3)		Writing skills: A for and against essay; developing ideas	
A radio documentary about the environment and global warming (11.1)	Illustrating a claim Talking about the causes and effects of global warming (11.1)	Key language: checking agreement	Write a short paragraph describing climate (1.2)	Meet the Expert: an interview with Dr Laura Baker, a meteorologist, about tracking and analysing storms (12.1)
A funding committee discussing a regeneration project proposal (1.3)	Problem-solving Discussion about ways to reduce waste (11.2)	Task: collaborating	Study skills: thinking critically about reading texts	
	Intonation in question tags (11.3)	Scenario: Allocating funds for local regeneration	Writing skills: Asking critical questions A report	
	Discuss the effects of the newsletter (11.4)			
Current affairs programme on TV (12.1)	Discussion about attitudes and approaches to sport (12.1)	Key language: answering complex questions	A summary paragraph of topical issues (12.2)	Meet the Expert: an interview with Rachel Pavlou, the Women's Football Development Manager for the English FA, about the rise of women's football (12.2)
Interview between a sports psychologist and a client (12.3)	Evaluating claims Discussion of topical issues related to football, sport and health and sports facilities in different countries (12.2)	Task: using a questionnaire	Study skills: Time Management; critical evaluation	
A tutorial about time management (12.4)	Intonation in lists (12.3)	Scenario: Doing a sports psychology survey	Writing skills: a formal email	

Audioscripts (p149-164) | Irregular Verb List (p165) | Phonetic Charts (p166)

1 Human planet
1.1 ONE WORLD

IN THIS UNIT

GRAMMAR
- present simple and present continuous
- action verbs and adverbs of frequency

VOCABULARY
- countries and regions
- modifiers
- adventure holiday activities

SCENARIO
- agreeing/disagreeing: holiday destinations
- making a choice

STUDY SKILLS
- understanding meaning (using a dictionary)

WRITING SKILLS
- describing a place (an online city guide)

'I change the world; the world changes me.' Libba Bray, 1964 – , US writer

SPEAKING

1a `1.1` **Discuss these questions with your partner and choose the correct answer. Then listen and check.**

1 How many different languages are there in the world?
   under 100   about 200   over 300
2 How many countries use English as a main language? Can you name any of them?
   15   30   60
3 What is the total number of English speakers in the world?
   1 billion   2 billion   3 billion
4 What percentage of the internet is in English?
   25%   55%   80%

1b **Why are you learning English? When do you use English in your life?**

READING

2a **Read the homepage *My world, our world*. What is the website for?**

2b **Answer these questions.**
1 What type of things are on the website?
2 The artist says 'the people of the world make this portrait of the world'. Why does he say that?
3 What language does the artist want the voice recordings to be in? Why?
4 Which sentence tells you how to see/find the photographs on the website?
5 Do you think the project matches the artist's aims?

my world, our world

Welcome to a photography project that brings the world's favourite places together in one place – in this website.

My world, our world is a portrait of the world in sound and images, and the people of the world make this portrait of the world. People take a photograph of a favourite place and share it on this website. With each picture, the photographer adds a voice recording about their favourite place.

I want this art project to give us a unique view of the world and to bring people together. Would you like to take part? Here's what to do.

- Take a photograph of your favourite place.
- Make a voice recording to go with your photograph. Say who you are and where you are, and tell the world about your favourite place. Please use English.
- Post your photograph and MP3 recording on the website.

To submit a photograph and recording, <u>click here</u>.
To view the online exhibition, <u>click here</u>.

LISTENING

3a 🔊1.2 **Summarise key points** Listen to three people on the website. Take notes to help you remember. After each recording, match the person with a picture on the website on page 6 and tell your partner what you can remember.

3b Listen again and answer these questions.

1 What do you think is the main reason Liu Shan goes to the park?
2 Why does Mo spend time at the top of the tower?
3 André plays beach football three times a week. True or false?
4 Transport to the beach is not a problem. True or false?
5 Which recordings and photographs do you find interesting? Why?

VOCABULARY
COUNTRIES AND REGIONS

4a Match these countries with the continents and regions.

| China | Canada | Saudi Arabia | Brazil | Thailand |
| Poland | Ghana | New Zealand | | |

| Europe | North America | South America | Australasia |
| the Arab World | East Asia | West Africa | South-East Asia |

4b What are the adjectives from the country and region nouns above?

China – Chinese

4c Do you ever visit other countries and regions? Do you know any people from other countries?

GRAMMAR
PRESENT SIMPLE AND CONTINUOUS

5a Which of these sentences are in the present simple (PS)? Which are in the present continuous (PC)?

1 Right now, people are dancing.
2 I'm studying science.
3 Currently, the beach is getting busy.
4 She comes to this park every week.
5 It is easy to get here.

5b Match these grammar notes (a–d) with the sentences above (1–5).

a This is a regular action or habit.
b This is an action happening now, or around now.
c This is a fact or general truth.
d This is a trend (i.e. a changing situation).

5c Find more examples of these grammar points in Audio script 1.2 on page 149. How do you make negative sentences with these tenses?

➡ *Language reference and extra practice, pages 102–103*

5d Complete these sentences. Use the present simple or present continuous of the verb in brackets.

1 I _____ at the café. Where are you? (wait)
2 She often _____ to the beach to relax. (go)
3 We _____ around Europe by train at the moment, before we go to university next year. (travel)
4 The sun _____ up in the east, and it _____ down in the west. (come, go)

GRAMMAR TIP

There are two types of verbs: state verbs and action verbs. State verbs usually describe feelings and situations, e.g. *be, have, know*. Action verbs describe activities and movements, e.g. *dance, play, hit*.

6a Underline the main verb in these sentences. Are they state or action verbs?

1 I'm a student.
2 The view is always different.
3 I'm playing football with my friends.
4 I love this part of the park.
5 She comes to this park every week.
6 People are taking photographs.

6b Which do you usually use for state verbs? Present simple or present continuous?

7 Complete this extract from *My world, our world*. Use the present simple or present continuous of the verbs.

Hi, I'm Lucy. I [1] _____ (be) English and I [2] _____ (live) in London. I'm here in Trafalgar Square, London – my favourite place. I [3] _____ (love) coming here because it's the centre of the city but it [4] _____ (have) a nice feeling. Right now, many people [5] _____ (look) around and they [6] _____ (take) photos. Everyone always [7] _____ (feel) relaxed here. I [8] _____ (study) photography at the moment, so I often [9] _____ (take) a lot of photos of people in this square. Also, the National Gallery [10] _____ (be) here, so I usually [11] _____ (have) a coffee in the square and then [12] _____ (visit) an exhibition at the gallery.

SPEAKING AND WRITING

8a Long turn taking Think of one of your favourite places. Draw a simple picture to represent it. Plan what to say in your short talk.

8b Work with a partner. Student A: give your talk while Student B listens, takes notes, then asks some questions. Then change roles.

8c Use your notes from your partner's talk to write a paragraph about his/her favourite place.

Ahmed's favourite place is the National Museum of Science. He goes there once a month because …

READING AND SPEAKING

1 Discuss these questions with a partner.

1 Are there seasons in your country? If so, what's your favourite season? Why?
2 Do you like winter? Why?/Why not?
3 What do you know about winter in Russia? What do you know about Siberia?

2a Understanding genre Quickly read the introduction to the text below. Where is the text from? Why do you think this?

1 a guidebook to Siberia
2 a book about climate change
3 a magazine about TV programmes

2b Read the rest of the text. What is the topic of each paragraph (A–J)?

paragraph A = the length of winter

2c Read the text again. Complete the gaps (A–J) with these interview questions.

1 Does winter last a long time?
2 And what's life like? Is it very difficult for people?
3 Really? Why do they do that?
4 How do people keep warm?
5 Is the climate changing? Are winters getting warmer?
6 Is it really cold?
7 What do Russians think about their cold winters?
8 I see. What about snow? How much snow is there in Siberia?
9 What about you? What do you think about winter in Siberia?
10 That's incredible! Why is it so cold?

Surviving Siberia

Wednesday 14 May 8 p.m. on Channel 7

Liam O'Connor is a familiar face in homes all over the country. Millions of us watch his documentaries. Now he's making a new programme about life in Russia. Here he tells Gaby Redmond about winter in Siberia.

A *Does winter last a long time?*
Yes, it does. Generally speaking, winter starts in September and lasts until May – so for about nine months. In the north, the sun never rises in December and January, and it's dark nearly all day.

B _____
Well, minus 30 or 40 degrees Celsius is normal, but in northern Siberia, the temperature sometimes drops to minus 60 or 70 degrees.

C _____
One reason is that, in the far north, the sun is always low in the sky and produces very little heat, so the ground stays cold all year. Another reason is that freezing winds come down from the Arctic because there are no mountains or trees to stop them.

D _____
It often snows, but it's rarely heavy. In the far north, snow cover lasts between 260 and 280 days.

E _____
Yes, they are. Definitely. Western Siberia is getting warmer faster than anywhere in the world. In fact, it's actually melting. And in some places in eastern Siberia, dangerous gases are rising from the ground. They're stopping the surface from freezing, even in the middle of winter. But it's still very cold!

F _____
They wear fur. In the West, we consider fur a luxury, but it's the only thing that keeps you warm when it's extremely cold.

G *And what's life like? Is it very difficult for people?*
Yes, it is. Without gloves, your fingers freeze. The little hairs in your nose freeze too. It's quite scary! The tyres of cars and lorries burst. Sometimes children can't go to school because it's so cold. They have lessons on TV!

H _____
Actually, they don't mind them. They enjoy a lot of outdoor sports. Ice-skating is the number-one sport – it's really popular. They also like cross-country skiing and ice-hockey. Reindeer racing is quite popular too. Some people swim in rivers and lakes in the sub-zero temperatures.

I _____
They say there are health benefits to swimming in icy water. It's a way to avoid colds. Also, it's a real community event. Everyone takes part – men, women and children.

J _____
Well, to tell you the truth, I love it! In my home city, Liverpool, the winters are usually cloudy and mild, and I don't like them much. You don't get many days when the weather's fine – you know, sunny and not raining. In Siberia, it's different. On bright sunny days, it's very beautiful.

3a Find words in the text (verbs, nouns and adjectives) that refer to winter weather.

cold, …

3b Complete these sentences with one or two words. Use the words you found above.

1 In my country, it _____ a lot in the mountains in winter.
2 The days are short, and it's already _____ at 4 p.m.
3 Driving on _____ roads is very dangerous.
4 When the _____ winds come from the north, it's very cold.

3c What other weather words do you know? Make a list of words to describe the weather in summer.

dry, clear, sunny …

VOCABULARY
MODIFIERS

4a Match these sentences with the pictures below.

1 It's extremely cold in Moscow in January.
2 It's very/really cold in Beijing in January.
3 In January, it's quite cold in London.

A	**B**	**C**

1°C	8°C	−7°C

4b Talk about the cities in the chart on page 134 using *extremely*, *very/really* and *quite,* and the weather adjectives from Exercise 3.

It's extremely hot in Dubai in July.

4c Talk about places and things you know, using these adjectives and a modifier.

crowded   dangerous   interesting   lively
popular   quiet   scary

My city is very crowded.

GRAMMAR
PRESENT SIMPLE AND CONTINUOUS QUESTIONS

5a Look at Exercise 2c. Which questions are in the present simple? Which are in the present continuous?

5b Match 1–3 with a–c to complete these grammar notes.

1 When *be* is the main verb, you make present simple questions
2 When the main verb isn't *be*, you make present simple questions
3 You make present continuous questions

a with the auxiliary verb *do/does* + subject + infinitive of the main verb.
b with the auxiliary verb *am/is/are* + subject + *-ing* form of the main verb.
c with *am/is/are* before the subject.

➡ Language reference and extra practice, pages 102–103

6a Choose the best word to complete these questions. Then answer them.

1 When *is / do / does* winter start in Siberia?
2 Where *is / are / do* dangerous gases rising from the ground?
3 *Is / Does / Are* winter in Siberia getting warmer?
4 *Are / Am / Do* your fingers freeze in the very cold conditions?
5 *Do / Be / Are* winter sports popular in Siberia?
6 *What / Why / Where* does Liam like Siberia?

6b Underline the question words in Exercise 2c. What other question words do you know?

6c Put these words in order to make questions.

1 sad / you / days / do / on / feel / cloudy / ?
2 wearing / your / teacher / what's / today / ?
3 English / are / fun / learning / you / for / ?
4 time / your / how / spend / free / you / do / ?
5 friends / doing / what / now / are / your / ?
6 holiday / you / how much / year / have / every / do / ?

6d Take turns to ask and answer the questions in Exercise 6c with a partner.

SPEAKING

7 Discuss these questions in a group. Listen to your partners' answers and ask them questions about their views.

1 What is life like for people in very hot countries?
2 Is it better to live in a very hot country or a very cold country?
3 What is the difference between *weather* and *climate*?
4 What, in your opinion, is the perfect climate?
5 Is the climate changing in your country?
6 How does the climate affect the way people live in your country?

WRITING

8 Write five sentences about the climate in your country and the way the climate affects people. Use your ideas from Exercise 7.

 ▶ **MEET THE EXPERT**

Watch an interview with James Moore, an expedition medical consultant, about living in extreme places.
Turn to page 126 for video activities.

SITUATION

1a Look at the advert below for Double Action Adventures. Why does the company have this name?

1b Match the different activities in the advert with the photos (A–J). What do you think of the activities?

2a Read this email from the boss of Double Action Adventures. What does he want his staff to do?

From james.ross@daa.com
To All staff

Dear all

We need your suggestions for two countries for our new holidays in Central and South America.

Remember, an ideal country offers a) a range of activities and locations, and b) something unusual or different.

Our main customers are adventurous young adults, but we're interested in some new customers:

- 'first timers' – people having an adventure holiday for the first time
- older adults (40–65) – active, rich, perhaps retired.

Let's have a meeting next week to discuss all your ideas.

James Ross

2b Look at these notes about southern Argentina. Do you think it is a good choice for Double Action Adventures? Why?/Why not? Refer back to the boss's email.

SOUTHERN ARGENTINA

LOCATION:	In the mountains	On the southern coast
ACTIVITIES:	• mountain trekking • horse riding	• three-day Antarctic wildlife cruise • sea kayaking with whales
HOLIDAY SEASON: November to February	windy	very cold

3a 1.3 Listen to Diana and Simon (two DAA employees) discuss southern Argentina. Do they have the same ideas as you? What do they think are the strong and weak points of this destination?

DOUBLE ACTION
adventures

One holiday, two adventures!

Choose an adventure holiday with us and get double the action. Spend your first week white-water rafting in the mountains. Spend your second week diving and snorkelling at the coast.

Other activities available:
mountain biking and trekking, sea kayaking, skiing and snowboarding, horse riding, wildlife watching and island cruises. Trips to North America, Australia and Europe. All equipment, training and guides included.

3b Listen again. Who has these opinions: Diana (D), Simon (S) or both of them (B)?

1 The Antarctic cruise is a good thing. *B*
2 The holiday season is not very long.
3 Horse riding is not a good activity.
4 It is OK to offer easy activities for first-timers.
5 The weather in the mountains is not good.
6 Argentina is a good place for older holiday makers.

KEY LANGUAGE
AGREEING AND DISAGREEING

4a **1.4** Listen and complete these sentences from the conversation.

1 D: I think the Antarctic wildlife cruise is a great idea.
   S: Mmm, _____ do I.
2 S: It's certainly something for older customers.
   D: I _____ with you.
3 S: I also think it's a good activity for our main customers.
   D: Do you? I _____. Our main customers like …
4 D: And whale watching is great.
   S: Yes, you're _____. So, are there any problems?
5 D: It's only four months long. I don't like that.
   S: No, _____ do I. It means we can't …
6 D: … everyone can go walking.
   S: Well, I disagree _____ you. I think …
7 D: Let's look at the other places, then decide.
   S: _____, so where are the other destinations?

4b In which sentences do they think the same? In which do they think differently?

PRONUNCIATION

5a **1.5** Showing interest Listen to this example twice. Which one sounds more interested in the discussion, the first or the second?

Mmm, so do I.

5b **1.6** Listen and do the same with these phrases.

1 I agree with you.
2 Do you? I disagree.
3 Yes, you're right.
4 No, neither do I.
5 Well, I disagree with you.
6 Don't you? I do.
7 Mmm, you're right.
8 OK.

5c Listen again and repeat.

6 Look at the activities in the box and tell your partner your opinions about them. Does he/she agree with you? Does he/she sound interested?

an Antarctic cruise   horse riding
sea kayaking   walking in a strong wind
white-water rafting   scuba diving

A: I don't think horse riding is interesting.
B: I disagree. I like it. / Neither do I.

TASK
MAKING A CHOICE

7a You work for Double Action Adventures. Turn to page 131 and read about three more countries.

7b Read the email from the boss in Exercise 2a again and think about these questions.

• What do you think of all four destinations?
• What do you think of the activities?
• How long is the best season for holidays?
• Is the weather OK?
• Do the holidays meet your boss's requirements?

Make notes and prepare to discuss with your partner.

So, what do you think?
It means …
The holiday season seems …

8 Compare your opinions with your partner and choose the best two countries for Double Action Adventures.

STUDY SKILLS
UNDERSTANDING MEANING

1 Many words in English have more than one meaning. Look at this dictionary entry for *cold*. Match the example sentences (a–c) below with the definitions (1–3).

> **C**   **cold** /kəʊld/ *adjective*
>
> ¹ something that is cold has a low temperature and is not warm or hot
>
> ² cold food is cooked, but is not eaten while it is hot
>
> ³ a cold person is not very friendly or kind

From Longman WordWise Dictionary

a   We eat a lot of cold chicken and salad in the summer.
b   Some people think that the British are cold.
c   The weather's really cold today.

2 The words in bold below describe the weather. Turn to page 132 and look at their other meanings. Write the number of the correct definition.

a   That's a really **cool** film.
b   Some Thai fish soups are really **hot**.
c   Gabriella's got very **dark** hair.
d   They always give visitors a **warm** welcome.
e   'How are you?' 'I'm **fine**, thanks.'
f   His writing isn't **clear**.
g   This shampoo is for **dry** hair.
h   She's a **bright** child.
i   I don't like **mild** cheese.

3 Definitions often give you more information than just the meaning of a word. Work with a partner and answer these questions. Then check your answers in a dictionary or turn to page 131.

1   What colour is a **cloud**?
2   When does it **snow**?
3   What happens in **autumn**?
4   What does the **sun** give us?
5   What kind of water is in the **sea**?
6   Think of two uses of a **horse**.

4a Dictionaries often tell us the opposites of words. Look at this entry for *rich*. You can see that the opposite (or antonym) of *rich* is *poor*.

> **C**   **rich** /rɪtʃ/ *adjective*
>
> ¹ someone who is rich has a lot of money or owns a lot of things ANTONYM **poor**: *He became rich and powerful.*

From Longman WordWise Dictionary

Think of the opposites of these adjectives from this unit. Check your answers in a dictionary.

1   long   4   easy
2   strong   5   quiet
3   interesting   6   popular

4b Complete these sentences with the opposites from Exercise 4a.

1   That's a really _____ question. I don't know the answer.
2   It's only a _____ distance to the coast.
3   I don't like _____ coffee.
4   That music's very _____. I can't study!

WRITING SKILLS
DESCRIBING A PLACE

5 Discuss these questions with a partner.
1   What are the good and bad things about living in a large city?
2   Do you like visiting large cities when you have a short holiday? Why?/Why not?

6 Look at this list of things you can find in a city guide. Can you add two or three more things to the list?
1   how to get there / travel around
2   information about the weather / when to go
3   information about the history of a place
4   places to visit / things to do

SEOUL
a fantastic mixture of the old and the new

INTRODUCTION

The capital of South Korea is a place of tradition and history, but it's also a busy, crowded and modern city. Twenty million people live in Seoul and the area around it. Seoul is great for shopping, eating and drinking, and you can do these things at any time of the day or night – it really is a 24-hour city. The transport system is excellent, and there is almost no crime.

7 Read the text below from an online city guide to Seoul and answer these questions.

1 Does the text tell us how many people live in the city of Seoul?
2 What are the two best seasons to visit Seoul? Why?
3 Name one place where you can go shopping very late in the evening.
4 Would you like to visit Seoul? Why?/Why not?
5 Think about where you live. Which things are similar to Seoul? Which are different?

8 Understanding text organisation In which part of the text (*Introduction, When to go* or *Things to do*) would you put this information?

1 It's a good time to visit if you enjoy skiing or snowboarding.
2 When you need a break from the noise of the city, take a walk along the 5.8km Cheong-gyechong stream – and listen to the water.
3 Seoul is 600 years old.

9a Linkers Words like *and, but, also* and *when* are linking words. You use them to join ideas. Underline examples of them in the text below.

9b Complete these rules with the words in the box.

different   fact   time   words

You use …

1 *and* to join two _____ or parts of a sentence.
2 *when* to talk about the _____ that something happens.
3 *but* to add something _____ or surprising.
4 *also* to add a new _____.

9c Choose the correct words.

1 The waiters are friendly *and / when / also* they speak good English.
2 The weather's good in spring. It's *and / when / also* good in autumn.
3 You can go white-water rafting *but / and / also* you can't go kayaking.
4 A good time to visit Venice is in winter *also / when / but* it isn't crowded.
5 The beach is beautiful *when / and* it's *and / also* a good place to go snorkelling.
6 You can buy souvenirs in the hotel *but / also / when* the prices are often very high.

9d Punctuation Do you need commas before *and* or *but* in the sentences above?

10 Write a description of your city, or a city you know, for an online guide. Use the text about Seoul as a model. Divide your description into different parts, e.g. *Introduction, When to go, What to do.* Make notes before you write.

WHEN TO GO

Seoul has four very different seasons. The best time to visit is in the autumn (September to November), when it's usually sunny. Spring, from April to early June, is also a beautiful season. Winter is dry but often extremely cold. Avoid summer – June to August is hot and wet.

THINGS TO DO

* Visit Gyeongbok Palace and learn about Korea's history.
* Bukchon village is an old part of the city with beautiful houses, cafés and restaurants.
* The famous Namdaemun market is hundreds of years old and is open day and night. You can buy anything here.
* Try *kimchi* (the national dish), but remember: it's quite hot!

2 People
2.1 DETERMINATION

IN THIS UNIT

GRAMMAR
- past simple: regular and irregular verbs
- past simple: negatives, question forms and short answers

VOCABULARY
- personality adjectives and nouns

SCENARIO
- describing people
- choosing a new flatmate

STUDY SKILLS
- learning styles and strategies

WRITING SKILLS
- a reflective blog (personal narrative)

"Always remember that you are absolutely unique. Just like everyone else.' Margaret Mead, 1901–1978, US cultural anthropologis

READING

1a Look at the photographs and the webpage. What is the webpage for? Why are these women on this webpage?

1b Read again. Are these sentences true or false?
1   Chimokel comes from a rich family.
2   She lives on her own.
3   Soula is a good example for people to follow.
4   She borrowed money to start her business.
5   Sarah used transport without engines and motors.
6   Sarah travelled with other people.

LISTENING

2a **2.1** Listen to each woman's story. Who needed special equipment? Who needed support from friends or family? Who needed digital media?

2b Put these events in the correct order for each person. Listen again and check.
1   get idea from a neighbour / marry Benjamin / run in the Nairobi marathon
2   work long hours / win an award / study graphic design
3   cycle across Asia / cycle across Europe / attempt to row across the Pacific Ocean

2c Use the information in Exercise 2b to retell the stories with your partner. Can you remember everything about each person?

International Women's Day Awards

The theme for this year is Outstanding Determination. We are looking for women who worked hard to achieve success in their field and did not give up when things were difficult.

The nominations for this year's award are:

Chimokel Chilapong: Chimokel is an ordinary Kenyan farmer, with a small family. She shows how determination can help other people. 'Go Chimokel! Go!'
Nominated by Eastern Kenya, Community/women's org.

Soula Zavacopoulos: Soula's a hard-working woman and a great role model. She started her own business from nothing. She invested all her savings and she worked extremely hard for a long time, but her business is a success now. She used her creativity and determination.
Nominated by UK, School community group

Sarah Outen: Sarah is the definition of determination! She travelled around the world alone by human power. She only used a bicycle, a kayak and a rowing boat. She faced many problems but she never gave up. She is a great example for us all.
Nominated by Matsumoto High School, Japan

3 Evaluation Discuss with your partner.
1   What are the similarities and differences between each story?
2   Can you choose the best one for the award? What are your reasons for your choice?

VOCABULARY
PERSONALITY ADJECTIVES AND NOUNS

4a **Find these adjectives in the text and in Audio script 2.1 on page 149. Who do they describe?**

determined   happy   creative   hard-working
kind   friendly   brave   confident

4b **Look again at the adjectives above. What are their nouns? Use a dictionary to check.**

determined – determination, happy – …

4c **Complete these sentences with words from above. Do you need a noun or an adjective?**

1 Dad is very _____. He's always at work.
2 I'm sociable and _____. I like meeting new people.
3 He's very _____; he often draws pictures.
4 _____ is more important than money.
5 _____ is the desire to continue even when it is difficult.
6 My sister says I'm very _____ because I love rock climbing and surfing.
7 My brother has a lot of _____. He is never nervous when speaking in English.
8 My mother is very _____, and she always helps people who have problems.

4d **Use the adjectives to describe people you know.**

GRAMMAR
PAST SIMPLE

5a **Match the beginnings and endings of these sentences. Who says each one?**

1 I married Benjamin   a last year.
2 I started my own business   b in 2011.
3 I won an award   c five years ago.
4 I travelled across Asia   d when I was 16.

> **GRAMMAR TIP**
>
> You use the past simple to talk about finished actions and situations in the past. You know, and often say, the time of the action or situation.

5b **Complete these grammar notes with the verbs in Exercise 5a.**

1 You add -ed to the infinitive to make the past simple of most verbs. These are regular verbs, e.g. _____ .
2 Sometimes you add -ed and make a small spelling change, e.g. _____ , _____ .
3 Many common verbs in the past simple are irregular. We don't add -ed. We use a different word, e.g. _____ .

5c **Find examples of the different types of verb spelling in the text and Audio script 2.1 on page 149.**

➡ Language reference and extra practice, pages 104–105

5d **Complete this description of Sarah's journey.**

I [1]_____(leave) Japan on 13th May, 2012 in my special rowing boat. At first, the weather was good and there [2]_____(be) no problems. However, after three weeks, there [3]_____(be) a terrible storm. The wind was very strong, and the sea [4]_____(become) very rough. The storm [5]_____(break) my boat and I [6]_____(use) my radio to ask for help. I [7]_____(stay) inside my boat and [8]_____(wait). This was an extremely difficult time for me. Finally, the Japanese rescue ship [9]_____(arrive) and [10]_____(save) me, but I [11]_____(lose) my boat. After that, I [12]_____(go) back to London, but I never [13]_____(give up). I [14]_____(start) my journey again in 2013.

6 Time expressions **Use these time expressions to make true sentences about you. Then compare your sentences with a partner.**

ten years ago   when I was 16   last year
last week   in 2005   last night   on Sunday

> **GRAMMAR TIP**
>
> You use *in* with years and months: *in 2006, in July*.
> You use *on* with days: *on Sunday, on Monday*.
> You use *at* with times: *at seven o'clock, at 8.15*.

PRONUNCIATION

7a **2.2** Voiced/unvoiced consonants **The past simple ending -ed has three possible pronunciations. Listen to these examples and repeat them.**

/t/ looked   /d/ travelled   /ɪd/ wanted

7b **2.3** **Work with a partner and put the regular verbs from Exercises 5c and 5d into the three groups above. Then listen and check your ideas.**

SPEAKING AND WRITING

8a **Do you know someone who has a lot of determination to do something or a story about great determination? Make notes to help you describe the person or tell your story.**

8b **Share your examples of determination with your partner. What are you personally determined to do?**

9 **Write a short story about determination, or a description of a determined person that you know.**

READING AND SPEAKING

1 Discuss these questions with a partner.

1   Are you creative, e.g. can you sing, draw, paint, dance, etc.?
2   Which famous creative people do you know or like?
3   What do you know about Japanese comics (manga)?

2a Read the text quickly. Write down two interesting things you remember. Compare with other students.

2b Correct these sentences about the text.

1   Osamu Tezuka was a Korean manga artist.
2   He drew his first comics during the Second World War.
3   His first success was with the comic 'Astro Boy'.
4   Tezuka wrote comics only for children.
5   Before Tezuka, many manga artists wrote long stories.
6   Tezuka created about 150,000 stories in his life.

2c Find words in the text that mean:

1   a building where workers make things. (paragraph 3)
2   using your imagination. (paragraph 4)
3   a machine that can move and do jobs like a person. (paragraph 4)
4   people in a book, film, etc. (paragraph 6)
5   we think that this is true, but we are not sure. (paragraph 6)
6   thought that someone is very good or clever. (paragraph 6)

3 Increasing your understanding Answer these questions with a partner.

1   Why do people call Tezuka 'the father of manga'?
2   Explain the influence of his parents on his work.
3   Why do you think manga is very popular these days? Do you read manga stories? Why?/Why not?

Ken's blog

15 September

These days, Japanese manga is everywhere, but they weren't always so popular. So how did it all begin? Today I want to write about Osamu Tezuka (1928–1989). He was a Japanese manga artist. People call him 'the father of manga'.

When he was a child, his mother often read stories to him, and she also took him to the theatre. His father showed animated films at home. These influences appeared in his later work.

He started to draw comics when he was about six years old. During the Second World War, at the age of 16, he worked in a factory, where he drew comics for the other workers.

After the war, he started his studies in medicine, but he didn't stop his creative work, and soon he had his first real success with comics like 'New Treasure Island'. In the early 1950s, he created the very popular boy robot – Astro Boy.

Tezuka didn't write for one age group; instead, he produced stories for everyone – from very young children to adults. He changed manga because he was the first artist to write very long stories – stories with the feeling of films.

People often ask why the characters in Japanese manga have very big eyes. Well, this was Tezuka's idea – but where did he get it from? Probably from Walt Disney. Tezuka really admired Disney; they say he watched 'Bambi' 80 times!

Over a period of 40 years, Tezuka created about 700 stories – over 150,000 pages of manga. He also worked on many animated films and TV programmes. He wasn't very old when he died – only 60 – and perhaps he worked too hard. Still, his last words were apparently: 'Let me work'!

Comment

This is really interesting. I didn't know anything about him. Where did you get this information? I want to know more. Did he work as a doctor? Why was Astro Boy so popular?

Seth 546

GRAMMAR
PAST SIMPLE NEGATIVE AND QUESTION FORMS

4a Underline all the negative sentences in the text. Then complete these rules.

1 With all verbs except *be*, you form the past simple negative with _____ + the infinitive without *to*.
2 You form the past simple negative of *be* with *was/were* + _____ .

4b Find all the questions in the text. Then complete these rules.

1 With all verbs except *be*, you form past simple questions with _____ + subject + the infinitive without *to*.
2 With *be*, you form past simple questions with _____ or _____ + subject.

➡ Language reference and extra practice, pages 104–105

4c Complete this conversation with past tense forms (positive, negative or question).

A: Tell me a little about Frida Kahlo.
B: She ¹_____(be) a Mexican painter. Many of her works ²_____(be) paintings of herself. In them, we can see her powerful feelings about herself and the world around her.
A: Apparently, she ³_____(have) a serious disease when she ⁴_____(be) young.
B: Yes, that's right. But she ⁵_____(not lose) hope. She ⁶_____(be) a very determined young woman. She ⁷_____(not have) an easy life, but she ⁸_____(become) famous.
A: When ⁹_____(do) her first paintings?
B: When she ¹⁰_____(be) about 18.
A: How many works ¹¹_____(produce) in her life?
B: About 200. Many people ¹²_____(admire) her work, including Pablo Picasso.
A: What ¹³_____(do) in her free time?
B: She ¹⁴_____(like) singing and telling jokes at parties!

5 Ask your partner what he/she did yesterday / the day before yesterday / on Thursday / last weekend, etc. Make a note of the answers. Then report to the class.

SPEAKING

6a 〔2.4〕 You are going to invite a famous person from the past or present to dinner. Listen to the example and complete these sentences.

ESPERANZA SPALDING

1 She is a jazz _____ and a musician.
2 Her early life _____.
3 She became interested in music _____.
4 She discovered the bass because she was bored _____.
5 She won a Grammy music prize for _____ in 2011.
6 'How _____ when you won the Grammy?'

6b Collaboration Work with a partner. Who would you invite? Research your person and make some notes under these headings:

• his/her life (early, later)
• personality
• his/her abilities, skills
• influence
• two questions you would like to ask him/her

6c Work in groups without your partner. Tell your group about your guest. Listen to the other students. Then choose two guests to invite.

▶ MEET THE EXPERT

Watch an interview with Karen Rubins, a comics artist, about manga.
Turn to page 126 for video activities.

PREPARATION

1a Work with a partner. Talk about where you live. Do you live with your family? Do you share a flat with friends?

1b Imagine you are looking for a flatmate. Choose five of the things in the box that are important to you. What other things are important in a flatmate? Compare your ideas with your partner.

have similar interests to me	not smoke	have a job
be friendly and sociable	be good-looking	be rich
do his/her washing-up	be quiet and polite	be tidy
be a good cook	be honest	be clever

A flatmate should have similar interests to me.

2 Match these opposite adjectives.

1	polite	a	shy
2	friendly	b	horrible
3	confident	c	rude
4	nice	d	miserable
5	cheerful	e	unfriendly
6	hard-working	f	stupid
7	clever	g	quiet
8	chatty	h	lazy

PRONUNCIATION

3a Word stress The word *confident* has three syllables: *con-fi-dent*. How many syllables are there in the adjectives in Exercise 2?

3b 2.5 How do we pronounce *confident*? Listen and check.

1 • confident　　2 • confident　　3 • confident

3c 2.6 Mark the stress on the adjectives in Exercise 2. Then listen and check.

3d Test your partner. Say one of the adjectives. Your partner tells you the opposite.

SITUATION

Robert (a PhD student from Poland) and Gao Ying (who works for an advertising company and is from Hong Kong) share a three-bedroom flat in London. They are looking for a new flatmate. Robert is in Poland at the moment and he missed the people who came to see the flat. Gao Ying telephones Robert and tells him about the different people.

4a 2.7 Listen to part of their conversation. Do you think Robert wants this person to be the new flatmate?

4b Listen again and complete Robert's notes. Write one word in each gap.

A Name/Nationality/Job
　　Martin, Canadian, ¹_____

B Personality
　　At first, not very ²_____.
　　Not ³_____.
　　Hard-working. Seems ⁴_____.

C Likes/Dislikes
　　Watching ⁵_____ on TV, cooking.
　　Hates ⁶_____

D Appearance
　　Looks ⁷_____.
　　Wearing ⁸_____ clothes.
　　Short ⁹_____ hair. Like Mr Bean.

E Gao Ying's opinion:
　　Happy to live with a ¹⁰_____ person.
　　Would like to share with a Canadian.

KEY LANGUAGE
DESCRIBING PEOPLE

5a [2.8] Complete these questions from the conversation. Then listen and check.

1 What's he _____?
2 What does he _____ like?
3 What _____ he like?
4 _____ you like to live with him?

5b Match the questions above with the sections A–E of the notes in Exercise 4b.

5c [2.9] Complete these sentences from the conversation. Listen and check. Which questions in Exercise 5a do they answer?

1 He's _____ short brown hair.
2 He _____ like the actor who plays Mr Bean.
3 He _____ honest.
4 He certainly _____ chatty.
5 He works long hours, _____ he's hard-working.
6 He _____ watching sport on TV.
7 He _____ nice clothes.
8 Yes, I think _____.

5d Choose someone you know, e.g. a friend or a member of your family. Prepare answers for the questions in Exercise 5a. Ask your partner about his/her person.

TASK
CHOOSING A NEW FLATMATE

6a You and your partner share a flat in London. You are looking for a new flatmate. There are three people to choose from: Martin, Isabelle and Toshi.

Student A: Turn to page 140 and read about Isabelle.
Student B: Turn to page 148 and read about Toshi.

6b Prepare to ask your partner about Toshi or Isabelle, and then to discuss who to choose for your flat. Look back at the language in Exercise 5a and the Useful phrases below.

USEFUL PHRASES

What do you think of …?
What about …?
I like / don't like … because …
I agree/disagree.
So do I. / Do you?
Neither do I. / Don't you?

6c Ask your partner about Toshi or Isabelle. Make notes under the same headings as in Exercise 4b. Then discuss the three people (Martin, Toshi and Isabelle) and choose your new flatmate. Who would you like to live with?

STUDY SKILLS
LEARNING STYLES AND STRATEGIES

1a People learn in different ways, and often one way isn't better than another. However, there are things you can do to improve your learning. One thing is to understand better *how* you learn, and to know your strengths and weaknesses.

Do the questionnaire on the right to find out your learning style. Give each statement a mark out of 5 (5 = Yes, a lot / easily, etc. 1 = No / Not at all, etc.). Then turn to page 133 to read the analysis of your answers and tips to improve your learning.

1b Look again at the section(s) where you got high scores. Think of one thing you can do to help you learn ten new words from this unit.

2a `2.10` Listen to two people talking about their experiences of learning a new skill and answer these questions.

1   What did they learn?
2   Did they enjoy learning it?

2b Listen again and answer these questions.

1   How did they learn the skills?
2   Was it easy or difficult to learn?
3   How did they feel when they could do it?

3a Work in a small group. Tell your partners about something that you learned successfully in your life (e.g. a school subject, to ride a bike, to drive). Use the questions in Exercises 2a and 2b to help you.

3b Write down one or two things that you learned from the experience you described.

What's your learning style?

A
1   Can you remember any of the photos in Unit 1 of this book?
2   Do you find it easy to understand charts and diagrams?
3   Are you good at using maps?
4   Have you got a good memory for people's faces?
5   When you get a new piece of equipment, e.g. a DVD player, do you read the instruction book carefully?
6   When you were a child, did you enjoy reading books in your free time?

B
7   Is it difficult for you to study in a noisy place?
8   Do you enjoy listening to books on CD?
9   When you think of a phone number, do you hear the numbers in your head?
10 When people tell you their names, do you remember them easily?
11 Do you enjoy listening to lectures and talks?
12 When you were a child, did you like listening to stories?

C
13 Do you learn best by doing things?
14 Is it difficult for you to study when there are many things happening around you?
15 Do you move your hands a lot when you're talking?
16 When you get a new piece of equipment, e.g. a DVD player, do you ignore the instruction book?
17 In your free time, do you like doing things with your hands, e.g. painting?
18 When you were a child, did you do a lot of physical activity in your free time?

WRITING SKILLS
A REFLECTIVE BLOG

It is a good idea when you are studying English to write a reflective blog. Writing gives you thinking time and helps you organise your thoughts, feelings and ideas. It also helps you to track your progress and development. In other words, writing can help you become a better learner.

4 Read the reflective blog below. Answer these questions.

1 When did Amy come to Spain?
2 What did Amy do on Wednesday?
3 What can you see late in the evening in Madrid?
4 In Amy's class on Saturday, what language does the teacher speak?

5 In a reflective blog, you can write about the things you do, things you see/hear, things you like/don't like, things you are thinking about, difficulties, problems or concerns, and/or things that change in your life. Find examples of these things in Amy's blog.

6 You can also comment on things you learn. Find examples of something Amy learns (or is learning) by:

1 watching/looking.
2 listening/hearing.
3 touching/using her hands.

7 Amy gives reasons for things. Find the reasons why she:

1 loves the Prado museum.
2 thinks it's important to see paintings in a museum – not in books or on the internet.
3 was worried about starting the jewellery class.

8 Inferring Answer these questions.

1 What subject do you think Amy is studying at Grey University?
2 Who is Alicia?
3 Is this Amy's first time abroad?
4 Do you think Amy is happy in Spain? Why?/Why not?

9 Linkers Study the examples of the linking words *until, at first, then, at the moment* and *afterwards* in the blog. Then choose the best word to complete these sentences.

1 *At first / Until* I was shy and didn't ask any questions. *At the moment / Then* I became more confident.
2 I'm enjoying my course in this country *at first / at the moment.*
3 *At first / At the moment,* I couldn't do the homework but *until / then* a friend explained how to do it.
4 We had a very long and difficult exam this afternoon. I felt really tired *afterwards / at first* and went to bed early.
5 I didn't use a Spanish–Spanish dictionary *at first / then,* but *then / at the moment* I realised that it was better than translating words.
6 I was working hard *until / afterwards* my flatmate arrived!

10 Start your own reflective blog. Try to write something every day or two. After about a month, read the blog from the beginning. Do you notice any changes in your English, in yourself or in the way you learn?

about *me* ▶▶▶

Hi! I'm Amy and I'm at Grey University in Chicago, USA. At the moment, I'm studying for four months in Madrid, Spain, as part of my program.

Wednesday May 10

Our class went to the Prado again. I love this museum—the buildings and the paintings are great. To be honest, I wasn't very interested in art until I came to this country. Now I realize it's important to see paintings in a museum—not just in books or on the internet. That's how they come alive. Afterwards, Alicia and I studied together for next week's exam on the development of the European Union.

Tuesday May 9

I really like the way people live here. In the evening, they have dinner late, around 10 or sometimes 11. The family is very important, and you see whole families eating together in restaurants, or walking in the streets. At first, I was surprised to see very young children out with their families at midnight, but then it became normal. Things like this are making me think about the differences between cultures. For the first time, I can see with my own eyes that some things are better in other cultures than in my own culture.

Saturday May 6

At the moment, I'm doing a jewellery class in my free time. It's a lot of fun. At first, I was worried—my fingers are very big—but I now know that I'm good at making things with my hands and I'm pleased with some of my work. The teacher speaks very fast, but my Spanish is also good now. When I came here in February, I didn't understand so much!

< previous next >

3 The media

3.1 THE INTERNET

IN THIS UNIT

GRAMMAR
- past continuous
- relative pronouns

VOCABULARY
- the media
- nouns (*photography/photographer*)
- TV programme genres

SCENARIO
- making suggestions
- designing a show

STUDY SKILLS
- collaboration: working with others

WRITING SKILLS
- a TV programme review

'Everybody gets so much information all day long that they lose their common sense.' Gertrude Stein, 1874–1946, US writer

VOCABULARY

THE MEDIA

1a Put these words into three groups: A (newspapers and magazines), B (television and radio) and C (computers and the internet). Some words can go in more than one group.

advert   article   blog   celebrity   channel
drama   email   front page   headline
homepage   journalist   presenter   programme
social networking site   spam   video

1b Use the words above to make collocations with these verbs.

1   to read *an article* …
2   to watch *an advert (on TV)*, …
3   to write
4   to listen to
5   to use/go on
6   to like/respect
7   to upload

1c Are these statements true for you? Discuss them with a partner.

1   I don't read newspapers.
2   I don't read articles about celebrities.
3   I like watching adverts on TV.
4   I think computer games are violent and expensive.
5   I read a lot of blogs.
6   I think journalists usually tell the truth.

1d Now use words from Exercise 1a to write two true statements about yourself. Then compare with a partner.

I don't like adverts on social networking sites.

READING

2a When (and how) do you think the internet began? Discuss with a partner, then read the text to check.

THE FIRST TIME

In 2009, about 1.7 billion people were using the internet. On January 1st 1994, there were 623 websites – in total. In the mid-1980s, email was beginning to change the world.

But when did the internet really begin? No one knows this
5   for sure, mainly because no one agrees on what, exactly, the internet is. But perhaps it was 29 October 1969.

This was the day Professor Leonard Kleinrock received a large metal box in his office. At the time, Kleinrock was working at the University of California in Los Angeles (UCLA). The box was
10   an IMP, or 'Interface Message Processor'. It looked like a fridge.

At 10.30 p.m., Kleinrock and his team connected a computer to the IMP, and the IMP made contact with a second IMP and computer, hundreds of miles away at Stanford Research Institute. They were planning to log in – from LA – to the
15   machine in Stanford. A student, Charley Kline, was writing the word 'LOGIN' when the system crashed after just two letters. Stanford only received the letters 'L' and 'O', so the first internet message was 'LO'.

2b Answer these questions.

1 When and where did Prof. Kleinrock receive the box?
2 What could it do?
3 What happened soon after Charley Kline started to write the word 'LOGIN'?

2c What do these words refer to?

1 it (line 6)
3 it (line 10)
2 this (line 7)
4 they (line 14)

2d Work with a partner. Take turns to retell the story without looking at your book.

LISTENING

3a [3.1] Listen to three people talking about the early days of the internet. Which of these topics – an internet café, a social networking site, a radio station, an ISP (Internet Service Provider), a computer game or a blog – do they talk about?

3b Which speaker(s):

1 started his/her own business?
2 didn't talk to customers face to face?
3 enjoyed what he/she did?
4 mentions the different names things had in the '90s?
5 tells us about his/her conversations in those times?
6 mentions an important visit?

3c Analysing the topic How do you think people felt at the time about these new developments in the internet? Which of the developments do you think was the most important for the future of the internet?

GRAMMAR
PAST CONTINUOUS

4a Use the past continuous to talk about a longer background action in the past, when a shorter action interrupts it or happens during it. Use the past simple for the shorter action. Match the time lines below with these sentences.

1 He was writing the word 'LOGIN' when the system crashed.
2 He received a large metal box in his office while he was working at UCLA.

Now

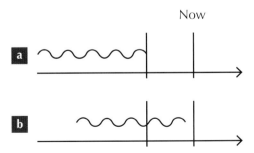

4b Find two more examples in Audio script 3.1 on page 150. How do we make sentences in the past continuous (affirmative, negative and questions)?

Use the past continuous on its own to talk about actions in progress in the past. You often use a time expression when you do this.

In 1992, I was working for an ISP.

*What were you doing **at 11 o'clock last night**?*

➡ Language reference and extra practice, pages 106–107

5 Complete these sentences, using a past continuous or past simple form of the verb.

1 I _____(send) an email to my sister when my computer _____(crash).
2 Sir Tim Berners-Lee _____(invent) the world wide web while he _____(work) in Geneva, Switzerland.
3 In 2004, Mark Zuckerberg _____(study) at Harvard University when he and three other students _____(create) Facebook.
4 I _____(finish) my homework, _____ (turn off) the computer and _____(go) to bed.
5 'Where _____(work) when they _____ (make) that discovery?'
'I don't know exactly. They _____(not work) in Europe – I'm sure of that.'
6 'What _____(do) at ten o'clock last night?'
'I _____(write) my blog.'

PRONUNCIATION

6a [3.2] *was/were* Listen to *was* and *were* in these sentences. How do you pronounce them?

1 I was living in a large house.
2 They stopped what they were doing.
3 'Was he working at UCLA?' 'Yes, he was.'
4 'Were you using the new computers?' 'Yes, we were.'
5 What were you doing at four o'clock yesterday afternoon?

6b Listen again and repeat the sentences above.

7 Choose a time (e.g. ten o'clock last night) and ask your classmates what they were doing at that time. Make a note of their answers. Then report to the class.

At ten o'clock last night, Kristina and Marina were doing their homework. Roman was doing online research.

SPEAKING

8 Interview your partner about how he/she uses the internet. Ask about these things and make notes of the answers. Do you use the internet in a similar way?
• when he/she first used the internet
• how long he/she spends on the internet every day – and at what times
• what he/she does on the internet – favourite websites / own blogs or website
• how he/she used the internet two years ago – is it the same as now?

READING AND SPEAKING

1 Discuss these questions in small groups.

1 How often do you watch the news on television? Which channels do you watch?
2 What are the big news stories at the moment?

2a What do you know about these news companies?

BBC World   Al Jazeera International
OneWorldTV   CNN   NowPublic

2b Read the article below from a British in-flight magazine and find out more about the news companies. Choose the best title (1–4) for the text.

1 The end of TV news
2 Choose the news
3 World news, global lies
4 Local news, real life

3a Complete these sentences with the names of the news companies in the text.

1 _____ and _____ are traditional, Western news broadcasters.
2 _____ is not a television company.
3 _____, _____ and _____ report some different stories from the western TV broadcasters.
4 _____, _____, _____ and _____ employ well-trained, professional reporters.
5 _____ does not usually pay its reporters.
6 _____ has a special interest in poor countries and their problems.

3b What do these words in the text refer to?

1 these (line 2)
2 both companies (line 8)
3 this company (line 14)
4 it (linc 16)
5 them (line 20)
6 this (line 21)

After a long flight, you finally arrive at the place where you can relax – your hotel room. You throw your bag on the bed, turn on the TV and watch an international news programme on a satellite channel that probably comes from the UK or the USA.

The main international broadcasters are BBC World and CNN. With an audience of over 1.5 billion people, **these** are popular channels that offer good-quality news programmes. In both companies, the journalists are experienced writers that produce journalism of a high standard.

5 However, there are alternative news channels which people watch because they want a less traditional or non-Western view on world events. Al Jazeera International, an Arabic company, and Russia Today are international channels that broadcast in English. **Both companies** say they give a fresh view on the big stories, and their experienced journalists often report from places where Western journalists do not
10 work, and so they give us stories that we don't normally see.

The internet offers more variety. OneWorldTV is an internet site where you can find stories about the developing world and human rights, rather than the usual stories about US politics and business. The writers for **this company** are often local people who
15 write the stories for free. This non-professional journalism is increasing, and **it** certainly offers more choice.

This increase in citizen journalism means that you too can write the news. Main news broadcasters often use photographs and eye-witness stories that members of the
20 general public send to **them**, especially when there is a dramatic breaking news story. Besides **this**, some blogs are popular sources of news, and the website NowPublic lets you write the stories with information that you get from anywhere, including from sites like Youtube, Flickr and Twitter.

25 So, next time you are in a hotel room, before you simply watch CNN, perhaps you should change channel, or turn on your laptop or even write the news yourself.

4 Personal reflection Discuss these questions with a partner. Give examples and explain your opinions.

1 Do you ever watch any of the international news channels or get your news from the internet? Do you follow the news in any other ways?
2 Which news channels or sites do you trust?
3 What are the advantages and disadvantages of non-professional journalism?
4 Do you have any experience as a citizen journalist?
5 Do you ever get your news from social networking sites?
6 What are the advantages and disadvantages of newspapers, TV and internet news?

VOCABULARY
NOUNS

5a Choose the correct word to complete each of these definitions.

1 A *journalist / journalism* is someone who writes reports for newspapers, news websites, television, magazines, television or radio.
2 *Journalist / Journalism* is the job of writing reports for television, news websites, magazines, newspapers or radio, or the subject that people study.

5b Put these nouns into two groups: A for the person and B for the job or subject.

art   artist   blogger   blogging   journalism
journalist   photographer   photography   politician
politics   psychologist   psychology   reporter
reporting   scientist   science

A: photographer

B: photography

5c 3.3 Mark the word stress on the words above. Then listen and check your answers.

GRAMMAR
RELATIVE PRONOUNS

6a A sentence can sometimes contain two pieces of information. This example tells us the journalists are experienced writers and the journalists produce journalism of a high standard.

The journalists are experienced writers that produce journalism of a high standard.

Identify the two pieces of information in each of these sentences.

1 BBC World and CNN are popular channels that make good-quality news programmes.
2 OneWorld is an internet site which has stories about the developing world and human rights.
3 The writers for this company are often local people who write the stories for free.
4 Their experienced journalists often report from places where Western journalists do not work.

6b Look at the sentences in Exercise 6a and complete these grammar notes.

1 You use _____ and _____ to link information about people.
2 You use _____ and _____ to link information about things.
3 You use _____ to link information about places.

6c How many more examples of this language can you find in the text?

➡ Language reference and extra practice, pages 106–107

7 Join these pairs of sentences.

1 Politicians are very important people.
  Politicians make the laws in a country.
2 The United Nations is a global organisation.
  The United Nations tries to solve world problems.
3 Nelson Mandela was a great leader.
  He made his country a fairer place.
4 I visited a hotel.
  Chairman Mao stayed in the hotel in 1965.

8 You often use relative pronouns to make definitions. Match 1–3 with a–c and join them using *who/that* or *which/that*.

1 A journalist is someone …
2 OneWorld is a company …
3 *Global* is an adjective …

a means 'international' or 'all over the world'.
b writes stories for television and newspapers.
c provides news about the developing world.

9 Work with a partner to complete a crossword.

Student A: Turn to page 139.
Student B: Turn to page 144.

SPEAKING

10a Prepare to tell your partner about a recent story from the news. Think about the people, places and events in the story. Make notes to help you remember the story and to organise your storytelling.

10b Tell your partner the news story. Try to use *who*, *which*, *that* and *where* to build your sentences. Take notes when you listen to your partner's story.

SITUATION

1 Do you watch these kinds of programme on TV? Describe some of your favourite ones.

game and quiz shows   current affairs programmes
cookery programmes   talent shows   chat shows
wildlife documentaries   lifestyle shows

2 **3.4** Listen to the introduction to a TV show, *Fame and Fortune*. Which of these things does the show include?

- Live music performance
- An interview with a politician
- Celebrity gossip
- Information about important businesses
- Consumer information

3 **3.5** Listen to the programme development team brainstorm ideas for *Fame and Fortune*. What ideas do they decide to include in the programme? What ideas do they decide not to include?

KEY LANGUAGE
MAKING SUGGESTIONS

4a **3.6** Complete the sentences below from the conversation in Exercise 3 with the words in the box. Then listen and check.

let's   any   about   don't   shall   anything
what   should   not

1 _____ ideas?
2 Why _____ we get some politicians on the programme?
3 Let's _____ interview them about politics.
4 _____ ask them about their lives.
5 _____ else?
6 We _____ have a live band on the programme.
7 What _____ interviewing rich people?
8 What else _____ we put in the programme?
9 _____ about something with animals?

4b Which of the sentences above *give* ideas or suggestions (G), and which *ask* for ideas (A)?

4c Look at Audio script 3.5 on page 151 and find more examples of this language. Notice the different sentence patterns after each key phrase. Then match the patterns in the box with the key phrases below.

subject + verb   verb (infinitive without *to*)
verb + *-ing*   noun phrase

1   Why don't + _____?
2   Let's not + _____
3   Let's + _____
4   We should + _____
5   What else shall + _____?
6   What about + _____?
7   What about + _____?

PRONUNCIATION

5a **3.7** Intonation in short questions **Listen to the two ways of saying** *Any ideas*? **Which one, a) or b), sounds most like a question?**

5b **3.8** **Listen and repeat these short questions.**
1   Anything else?
2   Any more ideas?
3   Any comments?
4   Any questions?

TASK
DESIGNING A SHOW

6a Work in a small group. You work in the programme development department of a TV channel. You are going to design a new weekly magazine show. The programme will be one hour long. Look at these groups and select your target audience for the show.

retired and elderly people   working adults
young teenagers   university students
foreign students and visitors   families

6b Individually, prepare for the planning meeting and get some ideas for your show. Look back at the language in Exercise 4a and prepare how you will give your suggestions.

USEFUL PHRASES	
Fine, but …	That's true.
I agree, but …	Perhaps that's not a good idea.
Exactly.	Great idea.
Really?	No, I don't think we should do that.

6c Regroup with your partners from Exercise 6a and have the planning meeting. Share your ideas and design the new show. Include a name for your show.

6d Tell other groups about your show. Make sure you explain your choices for the content of the show. Did the groups have similar or different ideas?

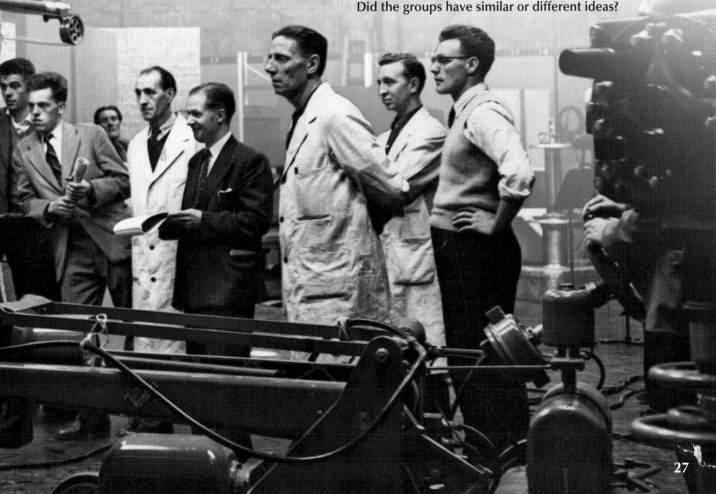

STUDY SKILLS
COLLABORATION: WORKING WITH OTHERS

1a Think about some of your experiences of working with other people outside the classroom. What did you like about working with others? Did you have any problems? How did you solve them?

I liked exchanging ideas with other people.

It was sometimes quite difficult for everyone to agree.

1b Think about some of the tasks in this book that you did with other students (for example, the scenario tasks in Units 1–3). Make a list of things you like about working in class with others, and things you don't like. Compare your ideas in small groups.

1c What should you do if you want to work well with others? Add two or three points to this list.

Listen carefully to others

Ask others for their opinions.

2 Body language is important when you work successfully with others. What do you understand by the term *body language*? Discuss with a partner.

3a ▶ 3 Watch the video without the sound. Look carefully at the speakers' body language. Do you think they are working well together? Why?/Why not?

3b Now watch the same video with the sound. What kind of things do the members of the group do when they want to speak?

4 Look at this list of things you do when you are working well in a group. Watch the video again and find examples of these things.

1   Checking that you understand something
2   Asking someone to explain something you don't understand
3   Agreeing with someone
4   Disagreeing (politely!) with someone
5   Showing interest in what someone says
6   Making suggestions
7   Asking others for their ideas
8   Asking others what they think about a topic
9   Remaining positive when the discussion is difficult

5 Evaluating How well do you think this group works together? Circle a number below, then summarise your answer in three or four sentences.

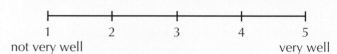

     1   2   3   4   5
not very well   very well

I think they are …

6a Sometimes you are asked to work with a partner or groups in your class. How can this help you to improve your English? Discuss in a group. Then turn to page 133 to check your answers.

6b What can you do to work better with others in future?

WRITING SKILLS
A TV PROGRAMME REVIEW

7 **Discuss these questions in small groups.**

1 What kind of TV programmes do you know?

news, drama, …

2 Where can you find reviews of TV programmes?
3 Do you read reviews of TV programmes?
Why?/Why not?

8 **We usually find these things in a review of a TV drama or film. What do you think is the best order for these things in a review? Discuss with a partner.**

1 a summary of the story
2 details of the main character(s)
3 a description of the place(s) where (and the time when) the action happens
4 a strong ending where the writer recommends (or does not recommend) the programme/series/film
5 comments on the actors' performances (and/or other opinions)
6 an interesting beginning

9a **The review on the right is about a political drama. Before you read it, check that you know the meaning of these words.**

government   leader   political party
general election   prime minister

9b **Read the review on the right. Is it positive or negative? Would you like to watch this series?**

9c **Read the text again and answer these questions.**

1 Do you think Nyborg is a pleasant character? Why?/Why not?
2 In what way are Nyborg and Fønsmark similar?
3 Why do you think BBC4 is showing this series again?

10a **Compare your answer to Exercise 8 with the review. Are there any differences?**

10b **What information do you find in each paragraph of the text?**

10c **A common mistake when writing a review is to write a lot about the story, but very little about your opinions of the programme. How many sentences in the review in Exercise 9b tell us the story of *Borgen*?**

11 **Summarising Look at the texts on the right about two TV programmes. Make them shorter by taking out two sentences from text 1 and three sentences from text 2. Keep the sentences with important information about each story.**

12 **Write a review for a website of a TV programme or series you saw recently. Alternatively, write a review of a film, play or book (novel).**

Borgen `BBC4`

Did you miss *Borgen* first time? Well, now there's another chance to see this first-class political drama from Denmark. *Borgen* means 'castle' in Danish, and refers to the building in Copenhagen which is the home of the government.

Borgen tells the story of Birgitte Nyborg, a 40-year-old politician who is the leader of the minor Moderate Party. After a general election, Nyborg shocks everyone – even herself – when she becomes Denmark's first female Prime Minister. But she must work successfully with others to stay in power.

Nyborg is an honest woman with a good sense of humour. She enjoys a warm family life, and the excellent scenes with her husband and two children are at the heart of the drama.

There are other strong female characters – for example, Katrine Fønsmark, the young TV journalist who interviews Nyborg.

Borgen is a modern and intelligent drama with great performances by the main actors, especially Sidse Babett Knudsen as Nyborg. See it – or see it again!

1

In the American comedy *A Fresh Start*, Cristina and DeeDee become good friends at work. Both of them are about 23 years old. They don't like their jobs – or their boss! Together, they decide to set up their own company.

2

There's a great new soap opera on Channel 6. *Then and Now* follows the lives of two families in the small town of Boxville. The town is famous for its many black cats. One of the families is quite poor, while the other is extremely rich. They live on opposite sides of the town. Before long, members of the two very different families meet – with surprising results!

4 Health

4.1 DOCTORS WITHOUT BORDERS

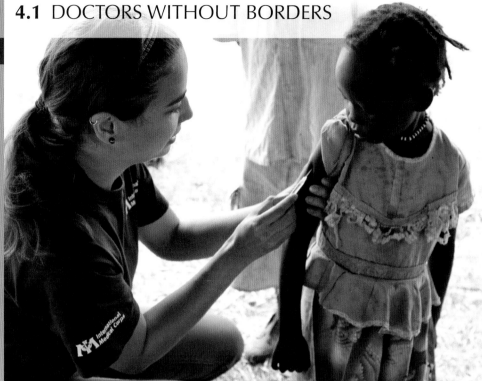

IN THIS UNIT

GRAMMAR
- present perfect (1)
- articles
- time expressions

VOCABULARY
- medical words
- reporting verbs
- health

SCENARIO
- giving advice and reasons
- giving advice about health issues

STUDY SKILLS
- guessing the meaning of unknown words

WRITING SKILLS
- an informal email (of thanks)

'The first wealth is health.' Ralph Waldo Emerson, 1803–1882, US writer

VOCABULARY
MEDICAL WORDS

1a Work with a partner. Which word is the odd one out in each group? Why? Use your dictionary if you need help.

1   a doctor   an optician   a clinic   a nurse
2   medicine   a dentist   an operation   a vaccination
3   a serious illness   a minor illness   a hospital   an injury

1b [4.1] Mark the word stress on the words above. Then listen and check.

READING

2a International Medi-Aid (IMA) is a healthcare charity that works in poor and disaster-hit areas of the world. On its website, there are regular audio reports from the places they are working in. Look at the list of podcasts for IMA and answer these questions.

1   Which podcasts are by and about people who provide care?
2   Which podcasts are about medical facilities?
3   Which podcast is about a financial problem?

2b Exploring facts Prepare your answers for these questions. Then discuss with your partner.

1   Why do you think:
    a)   Beverly often works for IMA in different countries?
    b)   IMA sometimes uses mobile clinics?
    c)   IMA is training local people in healthcare?
    d)   IMA training is only for treating minor illness?
2   What do you think are the positive and negative sides of the four facts in question 1?
3   What is your opinion of foreign charities and health workers providing healthcare in other countries?

International Medi-Aid

Podcast results 1–6

1   **Field diary: New life begins**
    A day in the life of one of our nurses, Beverly Timpleton, in Sri Lanka. She has worked in many different countries, but this is her most difficult position so far.

2   **Healthy teeth for the young**
    During their first week of action in rural areas, dentists in two new mobile clinics have treated more than 600 children.

3   **Working in the Congo**
    Miles Gallant, a doctor from London, talks about his current work with us in the Congo. He hasn't worked in a foreign country before.

4   **Hospital building continues**
    To date, our team in Sri Lanka has built four hospitals, providing healthcare to almost half a million people.

5   **Training local people in Kenya**
    During this year, we have trained 500 local people to care for people in their villages who have minor illnesses.

6   **Forced closure of mobile clinics in Ethiopia**
    We have closed our healthcare programme in Ethiopia because of a lack of funding.

LISTENING

3a 🔊 4.2 **Listen to four extracts and match them with the podcasts in Exercise 2 (1–6).**

3b Listen again and answer these questions.

1 How many IMA clinics were there in Africa last year?
2 How did Miles feel in the UK?
3 Why is the jungle clinic 'the only hope' for the villagers?
4 When did IMA decide to train local people?
5 When did the training course begin?
6 When does Vera's course end?
7 What caused the damage in Sri Lanka?
8 In how many clinics does Beverly work?

3c Look at Audio script 4.2 on page 151 and check your answers.

GRAMMAR
PRESENT PERFECT (1)

4a These sentences all describe completed actions. Underline the actions in each sentence.

1 I've worked in Kenya, Nepal and Peru.
2 On 1st January 2012, we decided to solve this problem.
3 So far, in my time here, I've probably saved about a hundred lives.
4 Last year, we ran ten health centres in Africa.

4b Answer these questions about the sentences above.

1 Which tense is each sentence in: past simple or present perfect?
2 Look at the past simple sentences. Which one is about a period of time in the past? Which one gives the exact time of the action?
3 Look at the present perfect sentences. Are they about finished or unfinished periods of time? What is the period of time in sentence 1? Do they give the exact time of the actions?
4 Match these time lines with the sentences.

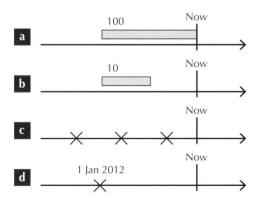

GRAMMAR TIP

You often use the present perfect to talk about actions that are completed before now. These actions are completed in a period of time that is unfinished. You do not say the exact time in the past of the action.

5a Time expressions **Which of these time expressions can we use with the present perfect?**

five months ago   last year   yesterday   this year
at five o'clock   today   in the last few days   never
this week   on December 20th   so far   to date

5b How do we make the present perfect (affirmative and negative sentences, questions and short answers)?

➡ Language reference and extra practice, pages 108–109

6 Complete these podcast summaries with the present perfect or past simple of the verbs in brackets. Underline the time expressions which helped you to decide which tense to use.

International
Medi-Aid IMA

Podcast results 1-6

1 A survivor's story One week ago, Asif _____ outside to collect some water. Seconds later, a bomb exploded. (go)

2 Training nurses So far this year, 110 local nurses _____ training courses in Aceh province. (complete)

3 Images of survival Last week, IMA _____ a special exhibition of photographs by survivors. (organise)

4 Healthier futures This year, we _____ two child nutrition clinics in Gaza and we hope to build two more next year. (build)

5 No deliveries Refugees in Darfur _____ any food supplies this month as the fighting continues. (not receive)

6 Soccer Aid Nearly 12,000 people _____ to raise vital funds for IMA at a charity football match on Christmas Day. (help)

SPEAKING

7a Complete the questions below with the verbs in the box. Ask and answer the questions with your partner.

see (x2)   read   give   visit

1 Have you _____ the dentist this year?
2 When did you last _____ an optician?
3 Have you ever _____ a doctor in another country?
4 Have you _____ stories in the news about organisations like IMA?
5 Have you ever _____ money to a charity?

7b You are going to find out about students' life experiences (what they have done in their lives). Turn to page 134.

SPEAKING AND READING

1 Discuss these questions in small groups.

1 Describe your usual diet. What do you eat that's good / not good for you?
2 When you were younger, was your diet different?

2a Sort these words into two groups: A (food and nutrition) and B (mental health and the mind).

carbohydrates   depression   poor concentration
junk food   vitamins   nuts   motivation
rice   brain   memory   salmon   mood
mental illness   sugar

2b The Scottish Health Authority (SHA) is planning a public health campaign about food and the mind. Read their report on this subject below and answer these questions.

1 Why does the SHA think this campaign is necessary?
2 Complete the summary below of the article with the words in the box.

concentration   healthy   illnesses   mental   research

Recent ¹_____ has shown that a ²_____
diet is good for your ³_____ health, from minor
issues such as ⁴_____ levels to serious
⁵_____ (e.g. depression).

3a Read the report again. How many of each thing (1–3) does the article mention?

1 types of food
2 mental health problems
3 research studies

3b Write a sub-heading for each paragraph in the *Research review* section of the report.

3c What do these words refer to in the report?

1 this food (line 9)
2 a serious mental health problem for the elderly (lines 21–22)
3 that (is probably not …) (line 27)
4 the two (lines 40–41)

VOCABULARY
REPORTING VERBS

4a Match the verbs in column A with verbs with similar meanings in column B.

A	B
say	feel
reveal	state
think	suggest
recommend	show

4b Find the examples of the above verbs in the report. Which word comes after the verbs?

FEED YOUR MIND

INTRODUCTION
We have known about the link between what we eat and our physical health for a long time. Recently, we have learned more about the link between our diet and our mind.

5 **RESEARCH REVIEW**
The Mental Health Foundation produced a report called Feeding Minds. The report states that the brain is a physical part of our body that needs the correct food to work properly, just like the heart. This food should contain
10 carbohydrates, vitamins and fish oil.

There is also research that shows how a good diet can improve the behaviour of children and their concentration (Tomlinson et al., 2009). Daniel Brown, the head teacher of Barnet School, says that after his school stopped

15 selling junk food, there was an increase in the students' concentration levels.

With regard to serious mental illnesses, Jacka (2010) and Sanchez-Villegas (2009) say that eating fruit, vegetables and fish helps to prevent depression, but eating a lot of sugar
20 makes depression more likely. Some research also reveals that a healthy diet can prevent Alzheimer's (a serious mental health problem for the elderly) (McCulloch and Ryrie, 2006).

However, many medical professionals feel that the research by Jacka and Sanchez-Villegas is early research,
25 and that we need to test their claims. Dr John Powell, a psychologist, thinks that although many of his patients with depression have a poor diet, that is probably not the reason for their illness.

4c Choose the best verb to complete each of these sentences.

1 The bar chart *shows / states* that sales changed over time.
2 The report *reveals / recommends* that we build a subway train system.
3 The numbers *think / show* that people travel more in the summer.
4 The author *feels / recommends* that things were difficult in the past.

5 Justifying opinion Discuss these questions in small groups. Use the language from Exercise 4 and your knowledge to justify your opinions.

1 Do you think there is a link between food and your mind? Do you know about any examples from your culture?
2 Does the food you eat sometimes affect your mood, e.g. a favourite dish, chocolate?
3 Do you eat much of the food mentioned in the report?
4 Is your usual diet healthy for both your mind and body? Can you improve it?
5 What other things do you think are good for your mind, e.g. sleep?

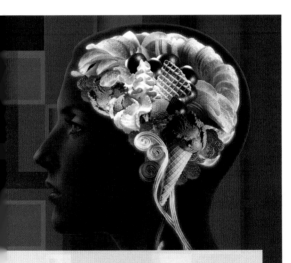

NUTRITION DETAILS

30 The research recommends that we eat particular food for particular mental health issues. To improve your memory, eat salmon and nuts. To improve your concentration, eat vegetables. If you have
35 problems sleeping, eat nuts. If depression is a problem, eat brown rice.

CONCLUSION

Overall, it seems clear that we need to eat healthy food for our mind. Although we do
40 not fully understand the link between the two, we suggest that we choose this as an important topic for publicity.

GRAMMAR
ARTICLES

6a Find these words and phrases in the report. Then use *a / an* or *no article* to complete the rules below and add examples.

a psychologist   an important topic   an increase
a report   junk food   vitamins

1 Use _____ with a singular noun (countable) to mention something for the first time.
2 Use _____ to talk about a person's job.
3 Use _____ with plural nouns, and uncountable nouns when they refer to people or things in general.

6b Find more examples in the report of when you use / don't use *a* and *an*.

> **GRAMMAR TIP**
>
> Use *the* when you talk about a specific/particular or unique noun.
> - *the brain*: unique (There is only one brain in our body.)
> - *the behaviour of children*: specific (Not everyone's behaviour)

6c Look at these examples from the report. Is *the* used because the noun is unique, or because it is specific?

1 the link between our diet and our mind (line 4)
2 the heart (line 9)
3 the head teacher of Barnet school (lines 13–14)
4 the students' (line 15)
5 the research by Jacka (lines 23–24)

↪ Language reference and extra practice, pages 108–109

7 Complete the gaps in these questions with *a/an/the* or leave them blank.

1 What was _____ last meal that you cooked or prepared?
2 Do you usually have _____ drink with your meals?
3 How often do you eat _____ chocolate?
4 In Britain, they say '_____ apple a day keeps the doctor away'? What does this mean? What _____ sayings and _____ traditions about _____ food and _____ health are there in your culture?
5 Do you agree with _____ conclusion of _____ SHA report? What _____ health publicity campaigns are there in your country?

SPEAKING AND WRITING

8 Ask your partner the questions in Exercise 7.

9 Write a short description of your typical diet. Include your healthy and unhealthy eating habits.

▶ MEET THE EXPERT

Watch an interview with Dr John Briffa, a doctor who specialises in nutrition, about brain food.
Turn to page 127 for video activities.

PREPARATION

1 Have you (or has someone you know) ever experienced any of these health and well-being problems? Do you know why you (he/she) had those problems? How did you (he/she) solve them?

- had headaches
- felt run-down – lacking energy and feeling tired
- felt homesick
- been unable to concentrate on studies or work
- felt stressed by exams or workload

SITUATION

2a `4.3` Universities often have Student Health and Well-Being Services which provide help and advice to students who have a range of worries, problems and minor health concerns. Mavis Much is a Health Officer at a university. Listen to two students talking to her, and complete Mavis's notes.

Name:	Abigail _____
Year:	Final
Subject:	_____
Problem:	Nervous about exams + not _____ well.
Background:	Studies all _____, _____ _____. Goes to bed at _____, gets up at _____. Has _____ meals a day. Drinks a lot of _____. Does _____ exercise.
Name:	Dane _____
Year:	_____
Subject:	_____
Problem:	Feels _____.
Background:	Not made many _____. Misses his mother and her _____. Only happy when goes to _____, goes there nearly _____ _____. Losing _____ in his studies. Wants _____ _____ _____.

2b What advice can you give the students in Exercise 2a?

2c `4.4` Listen to the advice which Mavis gives to the students, and complete her notes below. Was any of her advice the same as yours?

Reminders + −

ADVICE	REASON
Abigail	
Take more _____.	_____ a little.
Drink less _____.	
No coffee in the _____.	Coffee keeps you _____.
Don't take _____ pills.	
Dane	
Join a _____ club.	Make _____.
	Stop _____ _____ home.
_____ basketball.	American and _____
Change eating _____.	
Don't go to McDonald's	Need _____.
_____ _____.	
Join a cookery _____.	_____ to cook.

"I'M HERE TO HELP"

KEY LANGUAGE
GIVING ADVICE AND REASONS

3a **4.5** **Complete these sentences. Then listen and check.**

1 I think you _____ take more breaks during the day in _____ to relax a little.
2 You _____ drink a lot of coffee _____ it stops you from relaxing.
3 _____ drinking just two or three cups a day.
4 _____ you play sport, your mind will stop thinking about home.
5 And you _____ to change your eating habits.

3b **Answer these questions about the language above.**

1 Which phrases do you use to give a piece of advice?
2 Which phrases do you use to give the reasons for / explain your advice?

3c **Find more examples of these phrases in Audio script 4.4 on page 152.**

4a **Match these pieces of advice (1–6) with the reasons below (a–f). Then choose the correct linking word or phrase.**

1 You ought to eat some fruit every day *because / in order to*
2 You should go to the optician's *because / to*
3 You shouldn't play computer games all night *to / because*
4 Try changing your chair *in order to / because*
5 You should do some yoga *to / because*
6 Try eating a good breakfast *in order to / because*

a that gives you a lot of energy for the day.
b check your eyesight.
c it has a lot of vitamins.
d reduce your stress levels.
e that makes you tired in class.
f make your back better.

4b **Make logical connections. Which problems in Exercise 1 could the solutions above solve?**

PRONUNCIATION

5a Phrase stress and rhythm **Look at these phrases from Exercise 3a. Which words do you think are key words?**

1 during the day
2 drink a lot of coffee

5b **4.6** **Key words are usually stressed. Listen and check your ideas above.**

5c **4.7** **Which are the key words in these phrases? Listen and check. Practise saying the phrases.**

1 You should take more breaks.
2 If you play sport, …
3 Change your eating habits.
4 It has a lot of vitamins.
5 Reduce your stress levels.

TASK
GIVING ADVICE ABOUT HEALTH ISSUES

6a **Work with a partner.**

Student A: You are a health officer at a university. Prepare to interview and advise a student. Use the Key language and the Useful phrases on this page to help.

USEFUL PHRASES

What are you studying?
How can I help?
How long have you had this problem?

Student B: You are a university student. You are going to discuss your health problems with a health officer. Turn to page 148 and prepare to tell the health officer about your problems.

6b **Perform the role-play.**

7 **Change roles and repeat the role-play.**

Student A: Turn to page 140.
Student B: Prepare to be the health officer.

4.4 STUDY SKILLS
GUESSING THE MEANING OF UNKNOWN WORDS

1 Look at this statement. Do you think this is good advice?

Remember, when you're reading, you usually know a lot of words in the text. So be positive – concentrate mainly on those words. Don't panic about the words you don't know.

2a Which of these strategies do you use when you read a word that you do not know?

1   underline/highlight it
2   ignore it
3   try to guess the meaning and keep reading
4   immediately look it up in your dictionary
5   look it up in your dictionary if you see the same word two or three times and you can't guess its meaning
6   look it up in your dictionary if you can't guess the meaning, but you feel the word is important
7   ask your teacher or classmates
8   something else

2b Compare your methods with a partner. Which of the above are good ways of coping with new words, do you think?

3a Using grammar **Look at these sentences. What kind of word (noun, adjective, or verb) goes in each gap?**

1   This course has given me many _____ skills.
2   That doctor has probably saved about a hundred _____.
3   At the clinic, they _____ people with serious illnesses.

3b Think of some words that could go in the gaps above.

4a Sometimes you can understand if a sentence is positive or negative, even if you do not fully understand it. Look at these sentences. Which have a positive sense? Which are negative? Explain your choices.

1   She made a quick recovery, and the doctor discharged her two days early.

   quick recovery … two days early – positive

2   The scan shows that he has broken his arm.
3   The massive doses of painkillers made me sick.
4   Luckily, I found the crumpled prescription in my back pocket.

4b What kind of words (nouns, adjectives, etc.) are the words you do not know in Exercise 4a?

5 Using topic knowledge **Look at the nonsense words in these sentences. What do you think they mean?**

1   He survived the accident with only minor *gloobers*.   *gloobers = injuries*
2   She's very healthy. She has never spent a day in *tong* in her life.
3   I can't remember the exact details of his case. I need to check his medical *donks*.
4   Eating a good breakfast gives you a lot of *clest* for the day.

6a Read this text. What is the situation?

My health has been good in the last few years, but this morning I felt awful. I had a bad earache and a stomach ache and a pain in my chest, so I went to the local doctor. The waiting room was crowded. One man had a horrible red rash on his face. A woman was coughing all the time. A young man in a wheelchair had his leg in plaster. There were a lot of elderly people. They were probably waiting for their flu injections. I waited for ages. Finally, the doctor called my name. When I went into her room, she was sitting at the computer, with a stethoscope beside her.

6b Underline the words in the text that you do not know or are not sure about. Compare with a partner. Can you explain/ guess any words you don't know? Use the strategies on this page.

WRITING SKILLS
AN INFORMAL EMAIL

7 **Discuss these questions with a partner.**

1   How many emails do you receive a day? Do you read them all in full?
2   Tell your group about an email you received that made you happy.
3   Who do you send emails to? Why do you send those emails? How much do you usually write?
4   Do you pay attention to spelling and punctuation when you write emails?

8 **Inferring Read the informal email below and answer these questions. Use the ideas in this lesson to help you understand any difficult words or phrases.**

1   Why has Abi written this email?
2   Where do you think Abi is living at the moment?
3   What do you think is happening in Abi's bedroom at home?
4   What kind of relationship do you think Abi has with her mother?
5   How do you think Abi's mother felt when she read this email?

Subject: | Things are getting better   inbox 6

Hi Mum

Hope you're OK. Have you watched any of the tennis this week?

Thanks very much for that pile of mail. Most of it was junk, but there was one very important letter from the bank!

Anyway, this is basically to let you know I'm feeling a lot better about things now. On Monday, I went to see one of the Health Officers here at the uni. She was really helpful, though quite strict, too! She's given me some ideas to help me sleep. I've now cut out coffee in the evenings completely, and there's already a big difference. And ... guess what? I'm even thinking about doing some sport – but not until after the exams!

By the way, have those guys finished in my room yet? I can't wait to see what it looks like!

Thanks again for sending my mail. See you next month.

Love

Abi

---

9 **Which of these people can you send an informal email to?**

1   a brother or sister
2   a bank manager
3   a doctor
4   a friend

10a **Here are two features of informal writing:**

- informal vocabulary (e.g. *guys*)
- contractions (e.g. *I'm*)

Find other examples of these in the email.

10b **Find phrases in the email that you use when you want to:**

1   tell someone about something that you have just remembered
2   change the subject you are talking about.

10c **Can you find any other features of informal writing in the email?**

11 **Find one phrase in each box that we do not use in informal emails (or letters).**

Greetings

Hello   Hi   Dear Jane   Hiya   Dear Sir/Madam

Opening phrases

How's life?   How are things?   How are things going?
Hope you're OK/well.   How are you?
Thank you for your message of 26 May.
Hope everything's OK.   Hope all's well.

Endings

Take care   Yours faithfully   Bye for now   Love
See you soon   Cheers   With love   Love from

12a **Find the two examples of *thanks* in the email. Then decide if these statements are true or false.**

1   You use *thanks* with *for* + a noun (phrase) or a verb ending in *-ing*.
2   You can put other words after *thanks*, e.g. *very much, again*.

12b **After saying *thanks*, we often add another sentence for support. Match the phrases (1–4) with the supporting comments (a–d).**

1   Thanks for your advice.
2   Thanks for doing the shopping.
3   Thanks for dinner.
4   Thanks for the chocolates.

a   It's my turn next time!
b   They were delicious!
c   It was lovely.
d   It's been really useful.

13 **Look at these sentences. What does *'s* mean: *is*, *has* or the possessive (e.g. *Simon's health*)?**

1   She's had an operation.
2   It's a boy!
3   There's no problem with Danisha's eyesight.
4   The doctor's skills are very useful there.
5   John's broken his leg.

14 **Write an informal email to a friend. Choose either situation 1 or 2 below.**

1   Thank your friend for a present or for helping you to do something.
2   Tell your friend about something that has happened in your life recently.

5 Natural world

5.1 ISLANDS

A

IN THIS UNIT

GRAMMAR
• comparisons
• expressions of quantity

VOCABULARY
• landscapes: nouns and adjectives
• nouns and verbs (1) (*damage* n/vb)

SCENARIO
• discussing photo selections
• giving reasons and making choices

STUDY SKILLS
• correcting your writing

WRITING SKILLS
• writing paragraphs (comparative essay organisation)

'My mission is to create a world where we can live in harmony with nature.' Jane Goodall, 1934– , British naturalist

VOCABULARY

LANDSCAPES

1a How many of these things can you see in the photos (A–C)?

beach	cliff	coast	forest	hill
island	lagoon	lake	rock	peak
mountain	sand	wave	sea	river

1b Which of these adjectives do you often use with the words above?

cold	deep	high	long	sandy
steep	tropical	warm		

a sandy beach

1c Discuss these questions with a partner.

1   What do you think of when you think of an island?

I think of a tropical island with sandy beaches and a warm blue sea …

2   Which islands have you visited (in your own country or abroad)? Describe them.

3   Which islands would you like to visit? What do you know about them?

4   The places in the photos are all islands. Where in the world do you think they are?

READING

2a Read the text. Are these sentences true or false? If false, say why.

1   There is a single mountain.
2   The water in the lagoon isn't very deep.
3   The colour of the water is the same everywhere.
4   You can drive round Bora Bora very quickly because it's a small island.

2b Collaboration Work with a partner. Read the text again and use the information to draw a simple map of Bora Bora. Compare your map with the one on page 134.

> **TROPICAL ISLANDS**
>
> # Bora Bora
>
> *Many people have called it the most beautiful island in the world – a paradise of clear blue water and white sandy beaches in the Pacific Ocean.*

On the main island there are green hills and two impressive peaks. At 727m, Mount Otemanu is the highest point. The main island has a large ring of smaller islands around it. In between is the calm water of the lagoon.

The lagoon is the most important feature of Bora Bora and is three times bigger than the main island. The water is shallow and transparent, with an amazing number of different blues. You can go on trips to feed the sharks and friendly rays.

The town of Vaitape is on the east coast of the main island. There is an airport on a smaller island north of the main island. You can drive round Bora Bora in about an hour (it's only 6km long and 3.5km wide), but it's better to travel by bike. When you're thirsty, stop for a coconut drink. A man cuts off the top of your coconut with a huge knife!

LISTENING

3a 5.1 **Listen to a TV programme about islands. What do these numbers refer to?**

Greenland: 1,290; 85%; 1.5km; 55,000

Great Britain: 3; 60 million

Madagascar: 100 million; 18 million; 50

3b Look at these statements. Can you remember which island each one refers to? Listen again and check.

1 It's popular with tourists.
2 The animals and plants are different from other places.
3 There are big differences in climate between different parts of the island.
4 Its name doesn't describe it well.
5 There are big problems for the animals.

3c Which island(s) from the TV programme would you like to visit? Why? Discuss with two or three other students.

GRAMMAR
COMPARISONS

4 Underline the comparisons in the text on Bora Bora.

smaller islands   the most beautiful island

5 Complete these extracts from the listening with the comparative or superlative form of the adjectives in brackets. Then look at Audio script 5.1 on page 152 and check.

1 In the south, it's hot and dry, but the climate is _____ in the middle of the island. (cool)
2 The island's _____ animals are the lemurs. (famous)
3 Great Britain is _____ many of its European neighbours. (crowded)
4 Wales and the north of England are hilly, while the south and east of England are _____. (flat)
5 Greenland is _____ island in the world. (big)
6 Madagascar is _____ fourth _____ island in the world. (large)

⟼ Language reference and extra practice, pages 110–111

6a *as … as* **Look at this sentence and answer the questions below.**

About 50,000 people live around the coast, where the climate is not **as** cold **as** in the centre.

1 Which part of the island is cold?
2 Which part is *very* cold?

6b Choose the correct form. Look at Audio script 5.1 if necessary.

1 You use *as … as / not as … as* to say that two things are the same.
2 You use *as … as / not as … as* to talk about differences between things.

6c Complete these sentences using (*not*) as … as and the adjective in brackets.

1 Greenland is _not as green as_ Great Britain. (green)
2 The south of England is _not as hilly as_ the north of England. (hilly)
3 Parts of Great Britain are _as beautiful as_ its European neighbours. (beautiful)
4 In Bora Bora, the main island is _not as important as_ the lagoon. (important)

7 *Adjectives* **Talk about the four islands using the adjectives in the box.**

beautiful   calm   cheap   exciting   impressive
interesting   magical   peaceful   pleasant
popular   romantic   strange   wild

I'm sure Bora Bora is more romantic than Greenland.

I think Greenland isn't as wild as Madagascar.

SPEAKING

8a Long turn taking Think of two places you know and prepare to talk about them for one minute, describing and comparing their features.

8b Work in small groups. Tell your group about your places. Ask your partners about their places.

I'd like to tell you about two different parts of Spain. In the north, there are some high mountains and forests. The north is cooler and greener than the south …

READING

1 Can you name the animals in the photos (A–E) below? Have you ever seen any of these animals? What do these animals eat?

2a Read the magazine article below and choose the best summary.

1   It is about the problems that new animals face in new environments.
2   It is about how foreign animals affect local animals and environments.
3   It is about the similarities between the natural environment and the business world.

2b Read the article again and complete this table.

Animal	Where from?	Invaded where?	Problem caused?
grey squirrels			
red deer			
rabbits			
apple snails			

3a Read the article again and answer these questions.

1   What do you think happens to the small food shop when the supermarket starts business?
2   Is the red squirrel like the small shop or the supermarket?
3   How did the grey squirrel come to England?
4   Do all invasive animals cause the extinction of native animals?
5   Are there more large animal invaders than small ones?

3b Thinking beyond the text Discuss these questions.

1   Why do you think the apple snail doesn't cause many problems in Europe?
2   What do you think are the 'obvious reasons' for the fact that the amount of animal invasion is increasing?
3   Can you think of any examples of border controls?
4   Are there any problems with invasive species in your country?

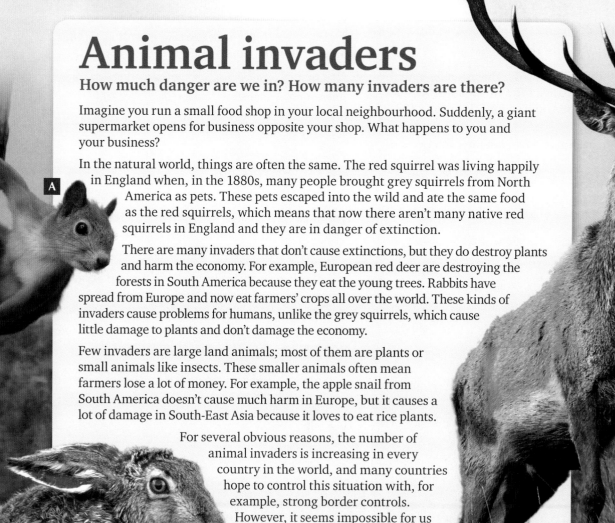

Animal invaders
How much danger are we in? How many invaders are there?

Imagine you run a small food shop in your local neighbourhood. Suddenly, a giant supermarket opens for business opposite your shop. What happens to you and your business?

In the natural world, things are often the same. The red squirrel was living happily in England when, in the 1880s, many people brought grey squirrels from North America as pets. These pets escaped into the wild and ate the same food as the red squirrels, which means that now there aren't many native red squirrels in England and they are in danger of extinction.

There are many invaders that don't cause extinctions, but they do destroy plants and harm the economy. For example, European red deer are destroying the forests in South America because they eat the young trees. Rabbits have spread from Europe and now eat farmers' crops all over the world. These kinds of invaders cause problems for humans, unlike the grey squirrels, which cause little damage to plants and don't damage the economy.

Few invaders are large land animals; most of them are plants or small animals like insects. These smaller animals often mean farmers lose a lot of money. For example, the apple snail from South America doesn't cause much harm in Europe, but it causes a lot of damage in South-East Asia because it loves to eat rice plants.

For several obvious reasons, the number of animal invaders is increasing in every country in the world, and many countries hope to control this situation with, for example, strong border controls. However, it seems impossible for us to bring such animal invasions to a stop, perhaps because changes are always part of nature.

VOCABULARY
NOUNS AND VERBS (1)

4a Many words are both nouns and verbs, without any change in form. Look at these examples. In each sentence, is *damage* a noun or a verb?

1 Grey squirrels don't **damage** the economy.
2 Apple snails cause a lot of **damage** in Asia.

4b These words can be both nouns and verbs. Are they nouns, verbs or both in the article? Underline the examples that you find.

shop	cause	harm	plant
hope	control	stop	change

4c Are the nouns in Exercises 4a and 4b countable (C) or uncountable (U)? What do you know about the grammar of countable and uncountable nouns? With which can you use *a/an/the*? Which have plural forms?

GRAMMAR
EXPRESSIONS OF QUANTITY

5a Which of these words and phrases mean a large quantity/number/amount, and which mean the opposite?

a lot of	few	little	several	many	much

5b You can use *a lot of* with both countable and uncountable nouns. When do you use the other words above? Find and underline the examples in the article.

6 Are these statements true or false? Use the examples you underlined in the article to help you.

1 You never use *much* in questions.
2 You often use *many* in positive sentences.
3 You don't usually use *much* in positive sentences. Instead, you use *a lot of*.
4 You never use *much* in negative sentences.
5 You can use *many* in questions and negative sentences.

➡ Language reference and extra practice, pages 110–111

7 Complete this paragraph with *much, many, a lot of, little* or *few*.

There are ¹ _many_ animals that are invaders, but perhaps there are ² _____, if any, invaders that are worse than humans. Two hundred thousand years ago, there were very ³ _____ humans; now there are nearly six billion of them. Unfortunately, there isn't ⁴ _____ information about the early history of this species, but it seems certain that the first humans came from Ethiopia in east Africa. After ⁵ _____ thousands of years (150–180), humans were living on every continent on Earth.

How ⁶ _____ damage have these invaders caused? Unfortunately, they have caused ⁷ _____ damage. They have destroyed ⁸ _____ native plants and animals. Before humans developed industry in the 19th century, there was ⁹ _____ pollution. Now, there is ¹⁰ _____ pollution and it is causing ¹¹ _____ harm to the global environment. It seems that humans need to change ¹² _____ things about their lifestyle in order to survive.

> **GRAMMAR TIP**
>
> In spoken and informal written English, you often use *not a lot of, not many* and *not much* instead of *few* and *little*, e.g. *There aren't a lot of students in my class. There aren't many cinemas in my city. There isn't much time left.*

SPEAKING

8a Compare your life with your partner's. First use the sentence beginnings (or similar ones) to make true sentences about you. If you need some help with ideas, turn to page 131.

In my country,	there are many / a lot of / few …
In my city,	there's a lot of / little …
In my college,	there aren't many / a lot of …
In my workplace,	there isn't a lot of / much …
In my house,	
I	have got many / a lot of …
People in my family	haven't got many / much …
	spend a lot of time …
	don't spend a lot of time …

8b Now turn your sentences into questions and interview your partner to find out if his/her life is similar to yours.

Are there many dangerous animals in your country? Give some examples.

What do you spend a lot of time doing? Why do you do that?

D

E

SITUATION

1a Look at the website on page 43. What kind of organisation is it for?

1 a business
2 a charity
3 an academic institution
4 a government department

1b Which link (A–E) do you click on for the following information?

1 people who kill animals illegally
2 special accommodation for animals
3 caring for ill animals
4 animals that are not free
5 saving animals from danger

2a 5.2 The AAI Website Manager, Neil, and the Communications Director, Katie, are choosing some photos for the new AAI website animal rescue page. They have each brought two pictures to discuss. Listen to their conversation and answer these questions.

1 In what order do they discuss the photos (A–D)?
2 Which two photos do they most like?
3 Which one of the links (A–E) on the website home page are they choosing a photo for?

2b Listen again and take notes. What comments do they make about each picture?

3a Work in small groups and discuss these questions.

1 What do you think of the reasons they give about using each picture? Are they good reasons? Why?/Why not?
2 Which picture from their first two choices is the best one to use, in your opinion? Why?

3b 5.3 Listen to Katie and Neil make their final choice. Is it the same as yours?

KEY LANGUAGE
JUSTIFYING CHOICES

4a 5.4 Complete these sentences from the conversation. Then listen and check.

1 … in this one, in the foreground, you can _____ three whales that are …
2 … there _____ some people who are trying to help them.
3 … in the background, loads of people are _____.
4 I like the _____ it shows a team of people who …
5 … they _____ very professional …
6 … this one _____ very unusual.
7 … we need to create the right _____ for our charity.
8 In the first picture, the message is _____.
9 I've got two pictures of people _____ are saving sea birds …

4b Answer these questions about the sentences above.

1 Which tense do we use to describe someone's actions in a picture?
2 What type of word do we use after the verb *look*?
3 Underline the phrases for describing the position of something in a picture.
4 Look at sentences 2 and 9. What are the two pieces of information in each?
5 Look at Audio script 5.2 on page 152 and find examples of comparatives and superlatives.

4c Which sentences in Exercise 4a give facts, and which give opinions or ideas?

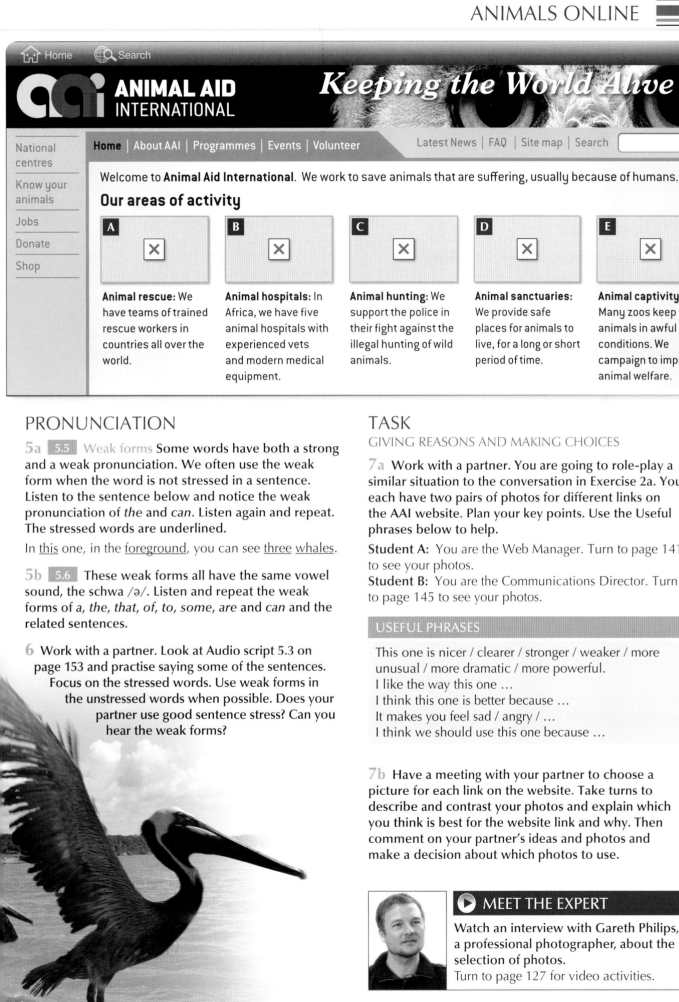

🏠 Home   🔍 Search

ai ANIMAL AID INTERNATIONAL

Keeping the World Alive

National centres	**Home**	About AAI	Programmes	Events	Volunteer	Latest News	FAQ	Site map	Search	

Know your animals

Jobs

Donate

Shop

Welcome to **Animal Aid International**. We work to save animals that are suffering, usually because of humans.

Our areas of activity

A ✕

B ✕

C ✕

D ✕

E ✕

Animal rescue: We have teams of trained rescue workers in countries all over the world.

Animal hospitals: In Africa, we have five animal hospitals with experienced vets and modern medical equipment.

Animal hunting: We support the police in their fight against the illegal hunting of wild animals.

Animal sanctuaries: We provide safe places for animals to live, for a long or short period of time.

Animal captivity: Many zoos keep animals in awful conditions. We campaign to improve animal welfare.

PRONUNCIATION

5a 〔5.5〕 Weak forms Some words have both a strong and a weak pronunciation. We often use the weak form when the word is not stressed in a sentence. Listen to the sentence below and notice the weak pronunciation of *the* and *can*. Listen again and repeat. The stressed words are underlined.

In <u>this</u> one, in the <u>foreground</u>, you can see <u>three</u> <u>whales</u>.

5b 〔5.6〕 These weak forms all have the same vowel sound, the schwa /ə/. Listen and repeat the weak forms of *a*, *the*, *that*, *of*, *to*, *some*, *are* and *can* and the related sentences.

6 Work with a partner. Look at Audio script 5.3 on page 153 and practise saying some of the sentences. Focus on the stressed words. Use weak forms in the unstressed words when possible. Does your partner use good sentence stress? Can you hear the weak forms?

TASK

GIVING REASONS AND MAKING CHOICES

7a Work with a partner. You are going to role-play a similar situation to the conversation in Exercise 2a. You each have two pairs of photos for different links on the AAI website. Plan your key points. Use the Useful phrases below to help.

Student A: You are the Web Manager. Turn to page 141 to see your photos.
Student B: You are the Communications Director. Turn to page 145 to see your photos.

USEFUL PHRASES

This one is nicer / clearer / stronger / weaker / more unusual / more dramatic / more powerful.
I like the way this one …
I think this one is better because …
It makes you feel sad / angry / …
I think we should use this one because …

7b Have a meeting with your partner to choose a picture for each link on the website. Take turns to describe and contrast your photos and explain which you think is best for the website link and why. Then comment on your partner's ideas and photos and make a decision about which photos to use.

▶ MEET THE EXPERT

Watch an interview with Gareth Philips, a professional photographer, about the selection of photos.
Turn to page 127 for video activities.

STUDY SKILLS
CORRECTING YOUR WRITING

1 Developing self-awareness **Which of these sentences are true for you?**

1 I always check my writing carefully when I've finished.
2 I read my teacher's comments and corrections carefully.
3 When my teacher gives back my work, the only thing I look at is my mark.
4 I look at my mistakes, but never remember them.
5 After my teacher gives back my work, I often rewrite it to make it better.

2 Match these common types of mistake with the sentences below.

grammar   vocabulary   spelling   punctuation
word order   leaving words out

1 That's an interesting idea.
(marked with ')

2 Greenland is the ~~bigger~~ island in the world.
biggest

3 Great Britain is ~~as not~~ cold as Greenland.
not as

4 These animals have caused a lot ∧ damage.
of

5 The situation is bad, but it isn't ~~useless~~.
hopeless

6 Their ~~advise~~ was very ~~helpfull~~.
advice   helpful

3a Word order **Change the position of one word in each sentence to make it correct.**

1 A mountain bigger than a hill is.
2 Are many dangerous animals there in your country?
3 Pollution damages the environment natural.
4 What you can see in the first picture?

3b Add one word to each sentence to make it correct. Are the missing words similar in any way?

1 It's fourth biggest island in the world.
2 These animals difficult to control.
3 Great Britain is crowded than many other countries.
4 This picture shows team of people.

3c Punctuation **Correct the punctuation in this piece of writing. Use full stops and capital letters, and take out unnecessary commas.**

the natural world is very important to us and we

must be careful, not to destroy it or damage it,

today, many beautiful places are in danger, from

greenland to madagascar

4a Look at this student's writing. The teacher uses a correction code. Correct the mistakes.

Gr = grammar   WW = wrong word (vocabulary)
Sp = spelling   WO = word order
∧ = missing word   P = punctuation

            Sp   *P*
Many mountins are impressive and magical, but its
                                  WW
important ∧ remember that they can also have
                            Gr
dangerous. If we climbing them, we should make sure,
           P   *WO*
for example that we have the equipment correct.

4b Read the rest of the student's work. Look for mistakes and write the correct symbol above the mistake. Then check on page 135.

The wether can change very quick and it's easy lose

your way. If you don't have much experiment, its

better go with someone who can you guide. If you

have any difficulties.

Eyjafjallajökull

WRITING SKILLS
WRITING PARAGRAPHS

5 Discuss these questions with a partner.

1 What is a paragraph?
2 How long are paragraphs?
3 Why do we use paragraphs when we write?

6 Look back at the texts on pages 38 and 40. How many paragraphs are there?

7 Discuss these questions with a partner.

1 Are there any volcanoes in your country? Are they famous?
2 Have you ever been up a volcano? What do you remember about it?
3 If not, would you like to go up a volcano? Why?/ Why not?
4 We use special terms to talk about volcanoes. Do you know what these words mean?

active   cone   dormant   erupt   an eruption

8 Paragraph organisation **Read this paragraph about a volcano in Iceland. Then put the points below (a–h) in the order they appear in the paragraph.**

> *Eyjafjallajökull* (pronounced: eh-a-fyat-la-yo-kutl) is an active volcano near the south coast of Iceland. It's 1,666m high. This means it's not in fact one of the largest volcanoes on the island. Also, it's not as dangerous as its neighbour, *Katla*, about 25km away. But in 2010, it erupted and caused a lot of problems for air traffic in Europe.

a how dangerous it is   e location
b effects of recent eruption   f name   *1*
c height   g size comparison
d date of recent eruption   h active or dormant?

9 How is the information in the paragraph organised? Put these points in the correct order. Why is this a good order?

a the eruption
b general information about the volcano
c comparison with other volcanoes

10a Topic sentences **The topic sentence of a paragraph tells us the topic of the paragraph. It is usually the first sentence of the paragraph. What is the topic sentence in the paragraph in Exercise 8?**

10b Look at these topic sentences. What information do you think we can find in the rest of the paragraph? Think of two or three points.

1 Russia is the world's largest country.
2 My favourite photo shows a family holiday when I was about ten years old.

11 Reference words **Look at the use of *it* and *its* in the paragraph in Exercise 8. Then improve this paragraph about Mount Fuji by using *it* and *its*.**

> Mount Fuji is perhaps the world's most famous volcano. Mount Fuji is about 100km from Toyko, in Japan. Mount Fuji is 3,776m high, and Mount Fuji's shape is almost perfect – a cone with quite steep sides. Mount Fuji is a dormant volcano which last erupted in 1707.

12 Use these notes to write a paragraph about the volcano Mauna Loa. Think about the best order for the points, then join them up, and use reference words (*it*, *its*).

> Location: Hawaii, Pacific Ocean
> Height: 4,170 metres
> Name: Mauna Loa
> Last eruption: 1984
> Active or dormant: active
> Shape: quite flat
> Size: largest active volcano in world

13 Write a paragraph about a natural feature in your country, or a country you know well, e.g. a mountain, lake or river.

Mount Fuji

Mauna Loa

45

6 Society and family

6.1 FUTURE OPPORTUNITY

IN THIS UNIT

GRAMMAR
- *will*, *might* and *may* for predictions
- first conditional

VOCABULARY
- nouns and verbs (2) (*consumer* vs *consume*)
- family
- negative adjectives (*un-* and *-less*)

SCENARIO
- expressing opinion
- having a discussion

STUDY SKILLS
- critical thinking

WRITING SKILLS
- a short article (answering a set question)

'I know I want to have children while my parents are still young enough to take care of them.' Rita Rudner, 1953– , US comedian

SPEAKING

1 Are these statements true about your country?

1 People retire at a younger age than 30 years ago.
2 More people go on holiday abroad than 20 years ago.
3 Nowadays, many people are using robots in their homes.
4 Most people spend more time on the internet than with real people.

READING

2a Read the IFA advert. Who uses the institute and its services: politicians, business people or academics? Why?

2b Find words in the advert that mean:

1 someone who studies the future
2 fashions, or changes over time
3 someone who puts money into a business
4 a chance to do something; a possibility of doing something

VOCABULARY

NOUNS AND VERBS (2)

3a Find these words in the advert. Are they verbs or nouns?

consumer	information	prediction	investor
improve	analysis	needs	advice ⁽ⁿ⁾ retire profit

advise (v)

3b What are the verbs for the above nouns, and the nouns for the above verbs?

consumer (noun, person), ...

3c Complete this description of the IFA with a noun or verb from Exercise 3a and 3c.

The IFA ¹p_____ future trends and ²a_____ business people so that they can ³invice well and ⁴improve their chances to make a good ⁵profit. The IFA ⁶analysis key data and ⁷information about society, e.g. the age of ⁸retirement and ⁹consumer behaviour, and it also considers what people are likely to ¹⁰need.

46

LISTENING

4a 🔲 6.1 **Listen to a meeting between Susan, a futurologist, and Patrick, a business investor. Tick the future changes she discusses.**

1 domestic use of technology
2 longer lives
3 use of the internet
4 people working from home
5 leisure activities and travel

4b **Listen again and complete Patrick's notes.**

* Main trends are about ¹_____ and ²_____.
* In 15 years' time, more than a ³_____ of people over 55, also people live ⁴_____.
* In 2030, more over-65s than ⁵_____.
* Fewer party and adventure holidays, more holidays on ⁶_____.
* Robots: to ⁷_____, to ⁸_____, to do the gardening.
* Currently, robot technology is⁹_____.
* ¹⁰_____ important in a few ways

4c **Contextualising information Discuss in groups.**

1 Does your country have any of the trends that Susan discusses?
2 Do you think older people want to travel and go on activity holidays?
3 Why does Susan use 'cruise ships' as an example?
4 What do you think of the three robot examples that she gives?
5 How is the internet important for the elderly?

GRAMMAR

WILL, MIGHT AND MAY FOR PREDICTIONS

5a 🔲 6.2 **Complete the sentences below from the meeting with the words in the box. Then listen and check.**

definitely (x2)   might   may   will
won't   probably

1 These older people _____ live for much longer – we know that from the statistics.
2 They _____ live until they're 95, or even 100.
3 That _____ won't be good for business.
4 I'm sure they _____ have much money.
5 These people will _____ need things to do with this extra time, for sure.
6 They _____ also want activity holidays, but that'll depend on their health.
7 They _____ won't go bungee-jumping.

5b **Answer these questions about the sentences in Exercise 5a.**

1 In which sentences is the speaker certain that his/her idea about the future is true?
2 In which sentences is the speaker less certain?
3 What verb form do you use after *will*, *might* and *may*?
4 Do you usually put adverbs (e.g. *definitely*) before or after *will*? Do you put them before or after *won't*?

➡ Language reference and extra practice, pages 112–113

5c **Correct the mistakes in these sentences.**

1 He might lives to the age of ninety.
2 Many people will probably to work from home.
3 I will live definitely in my own country.
4 There won't probably be big families.

6a **What do you think will happen to society in twenty years' time? Choose the correct word to complete your predictions.**

1 *More / Fewer* people than now will leave my country to find work.
2 People *will definitely / may* spend more time using the internet than watching TV.
3 *More / Fewer* people will probably live alone.
4 Most people *will / won't* retire at the age of fifty-five.
5 The differences between young and old people will probably be *greater / smaller*.
6 People will have *more / less* free time.

6b **Compare your ideas with a partner and explain your predictions. Which of the predictions are positive or negative for your country?**

SPEAKING

7a **Make some predictions for the future. Choose three or four topics from this box. What will your life, your country and the world be like ten years from now?**

education and work   technology and transport
health and lifestyle   sports and entertainment
business and trade   nature and the environment

7b **In small groups, discuss and explain your predictions.**

What predictions did you make about … ?

I think I'll buy an electric car this year or next.

More people will go to university, and they may study in English.

WRITING

8 **Write one or two paragraphs about your predictions for your society and country. Use your ideas in Exercise 7 to help you plan.**

VOCABULARY AND SPEAKING

1 Work with a partner. How many words can you think of for people in families? How many people are there in your (immediate) family?

parents, children, …

2a What age do you think these people are?

an adolescent   a middle-aged person   a young adult
a person in his/her mid-thirties   a child
an elderly person   a teenager   a retired person

2b What is the best age to:

1   move out of your parents' home?
2   have children?
3   be a grandparent?

READING

3a Match these words with their definitions below.

birth rate   childcare   employer
old-fashioned   responsible   suitable

1   not modern
2   you did it or caused it
3   a person or company that pays you to work for them
4   right for a particular purpose or situation
5   when someone looks after children while the parents are at work
6   the number of births for every 100 or 1,000 people in a particular year and place

3b Read the newspaper article below and complete this sentence in six or seven words.

This article is about …

3c How is the article organised? Put these topics in order (1–4).

a   reasons for the low birth rate
b   possible solutions to the problem
c   reaction to the possible solutions
d   facts about the low birth rate

3d Read the article again. Are these sentences true or false? Correct the false ones.

1   Only 40% of German female graduates have had children.
2   German women have an average of 1.41 children.
3   Few parents have more than one child.
4   A university professor believes that German employers do not have modern attitudes.
5   The government will pay parents 1,800 euros a month so the father can take time off work.
6   Ms von der Leyen's ideas are not popular with everyone.

4 Evaluating and predicting Answer these questions.

1   What do you think of Ms von der Leyen's plan?
2   What are the advantages and disadvantages of a small/big family?
3   How important is family life in your country?
4   How do you think the family will change in the future?

Germany: What future for the family?

Germany has one of the highest percentages of childless women in the world. Thirty per cent of German women have not had children, and this figure rises to nearly 40% among female graduates. Germany's Labour Minister, Ursula von der Leyen, has said that if the birth rate does not go up, Germany will die.

Germany's birth rate is one of the lowest in Europe, with an average of 1.41 children per woman, compared with 1.67 in Sweden and 1.91 in the UK. German mothers are also (with British mothers) the oldest, with an average age of 30 when they have their first child – and most parents choose to have only one child.

According to Professor Norbert Schneider of Mainz University, the reasons for Germany's low birth rate include poor childcare, a school day that still ends at 1 p.m. for many children, and old-fashioned attitudes among employers. In addition, many German women are already in their mid-thirties when they finish university and get a good job.

Ms von der Leyen, a mother of seven, believes that another difficulty is that some women cannot find a suitable man. 'Uncertain' men (who are unsure about becoming fathers) are also responsible for the low birth rate, she claims.

The minister has developed a plan to encourage people to have more children. First of all, if parents need private childcare, they will get help from the government, by paying less tax.

Secondly, families will get up to 1,800 euros a month from the government if men stay at home for two months after the birth of a new child.

But some men, even in the minister's own political party, are unhappy with this last idea. Professor Schneider says that in Germany it is acceptable for women to take time off to have children. However, if a man takes time off work to look after a new child, his career will be over. The typical family picture is very much alive in Germany, he said. Women look after the children while men go out to work.

VOCABULARY
NEGATIVE ADJECTIVES

5a We can use *un-* and *-less* to make adjectives. *Un-* means 'not' and *-less* means 'without'. Make negative adjectives of these words. Add an example if possible.

1 child*less*   6 hope*less*
2 *un*sure   7 kind
3 care*less* to make worse 8 lucky
4 *un*comfortable   9 use*less*
5 home*less*   10 *un*usual

childless: childless women, unsure: unsure about …

5b Choose an adjective from Exercise 5a to complete these sentences.

1 Big families are _____ in Germany.
2 It is dangerous for _____ people to sleep outside in winter.
3 The chairs in our living room are very hard – they're so _____!

5c Write questions with four of the negative adjectives. Then ask and answer the questions with your partner.

GRAMMAR
FIRST CONDITIONAL

6a You can use *if* to talk about the result of a possible future action. Look at the sentence halves below and match these labels with the two correct sections (1–3 and a–c).

main clause (result)   *if*-clause (condition)

1 If the father stays at home for two months,
2 If parents need private childcare,
3 If the birth rate does not go up,

a they will get help from the government.
b Germany will have a serious problem.
c families will get 1,800 euros a month.

6b Match the beginnings (1–3) and endings (a–c) above to complete three sentences.

6c Look at the sentences in Exercise 6a and complete these rules.

if-clause: *if* + _____
main clause: *will / will not (won't)* + _____ without *to*

> **GRAMMAR TIP**
>
> You can change the order of the *if*-clause and main clause in the sentence. Only use a comma when you start the sentence with *if*.

➥ Language reference and extra practice, pages 112–113

7 Complete these sentences with the correct form of the verbs in brackets.

1 If I _*see*_ (see) him, I _'ll tell_ (tell) him the news.
2 She _will be_ (be) ill if she _doesn't rest_ (not rest) more.
3 What _will you do_ (you do) if you _don't pass_ (not pass) your next exam?
4 We _won't arrive_ (not arrive) on time if we _don't hurry_ (not hurry) up.
5 If you _don't move_ (not move) your car, I _won't be_ (not be) able to park.
6 I _'ll do_ (do) the washing-up if I _have_ (have) time.

> **GRAMMAR TIP**
>
> Use *might* instead of *will* when you are less sure that something will happen.
> *If the birth rate does not go up, that country **might** die.*

PRONUNCIATION

8a `6.3` Contractions **Listen to the sentences from Exercise 7. Listen again and repeat.**

8b Think of things that you will, or might, do today / tomorrow / at the weekend, etc.

If I have time, I'll wash my hair tonight.
If I see Angelina later, I might ask her to the party.

LISTENING

9a `6.4` You are going to role-play some situations where people discuss problems and possible solutions. Listen to the example conversation and answer these questions.

1 What is Sam and Ellie's relationship?
2 What does Sam want to do?

9b Listen again and answer these questions.

1 What three problems does Ellie mention?
2 What are Sam's solutions?
3 What does Ellie think of Sam's plan?

SPEAKING

10 Work with a partner. Turn to page 135 and consider what you will do in the two situations.

SITUATION

Speak Out is a television talk show. Robert Hughes is the presenter, and the audience takes part in the discussions. This week, the topic of the show is problems and responsibilities in families.

1a Discuss these statements with your partner. Do you agree or disagree?

1 Mothers should stay at home with their young children.
2 Working men do not need to share the housework.
3 Children shouldn't watch many hours of TV a day.
4 Parents should let teenagers choose when to come home at night.

1b **6.5** Listen to an extract from the show. Which of the above issues do they discuss?

2a Look at the different points made on the show. Listen again and put them in order (1–8).

a Some mothers can't stay at home because they need money.
b A mother's love is important for her children. *1*
c Working mothers miss the best years of their children's lives.
d Some mothers work because they want to.
e TV is an everyday thing and children should know about it.
f Parents should not let children watch TV at all.
g Only let children watch a couple of hours of TV a day.
h TV is bad for children.

2b What do you think of the different arguments and points above?

KEY LANGUAGE
EXPRESSING OPINIONS

3a **6.6** Listen and complete these sentences.

1 _____, I think mothers should stay at home.
2 Well, I understand her _____, but sometimes mothers have no choice.
3 Well, that's a good _____, but I think some mothers work because they want to.
4 I agree _____ Sarah.
5 Well, _____ I think is that they shouldn't watch any TV.
6 Well, personally, I _____ disagree.
7 I think it's _____ if they know that TV is a normal thing.
8 Well, that's an interesting _____, but TV is different to phones.

3b Match the sentences above with these functions.

a giving an opinion
b accepting an opinion and then disagreeing

PRONUNCIATION

4a **6.7** Word linking Listen and repeat this phrase. What happens between words that end in a consonant and those that begin with a vowel?

Well, that's a good point, but …

4b **6.8** Which words do we link in these phrases? Listen and check.

1 Well, what I think is that …
2 Well, that's an interesting idea, but …
3 Well, I understand her opinion, but …

TASK
HAVING A DISCUSSION

6 Work with a partner. Think of as many arguments as possible for and against these statements.

1 Parents should pay children to tidy the house.

For: Stops arguments with the children. Children learn about work and money.

Against: Children need to learn about looking after a home. Money should not be part of family life.

2 It is not a good idea for a man to be a househusband.
3 A teenager can stay out late without permission.
4 Young children should get pocket money.
5 Families should look after their elderly members at home.
6 Children should not have computers in their bedrooms.

7a Work in small groups. You are on *Speak Out*. One student is the TV presenter. He/She chooses one of the statements in Exercise 6 and asks the guests for their opinions on that topic. Use the Key language, the Useful phrases below and your prepared arguments to help.

USEFUL PHRASES

Right, the next topic is, 'Working men should …'
So, what's your name, and what do you think?
Do you agree with him/her?
What do you say to that?
What's your opinion?

7b After the first discussion, another student becomes the presenter and chooses a new statement to discuss.

4c Practise saying the phrases in Exercises 4a and 4b.

5 Work with a partner. Use the opinions below and practise the key language. Student A gives an opinion; Student B accepts that opinion and then disagrees. Then change roles.

1 1st idea: Mothers should stay at home.
  2nd idea: Some mothers have no choice.

'Personally, I think mothers should stay at home with their children.'

'Well, I understand your opinion, but some mothers have no choice. They have to work.'

2 1st idea: TV teaches children about the world.
  2nd idea: Children should read books to learn things.

3 1st idea: Husbands should help clean the house.
  2nd idea: Men are tired after a day at work.

STUDY SKILLS
CRITICAL THINKING

1a Critical thinking Choose the best way to complete this sentence. Compare your answer with a partner.

'Critical thinking' means:

a thinking about very serious or important things.
b saying that you think a person or thing is bad or wrong.
c asking questions about what you see, hear or read.

1b ▶ 6.1 Watch the lecture to check your answer.

1c ▶ 6.2 Look at these questions and watch the first part of the lecture again. Which questions are examples of critical thinking?

1 How many children are there in your family?
2 Is it true that most people will live until the age of 90 in the future?
3 Why are German families small?
4 How high is Mount Fuji?
5 How do we know that the gap between rich people and poor people will increase?
6 What will you do if you don't pass your next exam?

1d ▶ 6.3 According to the expert, critical thinking can help you understand reading texts better. Watch the second part of the lecture again and name three things you can look for in a text. Make notes on what she says about each thing.

1 Look for reasons …
2 Look for …
3 Look for …

2 You can also think critically about events. Ask one or two critical-thinking questions about these events.

1 the first Moon landing in 1969

How do we know that someone really stood on the Moon's surface?

2 the day in 1990 when Nelson Mandela walked free
3 the Wright brothers' first flight in 1903

3 Judging reliability You should also ask questions about where information comes from, to know if it is true or reliable. Which of these sources do you trust most? Put them in order from 1–5 (1 = the most reliable).

1 Wikipedia
2 BBC News
3 a webpage from 2004
4 something your parents tell you
5 a government website

4a Considering evidence Look at these facts. How do you know they're true?

1 The population of Germany was nearly 82 million in 2011.
2 People cannot live without water.

4b Compare these claims. Which do you believe more? Why?

1 A mother's love is important for her children.
2 A mother's love is important for her children. Without it, it is difficult for a child to grow up into a normal, healthy human being. A number of studies over many years have shown this. These studies took place in several countries around the world, with very similar results.

5a Developing self-awareness You should ask questions about yourself, the reasons why you do things and the results of your actions. Look at these examples. Have you ever asked yourself these questions?

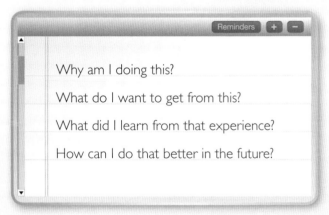

Reminders

Why am I doing this?

What do I want to get from this?

What did I learn from that experience?

How can I do that better in the future?

5b In Unit 2, you saw how it is possible to ask and answer questions like the above in a reflective blog. Look again at page 21. Then think of something you did recently, or are going to do in the future. Write three questions like those above, then answer them.

WRITING SKILLS
A SHORT ARTICLE

6a Discuss these questions with a partner.

1 Have you ever entered a competition?
2 Have you ever written anything for a competition?
3 Have you ever won anything?

6b Read this poster. How can you win a prize? How many people will win a prize?

INTERNATIONAL WRITING COMPETITION

What makes you proud of your society today?

The Global Council for Youth invites young people around the world to write about what makes them proud of their society today (maximum 200 words). The top 20 entries will receive a prize of 250 US dollars and will appear on the Council's website.

7 Read this competition entry. What do you think the judges liked and disliked about it? Think about ideas, organisation of ideas, etc.

What to choose? It's difficult to decide, as I feel proud of many things in my society today: for example, our education system, our creativity in the arts and our science. Two things, however, make me especially proud of my society. First, our big cities are very multicultural, so you see people of many different races, colours and religions. These people all live and work side by side. I think it's a great example of how people can come together and create a mixed, peaceful society. The second thing is less obvious, as it often happens out of sight. It's the fact that every day of the year, thousands of British people do voluntary work. They give up their time to help others for nothing. They help their local hospitals and communities, look after old people and do things to raise money for good causes. Because of these things, I feel proud of my society and see a positive future for it. However, I also want to contribute to it. In my life, many people have helped me, so now I would like to give something back.

Silvia Hussein, 20-year-old business student from Birmingham

8a Paragraph organisation Look at Silvia's answer again. It should be four paragraphs, not one. Divide it into four paragraphs.

8b What is the topic of paragraphs 2 and 3 of Silvia's answer?

8c What evidence does Silvia give for the two main things she is proud of?

9a Sentence structure Sometimes when there are three short, related sentences, it is possible to join them together to make one sentence. Look at this example and underline the repeated information.

They help their local hospitals. They look after old people. They collect money for good causes.

They help their local hospitals, look after old people and collect money for good causes.

9b Join these sets of sentences to make one sentence.

1 Silvia studies business at university. She lives with her parents. She helps in her parents' shop at weekends.
2 Her sister studies at school. She likes boy bands. She wants a car.

10 Linkers Study the use of the linking words *so, as, however* and *because of* in Silvia's answer. Then use them to complete the judges' report.

There were a very large number of entries (over 3,000), [1]_____ it took a long time to read them all. [2]_____, the judges' task was interesting, [3]_____ the young people wrote about a wide range of topics. The standard of entries was also very high, [4]_____ it was extremely difficult to choose the winners. After much discussion, [5]_____, the judges agreed on the top 20 entries.

The judges were impressed by Silvia Hussein's article, [6]_____ her modern vision and a feeling for other people. They also liked the style of her entry, [7]_____ she communicated her ideas very clearly. [8]_____, they were not happy with her paragraph organisation.

11 Write your answer to the question: *What makes you proud of your society today?* Use the model in Exercise 7 and the sentence starters below to help you. Think critically as you write and pay attention to your paragraph organisation.

Two things make me proud of my society …
First … The second thing is …

7 Science

7.1 CRIME LAB

IN THIS UNIT

GRAMMAR
- *should*, *must* and *have to*
- *had to* and *could*

VOCABULARY
- science and crime
- nouns, adjectives and verbs with prepositions

SCENARIO
- developing an argument
- making your case

STUDY SKILLS
- making notes (from presentations)

WRITING SKILLS
- describing charts (summarising key points)

A

'Be less curious about people, and more curious about ideas.' Marie Curie, 1867–1934, Polish scientist

READING AND VOCABULARY
SCIENCE AND CRIME

1a Match these captions with the photos (A–C).

2   Actors discuss evidence on the set of the latest TV crime drama about forensic scientists.

3   A worker in a lab prepares DNA samples for analysis.

1   Analysts collect important evidence at the crime scene.

1b Which words in the captions mean the following?

1   The place where a crime occurred
2   The things which show how the crime happened; clues
3   The person who does scientific tests to solve a crime
4   The place where scientists do experiments and tests

2a Read the two television programme reviews. Which is a documentary? Which is a drama? Which would you like to watch?

B

Crime Lab The crime scene investigation team has to solve two murders and a burglary tonight. Senior forensic scientist Karen Warner discovers a vital clue at a crime scene, her sister's DNA. She tries to keep her discovery secret, but her boss finds out and tells her she must leave the investigation. There's a burglary at the mayor's house, but there are no witnesses, and the burglar hasn't left any fingerprints. Because of this, laboratory assistant Dan Turner has to use a new piece of scientific equipment, with surprising results.

CSI – the reality This new series reveals the science behind modern police investigations. Iris Battle is a forensic scientist in a government crime lab. Her team examines the material from the crime scene – furniture, bullets, knives, cigarettes – to find things you can hardly see: fingerprints, hairs and DNA molecules. This series explains how scientists analyse the evidence in order to identify who has committed a crime. It's a fascinating programme about the lives and work of the real crime scene investigators – definitely one to watch, a must-see!

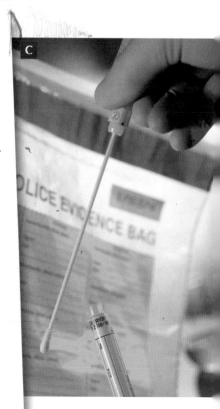

C

2b Read the reviews again and answer these questions.
1 Which programme does the reviewer prefer?
2 How many crimes are there in *Crime Lab* this week?
3 What problems does Dan Turner face?
4 What is the smallest thing that scientists analyse?

3 Find verbs or verb phrases in the reviews that mean:
1 find the answer to a problem
2 find or learn something that you did not know about
3 show something that you could not see before
4 examine something carefully in order to understand it
5 break the law; do something illegal or wrong

LISTENING

4a ⬛7.1 Listen to the first part of an interview between Iris Battle (a forensic scientist) and a researcher for the documentary programme. Which of these topics do they discuss?
a the two teams of employees
b work in the laboratory
c the researcher's main interest
d the effects of the TV dramas
e work at the crime scene

4b Listen again. Fill the gaps with information that Iris Battle gives.

Crime-scene analysts [1] _____ the evidence, but the forensic scientists [2] _____ in the lab. The analysts do not want to [3] _____ the evidence, so they wear rubber gloves. They take careful notes so that the scientists [4] _____ the evidence has come from. In reality, most of the crimes are burglaries, but on TV they [5] _____.

5a ⬛7.2 Look at the words in the box and check their meanings. Then listen to the second part of the interview and make notes.

patient   test results   rules   image   apply for a job

5b Work with a partner and use your notes to describe the work in the laboratory and the effects of the TV dramas.

6 Making personal connections Discuss these questions with your partner.
1 Which police and crime dramas do you watch? Do those programmes use forensic science?
2 Have you seen any documentaries about police work and about forensic science? What differences have you noticed between the dramas and the documentaries?
3 How do the police use science and technology in your country, e.g. DNA, CCTV cameras, speed cameras, computer databases and ID cards? What is your opinion about these things?
4 Would you like a career connected to science or technology? Why?/Why not?

GRAMMAR
SHOULD, MUST AND HAVE TO

7a Put the sentences below (1–6) from the interview into these five groups (A–E).
A It is a good or correct idea to do this.
B It is not a good or correct idea to do this.
C It is necessary to do this (there is no choice).
D It is necessary to not do this (there is no choice).
E It is not necessary to do this (there is some choice).

1 You must turn your phone off.
2 You should make that clear.
3 You don't have to study law.
4 We mustn't eat or drink in the lab.
5 You shouldn't ask me.
6 You have to study chemistry or biology.

7b Look at Audio scripts 7.1 and 7.2 on pages 154–155 and find more examples of this language. How do we make questions with *should*, *must* and *have to*?

➡ Language reference and extra practice, pages 114–115

8a Correct the mistakes in these sentences.
1 She have to check the evidence carefully.
2 We mustn't to eat or to drink in here.
3 As I'm a DNA expert, I haven't to know about guns.
4 They should to say sorry for being late.

> **GRAMMAR TIP**
>
> *Must* and *have to* are very similar in meaning in the positive form. You usually use *have to* when you talk about laws, rules, etc. You often use *must* when you give your opinion that something is important. However, you need to remember the negative forms of *must* and *have to* are different in meaning.

8b Complete the sentences below with the correct form of *must*, *have to* and the verbs in the box. (Sometimes both forms are possible.)

have (x2)   lend   make   wear (x2)

1 A forensic scientist *must have / has to have* a university science degree.
2 A police officer _____ a university degree.
3 A forensic scientist _____ a uniform.
4 A police officer _____ a uniform.
5 A forensic scientist _____ any mistakes.
6 A police officer _____ his/her gun to anyone.

8c Work with a partner. Make sentences similar to those above, comparing and contrasting these pairs.
• judge and lawyer   • student and teacher
• police officer and nurse   • artist and bank manager

SPEAKING

9 Work with a partner.
Student A: Turn to page 144.
Student B: Turn to page 148.

SPEAKING

1 Discuss these questions with a partner.

1 Which scientists do you know? Are there any famous scientists from your country?
2 What did they discover or do?
3 Look at the photos on the webpage below. Do you know anything about this man?

READING

2a Look at the webpage about Stephen Hawking. Why is he famous?

2b Complete this summary of Hawking's life. Write one word in each gap. (The words you need are in the text.)

Stephen Hawking was [1]_____ in Oxford, in 1942. He studied at the Universities of Oxford and Cambridge. He was still a young man when he [2]_____ that he had a serious disease. However, he married Jane Wilde, finished his PhD and got a [3]_____ at Cambridge University. From 1979 to 2009, he was Professor of [4]_____ there. In 1985, after an operation, he started to use special equipment to help him [5]_____. Three years later, his book A [6]_____ History of Time appeared and sold millions of copies. Hawking rewrote the [7]_____ in 2005. In [8]_____, he was part of the opening ceremony of the London Olympics. Surprisingly, Hawking believes that he is not an [9]_____ person. He is proud of his family and his work, and grateful for the [10]_____ that many different people have given him.

3 Justifying selections Read the webpage again. What are the two most interesting facts in the text? Tell your partner why you have chosen them.

VOCABULARY

NOUNS, ADJECTIVES AND VERBS WITH PREPOSITIONS

4a Complete these sentences with a preposition (e.g. to, of). Find the highlighted words in the text to check your answers.

1 The lab is separate _from_ the main building.
2 He's writing a history _of_ crime in the US.
3 She became very successful _in_ business.
4 Communicating is much easier now, thanks _to_ the internet.
5 They have received the report _from_ the police officers.

4b Look at the prepositions above. What other ones do you know?

4c 7.3 **Complete these questions with a preposition. Listen and check your answers.**

1 What are you interested _in_ ?
2 In your family, who do you have a good relationship _with_ ?
3 What are you afraid _of_ ?
4 What are you proud _of_ ?
5 What's the best thing that's ever happened _to_ you?
6 What do you spend your money _on_ ?
7 Which clubs or organisations do you belong _to_ ?

4d Work with a partner. Ask and answer the questions above. Give reasons for your answers.

I'm interested in science because I want to know how things work. I'm also interested in …

Born
8 January 1942, in Oxford

Education
▶ St Albans School
  (20 miles north of London)
▶ University College,
  Oxford (1959–62),
  studied Physics
▶ PhD, University of
  Cambridge (1966)

Career
▶ Institute of Astronomy,
  Cambridge (1968–73)
▶ Professor of Mathematics,
  Cambridge (1979–2009)
▶ Director of Research,
  Centre for Theoretical
  Cosmology, Cambridge
  (2009–)

Family
Married to Jane Wilde
(1965–1991, three children)
and Elaine Mason
(1995–2006)

Stephen William Hawking

Ideas and books

Stephen Hawking is one of the world's most famous scientists. He is well-known for his work on black holes, and has developed a number of new ideas about them. Hawking believes that the birth of the universe (the 'Big Bang') created many small black holes. Hawking also thinks that there is a sort of hole in the centre of a black hole. This hole leads to another universe, completely separate from our own.

Hawking's 1988 book, *A Brief History of Time: From the Big Bang to Black Holes*, sold one copy for every 750 people on Earth. However, many people could not really understand the book and they had to give up reading it. As a result, Hawking decided to write an easier version, *A Briefer History of Time* (2005).

In 'The Grand Design' (2010, with Leonard Mlodinow), Hawking argued that we should look for a different way to discover the deepest mysteries of the universe. Instead of trying to find one big new explanation for these mysteries, scientists should put together all the ideas that they already have.

At the opening ceremony of the London 2012 Olympics, Hawking said to a TV audience of 900 million people: 'Look up at the stars and not down at your feet … be curious.'

GRAMMAR
HAD TO AND COULD

5a Look at these sentences about the text. Then match 1–4 with a–d.

Until 1985, he **could** talk.

Doctors **had to** operate on him.

Many people **could not** understand the book.

He **did not have to** teach. He only **had to** do research.

1	had to	a)	was/were not able to do it
2	did not have to	b)	it was necessary to do it
3	could	c)	it was not necessary to do it
4	could not	d)	was/were able to do it

GRAMMAR TIP

There is no past form of *must*. Use *had to*.
You **must** work hard.   You **had to** work hard.

↦ Language reference and extra practice, pages 114–115

WHAT IS A BLACK HOLE?

A black hole is a place in space where gravity is very strong. Anything that falls into it never comes out. Nothing can escape from it, not even light. As a result, it is impossible to see a black hole.

Health, work and family life

Hawking learnt that he had the disease ALS (a disease that affects muscle control) at the age of 21, in his first year in Cambridge. He only expected to live a few years. However, he married Jane Wilde and found a job in Cambridge. In the early stages of his career, his illness got worse, but he was fortunate that he did not have to teach. He only had to do research, and this was easier for him.

Until 1985, he could talk, but in that year, doctors had to operate on him and he lost his speech. Soon, however, people developed equipment that allowed him to speak. In spite of his disease, Hawking does not consider himself an unlucky man. He says it has not prevented him from having a very attractive family, and being successful in his work. He says this is thanks to the help he has received from his family and a large number of other people and organisations.

5b Complete the text below from the webpage with the words in the box.

| had to | did not have to | could | could not |

After the operation

By 1985, Stephen's speech was getting worse, and only a few people who knew him well [1] _could_ understand him. But at least he [2] _had to_ communicate. In 1985, he [3] _had to_ have an operation on his throat. After that, he [4] _had_ have 24-hour care by nurses. For a time after the operation, he [5] _____ speak at all, so he [6] _had to_ communicate by spelling words. He [7] _could_ raise his eyebrows when someone pointed to the right letter on a spelling card. However, a computer expert in California (Walt Wotosz) heard of Hawking's problem and sent him a computer program. With this program, Hawking [8] _had to_ choose words from a menu on a screen. All he [9] _didn't have to_ do was press a switch in his hand. But he [10] _could_ also control the program by making a head or eye movement. In that case, he [11] _didn't have to_ press the switch. At first, he [12] _had to_ run the program on a desktop computer, but then a man called David Mason fitted a small portable computer to his wheelchair.

5c Describe some situations in your life when you had a problem, and explain how you solved it. Use this form: *I couldn't …, so I had to … .*

After my operation, I couldn't drive, so I had to go everywhere by bus.

I couldn't study at home because my baby sister was crying all the time, so I had to go to the library.

SPEAKING

6 Discuss these statements about attitudes to science in small groups.

1 Science has made modern life healthier and more comfortable.
2 My government should spend more money on scientific research and less on other things.
3 Science and technology can solve any problem.

WRITING

7 Research a famous scientist and write a paragraph about his/her life and work. Look back at the summary in Exercise 2b as a guide.

▶ MEET THE EXPERT

Watch an interview with Huw James, a scientist who specialises in astronomy, about black holes and astrophysics. Turn to page 128 for video activities.

PREPARATION

1a **Which of these things did someone invent, and which did someone discover?**

electricity   the internet   the printing press
DNA   the telephone   nuclear energy
global warming   the car

1b **Can you think of other important discoveries and inventions from the history of science and technology? Do you know who invented or discovered them? When and how? Why do you think they are important inventions or discoveries?**

SITUATION

Ideas and Innovations is an intellectual discussion programme on radio. For a special programme, they are choosing the most important inventions and scientific discoveries of the last thousand years.

2 **7.4** **Listen to an extract from the discussion. Julian Blake thinks the printing press is one of the most important inventions. Which of these reasons does he mention?**

1 People could make books and communicate ideas quickly.
2 Education became possible for everyone.
3 Libraries and universities increased in number.
4 Writing became a way to earn money.

3a **Read these notes. What do the different abbreviations mean, e.g. *PP, pdctn*? What is the purpose of the arrows (↓, →, ←, ↑)?**

3b **Listen again and complete the notes. Write one word or number in each gap.**

3c **Work with a partner and discuss these questions.**

1 Which of Julian's points are strongest?
2 Do you think there are any weak points?
3 Can you think of more reasons which support his claim?

KEY LANGUAGE
DEVELOPING AN ARGUMENT

4a **7.5** **In the notes in Exercise 3a, each arrow (↓, →, ←, ↑) shows a connection between two ideas. The arrows represent certain words and phrases like *caused, means that, so*, etc. Listen and complete the sentences below. Use the words and phrases in the box.**

caused   is connected to   led to
means that   meant that   so

1 I think this _____ a revolution in knowledge …
2 This _____ ideas could spread much more quickly than before.
3 It _____ education for everyone.
4 This _____ the fast production of books.
5 The written word became important at work and _____ people had to read.
6 The printing press _____ writers can make money.

Gutenberg invented PP in [1]_____
↓
revolution in knowledge, society, etc.
Why?

THE FIRST REASON
PP → books, large [2]_____ , quickly → ideas spread quickly
↓
great [3]_____ in society

THE SECOND REASON
PP → [4]_____ for all ← schools ← fast pdctn of books
↑
reading skills v.imp. ← written word imp. at [5]_____

THE THIRD REASON
PP → [6]_____ can make money → [7]_____ writers and journalists
↓
good for [8]_____

CRITICISM
Did PP → educ. for all? [9]_____ years between PP and schools

4b Look at Audio script 7.4 on page 155 and find more examples of this language.

5 Complete these sentences with your own ideas. Then compare with a partner.
1 The car means that …
2 The discovery of DNA led to …
3 Rapid global warming is connected to …
4 Television means people stay at home more, and so …
5 The discovery of electricity caused …
6 The invention of the refrigerator meant that …

PRONUNCIATION

6a 7.6 Word stress and the schwa Mark the key word stress on these phrases. Then listen and check.

the aeroplane
the telephone
the television
the internet

6b In each phrase, which vowels have the weak sound /ə/ (the schwa)? Listen again and check.

6c Answer these questions.
1 Does the stressed syllable ever have the schwa sound?
2 When does *the* not have the schwa sound?

6d 7.7 Mark the key word stress on these phrases. Which syllables have the schwa sound? Compare with a partner, then listen and check.

the computer   the fridge   the discovery of electricity
the refrigerator   the car   the discovery of DNA
the clock   the radio   the discovery of nuclear energy

6e Practise saying the phrases in Exercises 6a and 6d with your partner. Does your partner use word stress and the schwa well?

TASK
MAKING YOUR CASE

7a Choose three or four inventions and/or discoveries that you think are very important and make notes about them. Think about these questions.
- What are your reasons for choosing the inventions or discoveries?
- What do the inventions or discoveries mean we can/could do?
- What did they lead to? What is connected to them?

7b Work in small groups. Use the Key language from Exercise 4 and the Useful phrases below to explain and compare your choices. Agree on the top two.

USEFUL PHRASES

The main reason I've chosen this is because …
One reason it's important is that …
Another thing is that …
I completely agree with you.
I don't agree with that point.
Which shall we choose?

7c Tell the class about your two most important inventions and discoveries. Does the class agree?

STUDY SKILLS
MAKING NOTES

1 **Discuss these questions.**

1   What kind of notes do people make:
   - as students?
   - at work?
   - in other situations?
2   When and why do you make notes?

2a You are going to hear a talk about problems for women in science in the UK. What kind of problems do you think the speaker will mention? Discuss your ideas with a partner. Make a list of the problems.

2b **7.8** Listen to the talk, then answer this question: What were the main points of the talk? Choose from this list (1–6).

1   Schools are not doing enough to encourage girls to study science.
2   Male attitudes towards women in science are a problem.
3   One male colleague called the speaker 'the girl'.
4   The issue of children is another problem for women in science.
5   Women in science have to have more confidence.
6   Female scientists might feel uncertain about their careers and lives.

3 Look at these notes (A and B) that two students made during the talk. Find six mistakes and correct them.

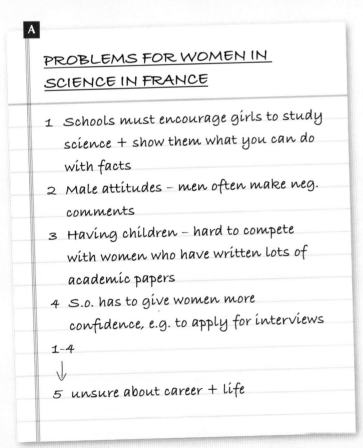

4 Compare the two styles of notes in Exercise 3. Which type do you prefer? Why?

5a Find examples of these things in the notes in Exercise 3. Why do the students do this?

1   words that the students have made shorter (e.g. *neg.*) and symbols (e.g. +)
2   places where words (e.g. *the*, *it*) are missing

5b Work with a partner and compare these phrases from the talk with the notes the students have made. What do you notice about the vocabulary? Why is this a good thing to do?

1   Schools are not doing enough to encourage girls to study science.
2   It's difficult to compete with men.
3   You might feel uncertain about where your career or life is going.

6a There is no right or wrong style for notes. You can even combine different styles. Look at the different styles on this page and choose one you want to practise.

6b Turn back to page 39 and look at Exercise 3a. Listen to the TV programme again (Audio recording 5.1) and make notes on the key points. Compare your notes with a partner. Are there any differences?

WRITING SKILLS
DESCRIBING CHARTS

7 **Discuss these questions in groups.**

1 Which university subjects are popular in your country with a) women and b) men?
2 Do you think the majority of science students in your country are men or women?

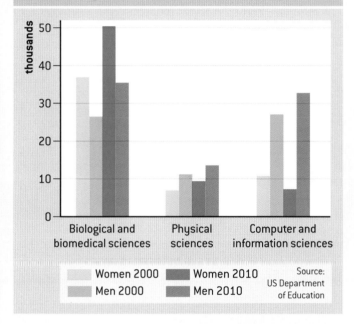

A **Number of Bachelor's degrees by selected fields of study: 2000 and 2010**

Women 2000   Women 2010
Men 2000   Men 2010

Source: US Department of Education

8a **Analysing data Look at bar chart A above. Can you find this information in the chart?**

1 the number of male and female graduates in psychology
2 the reason for the differences between the number of men and women who graduated in some science subjects
3 the number of students (men and women) who obtained Bachelor's degrees in some science subjects in 2000 and 2010.

8b **Complete this description of bar chart A.**

The chart shows the number of ¹_____ who obtained Bachelor's degrees in some ²_____ subjects in the ³_____ in 2000 and ⁴_____.

8c **Look carefully at bar chart A and decide if these statements are true or false.**

1 The orange bars show the number of men who obtained Bachelor's degrees in 2000.
2 The light blue bars show the number of women who obtained Bachelor's degrees in 2010.
3 In 2000, about 37,000 men graduated in biological and biomedical sciences.
4 In 2010, about 13,000 women graduated in physical sciences.

9a Describing bar charts **Look at these words and answer the questions below.**

an increase	fell	a rise	a decrease
decreased	rose	increased	a fall

1 Which are nouns? Which are verbs?
2 Which are about going up? Which are about going down?
3 Which words mean the same?

9b **What is the most interesting information in bar chart A? Discuss with a partner.**

9c **Complete this summary of the important information in bar chart A. Write one word or number in each gap.**

In biological and biomedical sciences, more ¹_____ graduated than men. On the other hand, the ²_____ of men who obtained Bachelor's degrees in physical sciences and in computer and information sciences was higher than the number of women.

Numbers ³_____ during the period both for men and women in all subjects, except for computer and information sciences, where there was a ⁴_____ in the number of female graduates, from about 10,500 in 2000 to about ⁵_____ in 2010.

Overall, more students obtained Bachelor's degrees in biological and biomedical sciences than in the other subjects. ⁶_____ sciences had the smallest number of graduates.

10 **Now write about bar chart B. Describe a) what it is about and b) some of the most important information. Discuss your ideas with a partner before you start writing. Use the summary of bar chart A in Exercise 9c to help you.**

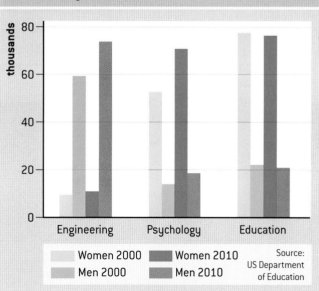

B **Number of Bachelor's degrees by selected fields of study: 2000 and 2010**

Women 2000   Women 2010
Men 2000   Men 2010

Source: US Department of Education

8 The night

8.1 SLEEP TIGHT

IN THIS UNIT

GRAMMAR
- verb patterns
- future intentions

VOCABULARY
- expressions with *sleep*
- *-ing/-ed* adjectives

SCENARIO
- discussing preferences
- making a future plan

STUDY SKILLS
- remembering vocabulary

WRITING SKILLS
- a narrative (describing an experience / a story)

'There is a time for words, and there is also a time for sleep.' Homer, 800–710BC, Greek poet

SPEAKING AND VOCABULARY
SLEEP

1 Are these statements true for you? If not, change them so that they are. Then compare with a partner.

1 I sleep for about six hours a night.
2 I usually have a lot of dreams.
3 I sometimes have nightmares.
4 I never talk in my sleep.
5 I often have sleepless nights.
6 I can sleep through a lot of noise.
7 On Saturdays, I usually sleep in.
8 When I go to bed, I fall asleep very quickly.
9 I feel sleepy after a big lunch.
10 I sometimes have a nap/doze in the afternoon.
11 I never go to sleep in class.
12 I had a good night's sleep last night.

how long does it take you to fall asleep?

READING

2 Abolaji is a student on a foundation course in Manchester before starting a science degree. Read the emails on the right and answer these questions.

1 Why has Abolaji written to Dr Wilson?
2 What is the relationship between them?
3 Do you think Dr Wilson's reply is helpful?
4 How do you communicate with your teachers? Do you use email?

Subject: End-of-course talk

Dear Dr Wilson

I think I've managed to find a good subject for the end-of-course talks next month. I'm thinking about doing a presentation on sleep and the brain (how much we need to sleep, stages of sleep, dreams, etc.). What do you think about this? Could you give me some advice? Could I come and see you about it later this week?

Thanks very much.

Abolaji

Subject: Re: End-of-course talk   inbox 28

Dear Abolaji

You seem to have a really interesting topic here.
You might also want to look at some of these things:

1 different types of sleep
2 how quickly people fall asleep
3 why people talk in their sleep
4 why some people suffer from insomnia
5 why some people are heavy sleepers, but others are light sleepers
6 how modern life affects our sleep, e.g. light pollution
7 when and why people take naps

I'm afraid I can't see you this week, as I've decided to go to the conference in Oslo that I mentioned on Tuesday. I'll be back on Monday. Perhaps we can talk after the class on Tuesday? In the meantime, keep reading about the topic!

Steve Wilson

LISTENING

3a [8.1] **Listen to the first part of Abolaji's talk. What does he say about these things?**

1 how long a one-year-old baby needs to sleep
2 how long adults need to sleep
3 the meaning of REM and NREM
4 what happens to the brain during REM sleep

3b [8.2] **Listen to the second part of his talk and answer these questions.**

1 How many stages of sleep are there?
2 What does NREM sleep do?
3 Why is it never completely dark?
4 Why can our modern way of life have a negative effect on our sleeping patterns?

3c Evaluating performance **Do you think Abolaji has given a good presentation? Why?/Why not?**

3d **Complete the summary below of the talk with the words in the box.**

brain	damage	darkness	dreams
less	organising	types	

As we get older, we need to sleep ¹_____, although not everyone needs the same amount of sleep. The two ²_____ of sleep are REM and NREM. About 80% of sleep is NREM sleep, when ³_____ activity slows down. REM sleep is when ⁴_____ happen and is important for ⁵_____ our memories. One of the problems we face today is that there is less ⁶_____ than in the past, and this could ⁷_____ our health.

GRAMMAR
VERB PATTERNS

4a **Look at these extracts from the emails.**

I'm thinking about doing a presentation on sleep and the brain …
… I've decided to go to the conference …
… keep reading about the topic!

Now put the infinitive of each of the verbs in this table.

verb + infinitive with *to*	verb + *-ing*	verb + preposition + *-ing*

4b **Find other examples of these verb patterns in the emails and Audio scripts 8.1 and 8.2 on page 156.**

GRAMMAR TIP

You can use some verbs (e.g. *like, hate*) with both the infinitive with *to* and with the verb + *-ing*. Often, there is not a big difference in meaning.

➡ Language reference and extra practice, pages 116–117

4c **Complete Dr Wilson's feedback comments with the correct form of the verbs.**

inbox 28

Dear Abolaji

I'm glad you ¹_____(decide/speak) about this interesting topic. Your presentation was excellent. You ²_____ (seem/have) a very good understanding of the subject, and you ³_____(manage/cover) a lot of key points. You also ⁴_____(succeed in/keep) the attention of the audience throughout. Perhaps you ⁵_____(need/give) a few more interesting examples. Anyway, it's clear that you ⁶_____(like/do) presentations and you were very confident. ⁷_____(keep/work) hard. You ⁸_____ (start/develop) into a first-class student. By the way, what are you ⁹_____(think of/do) for your next presentation?

5 **Complete these questions using a correct verb pattern. Then work with a partner, and ask and answer your questions.**

1 (What) do you want _____?
2 Do you like _____?
3 Why did you decide _____?
4 What do you hope _____?
5 Have you ever thought _____?
6 Do you enjoy _____?
7 (What) do you need _____?
8 Can you help me _____?
9 Did you apologise _____?
10 Do you remember _____?

SPEAKING

6 **Work in small groups. How much do you know about sleep? Do the quiz on page 135.**

READING

1a Which of these jobs regularly involve working when most people are asleep?

astronomer   baker   call-centre worker   cleaner
engineer   lorry driver   nurse   office worker
police officer   security guard   teacher

1b Ordering ideas Discuss these questions in pairs.

1   What do you think are the advantages and disadvantages of working at night? Make comparisons with working during the daytime. Make a long list if you can.
2   Compare your ideas with another pair of students. Put the different advantages and disadvantages in order of seriousness.

2 Read the first paragraph of an article about night workers. Does it mention any of your ideas from Exercise 1b?

3a Read the rest of the article about four people who work the night shift. What problem does each person have with their job?

3b Read the extracts again and match the people with these questions. (Sometimes more than one person is possible.)

1   Who couldn't get another job at first?
2   Who is doing a job that he/she loves?
3   Who wants to stop working at night?
4   Who enjoys working with his/her colleagues?
5   Who has a job helping people in another country?
6   Who talks about the money that he/she earns?
7   Who talks about people in other countries?
8   Who plans to use some of his/her work time to do something else?

3c Would you like to have any of these jobs? Why?/ Why not? Would you mind working a night shift? Do you know anyone who has worked on a night shift?

VOCABULARY
-ING/-ED ADJECTIVES

4a Underline the adjectives in these sentences and answer the questions below.

Night-shift work is tiring, so he is often tired.

I am bored because my job is boring.

1   Which adjectives describe how we feel, often because of something else?
2   Which adjectives describe what something is like?

4b Choose the correct adjectives.

1   We were *frightened / frightening* because the film was *frightened / frightening*.
2   The lecture was *interested / interesting*, so the students were *interested / interesting* in it.

Working *in the* dark

9–5: the standard working day. However, for some people, it's bedtime. These people are the night workers – nurses on the night shift, lorry drivers crossing continents and bakers preparing our breakfast bread. Working at night brings particular problems: family life is difficult, social life is limited, cafés are closed, there are few buses and it's bad for your health. With all these problems, who chooses to work the night shift, and are they planning to stay in their jobs?

Robert Moore

"I work at night because I'm fascinated by the stars, and I have been since I was a little boy. I'm happiest when I'm looking down my telescope. The stars are amazing, and it's great taking pictures of them. Honestly, I'm never going to change my job – I'm going to be an astro-photographer for life. Of course, my social life is poor, but I think I've found a solution to this problem. I'm going to bring my laptop to work and join a chat room online. I'm hoping to make friends with people abroad. They're the only people awake when I'm working!"

4c We can make *-ing/-ed* adjectives from verbs, e.g. *bore → bored/boring*. How many *-ing/-ed* adjectives can you find in the text in Exercise 3a? What are the verbs?

4d Complete these questions with the correct adjective. Then ask and answer the questions with a partner.

1   Have you seen an _____ TV programme recently? (interest)
2   What's the most _____ thing you have done? (excite)
3   When did you last feel really _____? (tire)
4   Is there anything that you are _____ by? (fascinate)
5   What's the most _____ thing you have seen? (amaze)
6   What's the most _____ thing that has happened to you? (embarrass)
7   When did you last feel _____? (surprise)
8   Is there anything you are _____ of? (frighten)

Tony Baggio

"My work involves repairing the railway tracks, so we have to work at night because they can't stop the trains during the day. It's not so bad, our team spirit is great, and we get paid extra. However, I'm going to leave this job soon. It's tiring and I have to find a normal job because my wife's pregnant. I haven't found a new job yet, but I'm hoping to be a builder. It's hard work, but no more nights!"

John Millar

"When I came to this country, the only work I could find was as a night security guard. This job is boring because it's so quiet, but I've decided to turn this problem into an advantage. Next month, I'm going to start a degree in literature by distance learning. I'm going to read my course books during the long quiet nights! I don't want to be a security guard all my life; I'd like to be a teacher. I'm going to apply for a teacher-training course when I finish my degree."

Indira Patel

"I work in a call centre in India, but I answer calls from people in the UK so I have to work at night. It's a good job with a good salary. It's also interesting because I use my English. But, to be honest, working at night is depressing – I miss my friends and family – so I'd like to leave this job soon. However, well-paid jobs aren't easy to find, so I don't know what I'm going to do, really."

GRAMMAR
FUTURE INTENTIONS

5a Who says these sentences in the article?

1 **I'm going to bring** my laptop to work.
2 **I'm hoping to make** friends with people abroad.
3 Next month, **I'm going to start** a degree in literature.
4 **I'd like to leave** this job soon.

5b Answer these questions about the sentences in Exercise 5a.

1 Which sentences describe a planned action in the future (i.e. a definite intention)?
2 Which sentences describe an ambition or dream for the future?
3 How do you make negatives and questions with this language?

5c Underline more examples of this language in the text.

➡ Language reference and extra practice, pages 116–117

5d Correct the errors in these sentences.

1 I am going buy a car next week.
2 He like to live in another country in the future.
3 You going to start your new job on Monday.
4 They not would like to eat out tomorrow.
5 Does he is going to sell his car?
6 We are going not to visit them next weekend.
7 Would you like go abroad on holiday this year?
8 Are you hope go to university in the future?

In standard speech, it is more natural to use contractions, e.g. *I'm going to buy a car*.

PRONUNCIATION

6a 8.3 Contractions **Look at these two sentences. Which do you hear?**

1 I am going to apply to university.
2 I'm going to apply to university.

6b 8.4 **Listen and repeat these sentences.**

1 I'm going to bring my laptop to work.
2 You're going to start university soon.
3 He's hoping to make friends around the world.
4 We'd like to work in a café.
5 They'd like to study abroad.
6 We're not going to change jobs.

SPEAKING

7a **Complete these sentences so that they are true for you. Compare your sentences with a partner.**

1 Next weekend, I'm going …
2 Next year, I'm hoping …
3 One day, I'd like …

7b **Think more about your future. What plans, hopes or dreams do you have? Think about future studies and work, as well as general life plans. Write five to ten sentences. Then find out about other students in the class.**

Do you have any plans for the rest of this week/month/year?

What future work and study plans do you have?

What hopes, dreams and ambitions do you have?

▶ MEET THE EXPERT

Watch an interview with Karen Fowler, a communications manager, about working in the dark in Antarctica.
Turn to page 128 for video activities.

PREPARATION

1 Do you do these things when you go out in the evening or at night? How often do you do them? What other things do you do? Discuss with other students.

go to a café   go to the theatre   go to the cinema
go to a fireworks display   go out for dinner
go to a sports event   go to a concert
go on a boat trip   go dancing   go to a museum

SITUATION

Every year, in January, there is a large arts festival in Sydney, Australia. There are classical and popular music concerts, large and small theatrical productions, comedy shows, films, dance shows, art events, talks and special events.

2 Look quickly at the festival events listing and answer these questions. At which event(s) can you:

1   see a film?
2   see a play?
3   hear some music?
4   see something with Australian performers?
5   see something from Asian countries?

3a `8.5` Listen to Paul, Christine and Emma plan a night out at the festival. Christine and Emma live in Sydney, and Paul is visiting from America. Which of the events do they decide to go to?

3b `8.6` Listen to an extract from the discussion about the evening events. Who has these opinions: Paul, Christine or Emma? Write *P*, *C* or *E*.

1   The film sounds fun.
2   He/She doesn't like the Bollywood film.
3   He/She doesn't like classical music.
4   He/She wants to visit the opera house after dark.

3c `8.7` Listen to an extract from the discussion about the night events. Who has these opinions: Paul, Christine or Emma? Write *P*, *C* or *E*.

1   He/She doesn't find Shakespeare funny.
2   A second music performance is not a good idea.
3   He/She thinks the drum show is something unusual.
4   He/She thinks the drum show will not be interesting.

SYDNEY FESTIVAL

EVENING EVENTS (6 P.M.–8 P.M.)

OPERA HOUSE CLASSICS
Great music, great orchestra, great location

Tonight: The Sydney Symphony Orchestra performs Beethoven's Symphony No. 9 in the world-famous Sydney Opera House.

MOVIES IN THE PARK
Enjoy movies from around the world in the festival's outdoor cinema – the popcorn is free!

Tonight: *Hum Tum* – an Indian film made in true Bollywood style. This is a romantic comedy filled with great songs and dances.

NIGHT EVENTS (9 P.M.–11 P.M.)

MINI-THEATRE
Powerful plays with the smallest of casts

Tonight: *Shakespeare – a writer's life*. Locally born actor Hugh Jackman returns to Sydney from Hollywood and performs the full story of Shakespeare's life. He acts as Shakespeare, his mother, father, his wife and even his children! You will laugh out loud.

WORLD BEATS
Music and dance from all round the world

Tonight: Japanese Taiko drumming. An incredible performance by 45 drummers that you'll never forget. Powerful and unique.

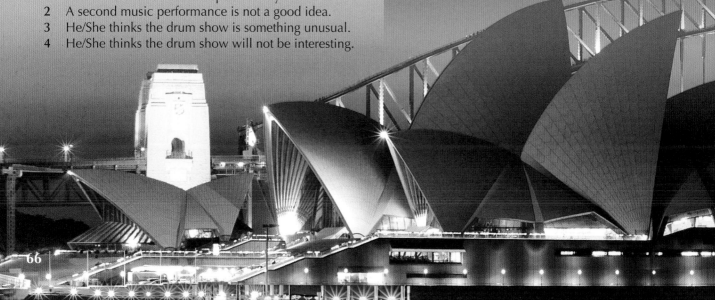

KEY LANGUAGE
DISCUSSING PREFERENCES

4a **8.8** Complete these sentences from the conversation with the words in the box. Then listen and check.

prefer (x2)   love   fancy   rather (x2)   keen   mind

1   What would you _____ to do, Christine?
2   I don't _____ the movie.
3   I'd _____ to go to the classical concert.
4   I'm not that _____ on the concert.
5   What would you _____ do?
6   Well, to be honest, I don't _____.
7   I'd _____ to see the drummers.
8   I'd _____ see that than a play about Shakespeare.

4b Which sentences above:

a   ask for someone's favourite thing or choice?
b   mean you like one thing more than another thing?
c   mean you don't like something?
d   mean you'd really like to do something?
e   mean you don't have a strong opinion?

PRONUNCIATION

5a Sentence stress: key words and clarity When giving information, it is important to speak very clearly. In a sentence or phrase, stress the key information words and organisational language. Underline the key information words and organisational language in these extracts.

1   There are two things to choose from.
2   So, first, the classical music concert is a Beethoven symphony.
3   Then, the open-air movie is an Indian film; it's a Bollywood film.
4   There's a music performance, called World Beats, and a one-man theatre show.
5   It says here that it's powerful and unique.

5b **8.9** Listen and mark the words with the strongest stress. Are they the same words that you chose in Exercise 5a? Are there any words with a weak pronunciation with schwa /ə/?

5c Listen again and repeat each sentence.

6a Which words should you stress to make these sentences clear? Compare your ideas with a partner.

1   OK, so, there are two choices.
2   The music tonight is by some Japanese drummers.
3   There are forty-five of them.
4   It's all about the life story of Shakespeare.
5   In this show, there's only one actor, but he plays many different characters.

6b Work with a partner. Practise saying the sentences.

TASK
MAKING A FUTURE PLAN

7a Work in groups of three to plan a night out at the Sydney Festival. You each have information for different time periods: 6–8 p.m., 9–11 p.m. or 11 p.m.–1 a.m.

Student A: Turn to page 140.
Student B: Turn to page 144.
Student C: Turn to page 148.

7b Prepare to give your information. Use the Key language and the Useful phrases on this page to help.

Student A: Turn to page 140.
Student B: Turn to page 144.
Student C: Turn to page 148.

USEFUL PHRASES

What shall we do tonight?	fun/boring/tiring
What about you?	great/unusual/interesting
I think we should …	

7c Regroup and share your information, discuss the different events and decide what you will go to in each time period.

8 Compare your plans with another group. Do you prefer your group's plan?

First of all, we're going to go to …

STUDY SKILLS
REMEMBERING VOCABULARY

1 We tend to forget things very quickly. Can you answer these questions?

1 What time did you go to bed last night?
2 What colour clothes were you wearing the day before yesterday?
3 Who was sitting next to you on your last bus or train journey?
4 What was the weather like on your last birthday?

2 What methods do you use to try to remember new words? Tell your partner.

3a Organising words One way we can remember words is by putting them in groups or ordering them. Look at these words for one minute. Then cover them. Write the words you can remember.

bus	star	nurse	café	bed	office worker
brain	cinema	baby	restaurant	teacher	
railway station	children	bread			

3b Now look at this list of words from Unit 7. Organise them into groups. Then compare your groups with your partner's. Are they the same?

book	clock	equipment	notes	television	
car	hair	uniform	Earth	phone	lab
black hole	computer	aeroplane			

4a Association Another way we can remember words is by imagining them in a particular place (e.g. in your house or room). Look at these words (from Lesson 8.2) for different kinds of people.

a call-centre worker	a cleaner	a baker
a lorry driver	a police officer	a security guard

Choose one and imagine this person in different places in your house. You can add surprising or funny details, e.g. imagine a call-centre worker sitting in your living room answering your phone and putting your friends on hold. These associations and connections can help your memory.

4b Look at the other people in Exercise 4a and think of a place in your house where you can 'see' them. Add some details to the scene. Tell your partner about your house.

5 It can also be a good idea to make up stories using new words. Imagine you want to learn the words in this box. You could make up a story like the one below.

presentation	weekend	sleepless nights	festival
dinner	museum	engineer	cousin

*Last week, I had a lot of **sleepless nights** because I had to do a **presentation** on Thursday. The **weekend** was good, though. My **cousin**, who's an **engineer**, came to stay with me. On Saturday, we went to the Science **Museum** and then we had **dinner** together in the evening. On Sunday, we went to a beach **festival**.*

Find between eight and ten words in this unit that are difficult or important for you. Make up a story using these words. Tell your partner your story.

6 Test your learning. How many of the words can you remember:

1 from the yellow box in Exercise 3a?
2 from the words in the blue box that you grouped in Exercise 3b?
3 from your house or room in Exercise 4?
4 from the story you made up in Exercise 5?

7a Evaluating methods Which of these methods for remembering vocabulary were new ideas for you? Which do you think will be the most useful for you?

7b How often do you review new vocabulary? Do you think this is enough? Why?/Why not?

WRITING SKILLS
A NARRATIVE

8 Work in small groups.

1 Tell your partners what you did last weekend.
2 Tell your partners about a frightening experience you had.

9a Prediction Read this story. How do you think it will end?

It was a cold winter that year, but – at last – spring arrived. One day, my friends and I decided to go camping in the desert. Perhaps I should explain: most of my country is desert – and too hot for camping in the summer.

Anyway, we drove about 70 kilometres from the capital – where we live – to a very beautiful place near a small lake. There, we set up our camp. At first, it was difficult to put up the tents, but we finally managed to do it. After that, we had a light lunch, and then relaxed until dinner.

After dinner, we sat outside in the bright moonlight, and talked about many different things. In the end, we started to talk about ghosts and before long, we were telling each other ghost stories. One of my friends was in the middle of telling us a very scary story when suddenly we saw something moving in the distance. We couldn't see clearly what it was – but it was white, and it was coming slowly towards us! We were really frightened! 'What should we do next?' we thought.

9b 8.10 Dictation Listen to the end of the story. Write down the words you hear. You will hear each phrase twice, with the punctuation.

9c 8.11 Listen to the end of the story a final time. Then turn to Audio script 8.11 on page 158 to check.

9d Discuss with a partner.

1 Did you like this story? Why?/Why not?
2 Do you like ghost stories in general? Why?/Why not?
3 What kind of stories do you like?

10 Match these headings with paragraphs 1–4 of the story. (This includes the ending on page 134.)

a later events
b final events/conclusion
c background information
d first events

11a Time expressions Underline all the time expressions in the text (e.g. *soon, later*).

11b Choose the best word or phrase to complete each sentence.

1 I was lying on the sand with my eyes closed. *Soon / After some time / Suddenly* something jumped on top of me.
2 I had so many sleepless nights that *in the end / next / then* I went to the doctor.
3 We saw a lake in the distance. *At that moment / Soon / Suddenly* we were standing next to the water.
4 I phoned her several times last night. *At first / Before long / Finally*, around 11 p.m., she answered.

12a You can use adjectives to make a description more interesting. Underline all the adjectives in the text in Exercise 9a, including the ending on page 136.

12b Add these adjectives to the sentences below. (More than one answer is sometimes possible.)

beautiful	bright	different	difficult	frightened

1 At night, you could see the lights of the aeroplanes several kilometres away.
2 Twenty men and women made the journey.
3 The children ran away from the dogs.
4 Last summer, I stayed in a town in the mountains.

13 Write a story about one of these topics:
• a ghost story
• a strange dream
• the worst night of your life.

Use the paragraph structure in Exercise 10 and some of the time expressions you underlined in Exercise 11a. Make your description interesting by using adjectives.

14 Show your work to another student. Ask them to check it, and to add three adjectives and/or time expressions in suitable places.

9 Work and industry

9.1 EMPLOYMENT

IN THIS UNIT

GRAMMAR
- *used to* + *before not now*
- present simple passive

VOCABULARY
- work
- compound nouns

SCENARIO
- making offers and proposals
- having a negotiation

STUDY SKILLS
- giving a short talk

WRITING SKILLS
- describing a process

'I like work; it fascinates me. I can sit and look at it for hours.' Jerome K. Jerome, 1859–1927, British writer

SPEAKING

1a What is your perfect job? What kind of skills or knowledge do you need to do this job?

1b What do/will you look for in a job? Put these things in order of importance (1 = the most important; 8 = the least important). Compare in small groups.

a well-known company   good pay   good managers
having fun   learning new skills   friendly colleagues
pleasant working conditions   opportunities to travel

1c In general, what kind of skills, experience and personal qualities do you think employers are looking for in the people who work for them?

READING

2a Read the email on the right. What do the managers want to know? How will they get this information?

2b These employees all quickly read the email. Which of them have not understood it?

1   I'm interested, and I can do it, because I started here four years ago.
2   I don't want to do it, because I don't want to discuss these matters with the company. They might use it against me later.
3   There's no point, because they never tell you the results of these surveys.
4   It sounds really interesting. I'll give Melanie Chadwick a call on Wednesday 12th.

From:	Head of Human Resources
To:	All staff
Subject:	Staff survey

At Maxicomp, managers welcome the views of staff on a wide range of company matters. We believe that listening carefully to our employees over many years has helped us to maintain our position as the market leader.

For this reason, we would now like to find out if, and how, staff think that Maxicomp has changed in the last few years. We want to know how staff used to feel about the company and their jobs, and how they feel now.

An external organisation, Swift Consulting, will do the research, including interviews with a number of employees. All staff who have worked for the company for more than five years can take part. The discussions will be completely private, and Maxicomp will not be able to identify staff from their comments at any stage in the process. We will inform staff of the results in a future report.

If you are interested in taking part, please contact Melanie Chadwick of Swift Consulting, m.chadwick@swift.con (0228 6320 1244) by Friday 14th May.

m MAXICOMP

LISTENING

3a `9.1` Listen to Swift Consulting interviewing two Maxicomp employees and answer these questions.

1   Who thinks that the company has changed the most, Anita or Tom?
2   Who thinks that he/she has changed the most?

3b Listen again and choose the best answer to complete these sentences.

1   Anita thinks that she is less enthusiastic now because she *started working for the company six years ago / is older / works longer hours*.
2   The company has helped her to *learn new skills / achieve more / travel*.
3   Tom *was more friendly in the past / ate more 15 or 16 years ago / doesn't have long for lunch these days*.
4   Tom thinks that he is still working for the company because *he can learn new skills / it is more professional / the pay is better*.

3c Exploring the topic Discuss these questions in small groups.

1   Do you think Maxicomp is a good company to work for? Why?/Why not?
2   Would you like to work for a company for a very long time, like Tom? Why?/Why not?
3   Do workers in your country work longer or shorter hours than in the past? What are the reasons for this?

VOCABULARY

WORK

4a Find these words and phrases in Audio script 9.1 on page 158 and the email. Work with a partner and explain their meaning.

employee   long service record   lunch break
market leader   department   promotion
staff   training course   work as a team

4b Complete these sentences with words from the box above.

1   The ___employee___ received an award for her extremely long service record.
2   I low long is the ___lunch break___ on the ___training course___?
3   Thanks to the way we work as a team, we have become the ___market leader___.
4   About six members of ___the staff___ have moved to another ___department___ in the company.

4c Discuss these questions in a group.

1   How long should employees have for their lunch break?
2   What should you do if you want promotion?
3   Can you think of three companies that are market leaders? What makes them market leaders?

GRAMMAR

USED TO

5a *Used to* can describe past habits and past states. Look at these two sentences and decide which is about a) a past habit and b) a past state.

1   Tom used to travel a lot.
2   I used to be more enthusiastic. *= enjoy , happy to do something*

5b Look at Audio script 9.1 on page 158 and find examples of *used to*. How do you make the negative and ask questions with *used to*?

> **GRAMMAR TIP**
>
> You can always use the past simple instead of *used to*, e.g. *He used to travel a lot when he was younger.*
> (= He travelled a lot when he was younger.)
> You cannot use *used to* for single actions in the past, e.g. *She used to finish work early yesterday.*

➡ Language reference and extra practice, pages 118–119

5c Complete these sentences about the interviews with *used to*, *didn't use to* or *use to*.

1   Anita ___used to___ feel the same way about the job.
2   Did she ___use to___ go home after 7 p.m. every day?
3   Tom and his colleagues ___didn't___ use the gym together.
4   Did Tom ___use to___ have long lunch breaks?
5   They ___used to___ work more as a team.
6   They ___used to___ have many opportunities to learn new skills.

PRONUNCIATION

6a `9.2` *used to* Look at Audio script 9.2 on page 158 and listen. How does the speaker pronounce *use* and *used*?

6b Listen again and repeat.

7 Write six sentences about you, your family and friends. Use *used to* (x3) and *didn't use to* (x3) and the verbs in the box. Then tell your partner.

be   eat   feel   finish   go out   have   help
know   listen   think   travel   work

SPEAKING

8 In a group, compare the way people live and work today with the past.

A long time ago, most people used to work on the land – now a lot of people work in offices.

Thirty years ago, most people didn't use to have mobile phones …

WRITING

9 Write a paragraph about the ideas you discussed in Exercise 8.

READING

1a Discuss these questions with a partner.

1 What things do people have that are gold (e.g. jewellery)?
2 Which do you prefer, gold or silver?

1b Making informed guesses Look at the items in this box. Which items often have gold in them? Discuss with a partner, then read the webpage below to check.

cars   spacecraft   teeth   pens   perfume bottles
washing machines   bathrooms   computers

1c Read the webpage again and match the sentence beginnings (1–4) with the endings (a–g). (You can use them more than once.)

1 Pure gold
2 Gold wire
3 Gold in teeth
4 Gold leaf

a is an alloy.
b is in many electrical products.
c is not very thick.
d is not very hard.
e contains 62–78% gold.
f lasts longer than some other materials.
g is not difficult to use.

1d Find words in the webpage that mean:

1 when something allows heat or electricity to travel along or through it: verb (paragraph 2)
2 the places where two things join: two words (paragraphs 2 and 3)
3 you can trust someone or something to do what you want (paragraph 2)
4 when you mix two or more metals together so that they combine and become a single metal (paragraph 4)
5 pretty or attractive, but not always necessary or useful (paragraph 5)

VOCABULARY
COMPOUND NOUNS

2a Two nouns can be joined together to make a compound noun. They are sometimes found as one word (e.g. *bathroom*), sometimes as two words (e.g. *credit card*). Find examples of compound nouns in the text.

2b Make compound nouns using a word from each box. Then use the compound nouns to complete the sentences below.

chair   coal   family   head   quarters (centre of comp)
job   office   work

job   quarters   force   mine   workforce (staff)
security   business   person

1 Is it better to work in a factory, or to do a(n) _____? job office job
2 What is the best way for a company to keep its workforce happy?
3 What do you think it's like to work in a _____? coal mine
4 Is job security a thing of the past?
5 What is the best location for a large company to have its head quarters?
6 In a meeting, is it a problem if the chairman is younger than all the other people there?

2c Discuss the questions with a partner.

WORLD GOLD COUNCIL

Uses of gold in industry

Where is gold used in industry?

1 Gold is used almost everywhere, from our homes to outer space.

Why is it used?

2 Gold has a number of advantages over other metals. It is soft, so it is easy to use. It conducts heat well. It lasts a long time and it is not damaged by the environment. Gold connections are very reliable, so they are used where safety is important. In addition, gold is a popular material in industry because of its special appearance, colour and beauty.

How is it used?

3 It is used in a wide variety of ways. The main use is in electronics – computers, pocket calculators, washing machines, televisions, recordable CDs, cars, credit cards and spacecraft. The Columbia space shuttle, for example, used nearly 41 kilograms of gold. Gold is the perfect material for contacts. An ordinary telephone contains 33 gold contacts. In some electronic equipment, very fine gold wires are used to connect different parts of the equipment. Each piece of wire is made of very pure gold (99.99%) and thinner than a human hair.

4 The second most important use of gold is in teeth. However, pure gold is not used, as it is very soft to use on its own. It is mixed with other metals to make an 'alloy'. A typical alloy contains 62–78% gold.

5 Decorative uses of gold include jewellery, pens and pencils, watches and glasses – even in cooking! It is found in bathrooms, on plates and especially on perfume bottles. The most impressive use of gold is gold leaf. This is an extremely thin sheet of gold. Generally, it is produced by hand and is used by builders, glass makers, artists and chefs. It can be applied to the roofs and ceilings of public buildings, and lasts much longer than paint.

GRAMMAR
PRESENT SIMPLE PASSIVE

Handwritten annotations:
S + was + V (past participle) → passive voice
here
S + is/am/are + V → present passive (pp passive)

3a Look at these sentences (a–c) and answer the questions below.

a   Pure gold is not used in teeth.
b   It is mixed with other metals.
c   Gold wires are used in electronic equipment.
1   Underline the main action verb in each of these sentences.
2   Do the sentences say who or what does the action (the agent)?

> **GRAMMAR TIP**
>
> Use the passive when you don't want to focus on the agent of the action. The agent may be unnecessary or unknown, e.g. *Pure gold is not used in teeth.* (It isn't necessary to talk about the dentists.); *It is mixed with other metals.* (We do not know who mixes it.)

3b Look at these sentences (a–b) and answer the questions below.

a   Gold is not damaged by the environment.
b   The environment does not damage gold.
1   Which sentence focuses our attention on gold?
2   Which sentence emphasises the environment?
3   Which word do we use in a passive sentence to introduce the agent of the action?

3c You form the present simple passive with *is/are* and the past participle of the verb. Find other examples of passive forms in the text on page 72. How do we make questions in the passive?

➥ Language reference and extra practice, pages 118–119

4 Complete this text with the present simple passive of the verbs.

Oil is sometimes called black gold, because it is extremely valuable. Oil ¹_____ (make) by very small plants and animals that died on the sea bed millions of years ago. When oil ²_____ (find) in the sea bed, an oil rig ³_____ (move) into the right position, and the oil ⁴_____ (take out). Over 50% of the world's oil is in the Arab World. Oil ⁵_____ (use) for fuel (e.g. in car engines) and to make electricity. We also make plastics with it. About 9,000 million litres of oil ⁶_____ (consume) every day.

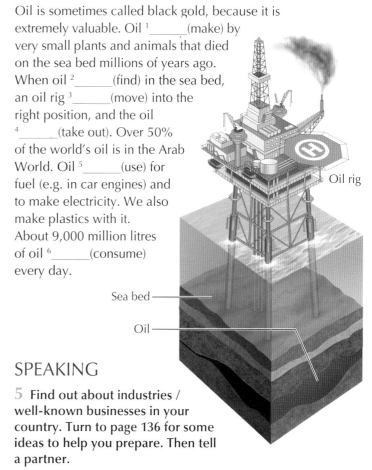

Oil rig

Sea bed ———

Oil ———

SPEAKING

5 Find out about industries / well-known businesses in your country. Turn to page 136 for some ideas to help you prepare. Then tell a partner.

There are a lot of big factories around the capital. Most of them are new. A lot of electronic equipment is made there, and then it's sent all over the world. In the north, they still build ships …

73

PREPARATION

1a Discuss these questions with a partner.

1 Do shops in your country often have sales? How much discount do they generally offer? Have you bought any bargains recently?

2 Do you ever buy things at a market? Do you ever bargain for a lower price?

1b Complete the sentences below with the words in the box. Use your dictionary if necessary.

---

supply   import   buyers   exports
manufacturers   retailers

---

1 We have to _____ these machines because we can't find them in our country.

2 Coffee is one of our main _____. We sell a lot to Europe.

3 We are _____ of clothes that are sold abroad.

4 We sell car parts to Ferrari and Fiat. They are our most important _____.

5 Tesco and Marks & Spencer are British _____ that have shops abroad.

6 We _____ electrical items to shops and supermarkets; we don't sell to the general public.

SITUATION

2 Look at the business advert below and answer these questions.

1 What does Route One do? Choose the correct answer.
   a   It manufactures electrical goods.
   b   It sells electrical goods to the public.
   c   It sells electrical goods to shops.

2 Where is it based, and where does it import from?

3a Route One wants to import some digital music players from Guangdong Digital (an electrical goods manufacturer in China). Richard Fallows, Purchasing Manager for Route One, is making a deal with Lu Han, a Sales Representative for Guangdong Digital.

Before you listen to their negotiation, look at these questions. Who usually says each one, a buyer or a seller?

---

1   Price
What's the price per item?
How much are they per item?
How much would you like to pay?

---

2   Delivery time
What's your normal delivery time?
We need delivery in two weeks. Can you do that?
When would you like us to deliver?

---

3   Quantity and discounts
How many would you like to order?
Can you offer me a discount?
What discount can you offer?

3b 9.3 Listen to the negotiation between Richard and Lu Han. Tick (✓) the questions above that you hear.

3c Listen again and circle the correct details of the negotiation. Who do you think gets the best deal?

Route ONE
Discount Electrical Goods Supplier

○ *New brands from Asia*
○ *Fast delivery*
○ *Large orders welcome*
○ *Suppliers to major retailers*

Route One: the fastest way to get new products into your shop

0794 8345586

www.route1r1.ca info@route1r1.ca
Unit 57, Harbour Business Park, Ontario, Canada

Starting price:
1 $100 / $85 per item

First quantity wanted:
2 515 / 550

First discounts offered:
3 5% / 13% (orders > 500)
4 13% / 18% (orders > 1,000)

Final quantity ordered:
5 815 / 850

Final price:
6 $87.50 / $87 per item

Final delivery time:
7 30 days / two weeks after order

PRONUNCIATION

4a | 9.4 | **Numbers** Listen carefully. When we say these numbers – 127 and 205 – what word comes immediately after *hundred*? Is the word after *hundred* stressed?

4b Work with a partner and practise saying these numbers. Listen carefully and check your partner's pronunciation. Pay attention to the stress pattern.

145   278   304   450   599

5a | 9.5 | Listen and circle the number you hear.

a   13   30
b   14   40
c   15   50
d   16   60

5b Listen again. Which syllable is stressed each time, the first or the second? What is the difference between the two types of number?

5c Work with a partner and practise saying these numbers. Listen carefully and check your partner's word stress and pronunciation.

13   30
17   70
18   80
19   90

KEY LANGUAGE
MAKING OFFERS AND PROPOSALS

6a | 9.6 | What are the missing words below? Listen and check.

1   $100? That _____ quite high.
2   I see. Well, I'm not _____ that we can go that low.
3   If you order 1,000, we can _____ 18%.
4   What about if we _____ 750?
5   How _____ 13%?
6   No, I'm _____ we can't do that.

6b Which of the sentences in Exercise 6a are:

a   suggestions, offers or proposals?
b   reactions or replies to offers and proposals?

7a Work with a partner. Write this negotiation from the prompts.

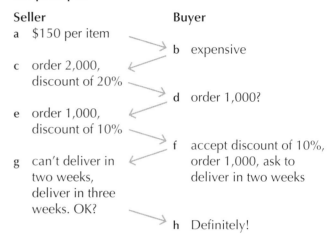

Seller	Buyer
a $150 per item	b expensive
c order 2,000, discount of 20%	d order 1,000?
e order 1,000, discount of 10%	f accept discount of 10%, order 1,000, ask to deliver in two weeks
g can't deliver in two weeks, deliver in three weeks. OK?	h Definitely!

7b Practise the negotiation with your partner.

TASK
HAVING A NEGOTIATION

8a Work with a partner to negotiate a deal. Use the Key language and Useful phrases on this page to prepare.

Student A: Turn to page 139.
Student B: Turn to page 140.

Student A: Turn to page 139.
Student B: Turn to page 140.

> **USEFUL PHRASES**
>
> Which of our products are you interested in?
> What's the price per item?
> That's a deal!

8b Negotiate the deal. After your first negotiation, change roles.

STUDY SKILLS
GIVING A SHORT TALK

1a Louise works for a company that makes chocolate. Part of her job is to give talks about the company. You are going to see a video of her talk but before you do, here are four questions she always asks herself before she starts to prepare a talk. How do you think she answers them?

1 What is the topic of my talk?
2 Why am I going to say it (e.g. to inform, persuade, amuse)?
3 Who am I going to talk to?
4 How much time do I have for the talk?

1b ▶9.1 Watch the beginning of her talk and answer the questions above.

2a ▶9.2 Watch the second part of the talk and complete these notes. Write one or two words/ numbers in each gap.

History of chocolate

Mayans discovered chocolate in about ¹_____ AD.

They made a ²_____ from roasted cocoa beans – 'chocolatl'.

Spread to Aztec civilisation (modern ³_____).

In ⁴_____, Hernán Cortés drank chocolate with Moctezuma.

Cortés returned to Spain in ⁵_____, taking cocoa beans with him.

Chocolate became popular with ⁶_____ in Spain.

It took nearly ⁷_____ to spread across Europe because the Spanish kept it a ⁸_____.

In 17th century, chocolate ⁹_____ became popular in London.

In 19th century, chocolate became ¹⁰_____ and the first eating chocolate appeared.

2b ▶9.3 Non-verbal features Watch the whole video. Below are some typical mistakes people make when giving presentations. Does Louise make these mistakes? If not, change the sentences to explain what she does.

1 She looks down at her notes all the time.
She looks up at her audience.

2 She makes eye-contact with only one or two people, often on one side of the room.
3 She makes a lot of nervous movements or gestures (e.g. pushing her hair back with one hand).
4 She's wearing old, scruffy clothes.
5 She stands in front of the screen, so the audience can't see her slide show.

2c Look at Video script 9.3 on page 159 and find the phrases Louise uses to:

1 introduce the first topic.
2 finish a topic.
3 summarise/conclude a topic.
4 start a new topic.

2d Match these phrases with 1–4 above.

To summarise, …	First, I'd like to talk about …
Turning now to …	That's all I want to say about …
In conclusion, …	Let me begin by -ing …
To conclude, …	I'd like to start by -ing …

3 Look at the list of things below you should do when you prepare a talk. Complete the gaps with the words in the box.

charts   information   notes   order
practise   pronunciation

1 Find out some interesting _____.
2 Put your ideas in the best _____.
3 Make some _____ to help you to remember things in the talk (including key vocabulary).
4 Prepare some pictures or _____ to make your points clearer.
5 Check the _____ of difficult words.
6 _____ the talk.

4a Prepare a short talk of about two minutes on one of these topics.
- your life story
- the history of your family/university/town/city/company

Use the points in Exercise 3 and the phrases in Exercise 2c and 2d to help you.

4b Analysing performance Work in groups. Take turns to give your talk. When you listen, look at this list. How well does the speaker do these things: *very well, OK* or *needs to improve*?

He/She …

1 welcomes the audience.
2 tells the audience what he/she is going to talk about.
3 speaks slowly and clearly.
4 sounds interested in what he/she is saying.
5 tries to build a relationship with the audience.
6 chooses vocabulary that he/she thinks the audience will know, and explains any difficult words.
7 uses language (grammar and vocabulary) that is generally correct.
8 looks at everyone in the group.

 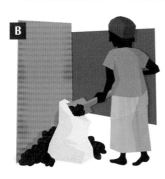  

THE EARLY STAGES OF MAKING CHOCOLATE

– a traditional family business in West Africa

To begin with, cocoa pods are cut from cocoa trees with large knives. The women of the family collect the pods in large baskets, which they carry on their heads. Next, the pods are cut open with a knife and the beans are taken out. Following this, wet cocoa beans are put on banana leaves, in a circle on the ground. More banana leaves are put on top of the beans. The wet beans are dried in the sun – this takes five to six days. Lastly, the beans are put into sacks for transport all over the world.

WRITING SKILLS
DESCRIBING A PROCESS

5 The pictures above show the early stages of making chocolate. What do you think is the correct order? Read the text and check.

6a Linkers Sequencing phrases (e.g. *to begin with*) tell us the order in which things happen. Underline the sequencing phrases in the text.

6b Which other sequencing phrases do you know?

7 The passive is often used to describe a process. Underline the examples of the passive in the text above.

8 The pictures below show the later stages of producing bars of milk chocolate in a factory. Write a paragraph describing the process, using the words next to each picture.

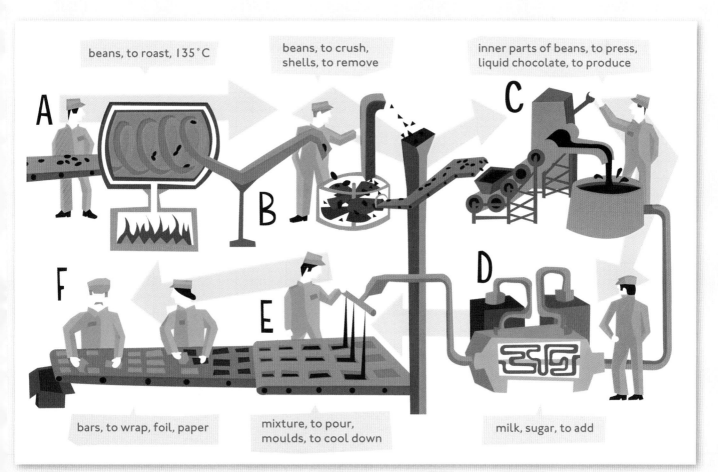

beans, to roast, 135°C

beans, to crush, shells, to remove

inner parts of beans, to press, liquid chocolate, to produce

bars, to wrap, foil, paper

mixture, to pour, moulds, to cool down

milk, sugar, to add

10 Global affairs

10.1 UNITED NATIONS

IN THIS UNIT

GRAMMAR
- present continuous for future arrangements
- past simple passive

VOCABULARY
- people and organisations

SCENARIO
- giving examples to strengthen points
- giving a presentation

STUDY SKILLS
- improving your listening

WRITING SKILLS
- a for-and-against essay

'Peace at home is peace in the country. Peace in the country is peace in the world.' Kemal Atatürk, 1881–1938, Turkish statesman

SPEAKING

1a What do you know about the United Nations (the UN)? Discuss these questions with a partner.

1 When and why was the UN founded?
2 How many countries are now UN members?
3 Where are the UN headquarters?
4 How often does the UN have a new Secretary General?
5 Which activities is the UN *not* involved with:
- Aid and peace keeping
- Children's rights
- Religious education
- Economic development
- International justice
- Entertainment

1b 10.1 Listen and check your answers. What other things do you know about the UN? Do you have a personal opinion about the UN and its work?

READING

2a Read the entry on the right from an encyclopaedia. What is the main subject of the text?

2b What do these phrases refer to in the text?

1 its (line 2)
2 this UN department (lines 4–5)
3 this work (line 13)
4 these people (line 16)

The United Nations is an organisation that works in many different areas. In order to carry out its work, the UN has a large department of international civil servants (the Secretariat). The head of this UN
5 department is the Secretary General and there are about 9,000 other staff members. The Secretary General is responsible for the day-to-day organisation of the UN and its many projects.

As well as these work responsibilities, the Secretary General
10 is a symbol or face of the United Nations. He or she is also a spokesperson, or representative, for the people of the world and can ask the UN to help with difficult situations in the world. In this work, he or she meets national presidents and ambassadors to discuss world problems.

15 The Secretary General also chooses the Messengers of Peace. These people publicise the work of the UN and they are chosen from the fields of arts, literature and sports. Messengers of Peace have included George Clooney (actor), Midori Goto (violinist) and Muhammad Ali (boxer).

2c Are these statements true or false, or does the text not say?

1 The UN helps protect endangered animals.
2 The Secretariat manages the UN's daily business.
3 The Secretary General is very well paid.
4 The Secretary General can request that the UN solves a problem.
5 The countries in the United Nations select the Messengers of Peace.
6 The Messengers of Peace tell the world about the UN's work.

3 Evaluating opinions Read these different opinions on and comments about the UN (a–e). Then answer the questions below (1–3).

a The Messengers of Peace should not only be celebrities.
b The UN talks a lot, but it doesn't do a lot.
c Ten powerful countries control the UN.
d The UN should focus on emergency disaster aid and not work in other areas such as human rights and peacekeeping.
e The UN was created in the '50s. We don't need it now.

1 Have you heard these opinions before?
2 Can you think of any reasons for these opinions?
3 Do you agree or disagree with these opinions?

VOCABULARY
PEOPLE AND ORGANISATIONS

4a Put these words into two groups: A for individuals and B for groups of people.

ambassador   assistant   civil servant   committee   department
head of a department   minister   president   spokesperson   staff

4b Which of the words can you find in the text?

4c Match some of the words above with these definitions. Write definitions for the other words.

1 a group of people who meet regularly and make important decisions
2 a politician with an important government job
3 one part of a company or an organisation
4 someone who represents and speaks for a group of people or an organisation
5 someone who helps a more senior colleague

4d 10.2 Mark the word stress on the words in Exercise 4a. Listen, check and repeat.

LISTENING

5a 10.3 Listen to a meeting between Liz, a UN staff member, and Geoff, a UN Messenger of Peace. They discuss the schedule for his future trip to Ghana. How many meetings/appointments do they discuss?

5b Listen again and answer these questions.

1 When is the trip to Ghana?
2 How many trips has Jeff done before?
3 On what day is he flying to Ghana?
4 What type of school is he visiting on Monday?
5 When is the student performance?
6 What time is the press conference?
7 Who is Sandra Ominga?
8 At what time does the meeting with the Minister for Children finish?
9 What is Geoff doing at 8 p.m.?
10 When and where is the TV interview?

GRAMMAR
PRESENT CONTINUOUS FOR FUTURE ARRANGEMENTS

6a Look at these two sentences (a–b) and the statements below (1–5). Are the statements true or false?

a At four, you're giving a press conference.
b Next Friday, Midori Goto's doing six different events.

1 These sentences are about the present.
2 They describe actions, not states.
3 The future time of the action is clear.
4 The future action is not certain to happen.
5 They describe meetings, appointments and arrangements.

6b You can use the present continuous to talk about fixed future arrangements and meetings. These arrangements often involve other people, so the time or place of the action or event is usually given. Look at Audio script 10.3 on page 159 and find examples.

GRAMMAR TIP

When you talk about future plans, you can use either the present continuous or *going to* with little change in meaning. When you want to show the plan is more arranged or fixed, you use the present continuous, especially when you give the exact time of the arrangement.

Language reference and extra practice, pages 120–121

7 Yo-Yo Ma (a musician) and Paulo Coelho (an author) are UN Messengers of Peace. Complete their appointments diaries for next week.

Student A: Turn to page 142.
Student B: Turn to page 146.

SPEAKING AND WRITING

8a Interview your classmates to find out what they are doing this week. Make notes of their answers.

What are you doing tonight / on Friday / this weekend?

I'm going to the cinema on Saturday and on Sunday, I'm …

8b Write a paragraph to summarise your class's social arrangements.

Five people are going to the cinema at the weekend. Two of them are going on Sunday, and three of them are …

SPEAKING

1 **Look at this list of companies and answer the questions below.**

Toyota Coca-Cola Volkswagen Nestlé
McDonald's Samsung Google Zara
PetroChina Shell Apple Roche HSBC

1 What does each of them do/produce?
2 In which country did each of them start?
3 Are there any other companies like this in your country?
4 Would you like to work for any of these companies? Why?/Why not?
5 Which companies can you see in the pictures on these pages?

READING

2a **Read the text about Apple. How did Apple change between 1976 and 2012?**

2b **Which century – 20th, 21st or both – do these statements go with?**

1 People thought that Apple was the best company in the USA and in the world.
2 Steve Jobs spent some time away from Apple.
3 Sales of a particular product were very good.
4 Apple became interested in more products than just computers.
5 Different people wanted to control the company.
6 Apple started selling its products directly to the public.

3 **Find words in the text that mean:**

1 small and easy to carry
2 got a new person or thing, instead of the one you had
3 problems with a machine or a piece of equipment that stop it working properly
4 a short, clever phrase that is used in advertising
5 the programs that a computer uses to do different jobs
6 made a new product available (two words)

4 **Identifying key dates** What do you think were the three most important years for Apple?

Growth of a global giant

Today, Apple employs 80,000 people around the world. In 2012, it had nearly 400 stores in 14 countries and was the most valuable (and most admired) company in the world. But it wasn't always that way …

The 20th century

1976 Apple was set up by Steve Jobs, Steve Wozniak and Ronald Wayne, although Wayne soon left the new company. Apple's first headquarters was Jobs's parents' house in Los Altos (California, USA) where Apple I personal computers were built in the garage.

1977 The famous Apple logo was created, which was used until 1998. Also, a new, improved machine, the Apple II, was presented to the public. Over time, millions were sold.

1980 Apple became a public company. The Apple III was released, but it had a number of faults, such as becoming too hot.

1981 Steve Wozniak was injured in a plane crash and gradually withdrew from the company. So, from the original trio, only Jobs remained.

1984 The Macintosh personal computer was launched, using a brilliant TV advert directed by the film-maker Ridley Scott. The Mac was easy to use and cheap, but not very powerful.

1985 A power struggle developed in the company because sales of the Mac were falling – as a result of strong PC competition. Jobs's responsibilities were taken away from him. He decided to leave Apple and start a new company (NeXT).

1987 Apple registered the name Apple.com; it was one of the first 100 companies to register a .com address on the new internet.

1996 Jobs returned to Apple when NeXT was bought by Apple, and a new era began.

Into the 21st century

2001 The iPod was launched with the slogan 'iPod therefore iAm'. This portable music player could store about 1,000 songs. The first Apple retail stores were opened in the USA.

2003 The online iTunes Music Store was opened, selling songs for 99 cents each. For the first time, consumers could get legal digital music.

2007 Apple launched a smartphone – the iPhone. The name of the company was changed from 'Apple Computer, Inc.' to 'Apple Inc.', as it was now concentrating on mobile electronic devices.

2008 Apple was named the most admired company in the US by *Fortune* magazine. The online App Store was opened.

2010 The iPad tablet was released, and 300,000 were sold on the first day.

2011 iCloud was launched – an online service for storing music, photos, files and software. In August, because of ill health, Jobs was replaced by Tim Cook as CEO of Apple. On October 5th, the death of Steve Jobs was announced.

2012 The iPad Mini was released. This small tablet could fit in a jacket pocket. At this time, Apple was considered a company that set trends – able to predict the future of computing. However, with growing competition from Samsung and other technology giants, it will be interesting to see who is the market leader in years ahead.

GRAMMAR
PAST SIMPLE PASSIVE

5a Use the past simple passive to talk about the history of something (e.g. an organisation), especially when you are more interested in 'what happened' than in 'who did it'. Look at these examples, then find other examples of this grammar in the text.

*Apple **was set up** in 1976.*

*The iPad **was released**.*

*The computers **were built** in the garage.*

5b You form the past simple passive with *was/were* and the past participle of the verb. How do you make negatives and questions?

↳ Language reference and extra practice, pages 120–121

Apple, Mac, iPod, iTunes, iPhone, iPad and iCloud are trademarks of Apple Inc., registered in the U.S. and other countries.

6a Use these prompts to make questions about Apple.
1 Why / name Apple / choose / for the new company?
2 How many Apple I computers / build?
3 Who / Apple logo / create by?
4 Why / the advert for the Macintosh / like / by many people?
5 When / first Apple store / open / outside the USA?
6 Which other companies / admire / in 2012?

6b `10.4` Listen and check. How do you pronounce *was* and *were* in the above questions?

6c `10.5` Listen and note the answers. Then compare with a partner.

7 Complete this text about the Korean company Samsung with the past simple passive or active form of the verbs in brackets.

Samsung ¹ was ~~set up~~ (set up) in Taegu, South Korea, in 1938 by Byung-Chull Lee. At that time, Samsung General Store (its original name) ² sold (sell) dried fish, vegetables and fruit to China. Samsung (which means 'three stars' in Korean) ³ was grown (grow) quickly.

In the 1970s, Samsung ⁴ moved (move) into industry, and many new Samsung companies ⁵ were created (create), e.g. Samsung Shipbuilding. During this decade, Samsung also ⁶ developed (develop) its home electronics business. In 1976, the one millionth black-and-white TV ⁷ was produced (produce). The next year, colour televisions ⁸ were exported (export) for the first time.

In the 1980s, Samsung ⁹ put (put) its energies into technology, and new products ¹⁰ were introduced (introduce) to the global market. Today, most people know the company for its TVs, smartphones and tablets, but there are in fact about eighty different companies in the Samsung group – or 'chaebol' in Korean.

SPEAKING

8 Exploring the topic Discuss these questions in small groups. Give reasons for your answers.
1 In what way do the companies on these pages affect your life?
2 How can a company become very large and successful? What does it need to do this?
3 Do you think big companies are good or bad for society?
4 What do you understand by the term *globalisation*?

▶ MEET THE EXPERT
Watch an interview with Nick Cooper, a brands specialist, about what makes a global brand.
Turn to page 129 for video activities.

PREPARATION

1a Where was the last Summer Olympic Games held? Did you watch any of it? Did your country win any medals?

1b Which of these cities have *not* hosted the Summer Olympic Games? Check your answers on page 136.

London	Los Angeles	Paris	Mexico City
Nairobi	New York	Abu Dhabi	Moscow	Seoul

SITUATION

The International Olympic Committee (IOC) decides which city will host the Olympic Games. Cities that want to host the games have to give presentations to the IOC about how they will organise and deliver a successful Olympic Games.

2 10.6 The British Olympic Committee gave a presentation to win the chance to host the 2012 Olympic Games. Listen to the opening of the presentation. Which of these topics are parts of the presentation?
- transport
- catering facilities
- sports facilities
- accommodation for athletes
- facilities for media companies
- London's special ambition for the Games

3 Look at these statements and analyse them. If a country wants to host the Olympics, are these points strong or weak to use in the presentation?

1 There is a comprehensive and efficient public transport system.
2 The athletes will live one hour from the Olympic Park, where the main sports venues are.
3 A famous architect will design an amazing new athletics stadium.
4 The Olympic Park will have the largest fast-food restaurant in the world.
5 The city has many famous tourist attractions and sites.
6 The city has never hosted a global sporting event before.

4a 10.7 Listen to the rest of the presentation and take notes for each of the topics in Exercise 2. Note key points and examples.

4b Work with a partner and compare your notes with the points in Exercise 3.

4c Use your notes to answer these questions.

1 Where will they build the Olympic Park?
2 How many examples of existing sports venues are given?
3 What kind of facilities will the rooms have?
4 How many bus routes are there in the same area as the Olympic Park?
5 How long will the journey to the city centre on the high-speed train take?
6 Who will be able to travel for free on public transport?

KEY LANGUAGE
GIVING EXAMPLES

5a 10.8 In the presentation, the speaker gives many examples in order to support his claims and promises. Complete these sentences. Then listen and check your ideas.

1 For _____, children will be the main performers …
2 _____ instance, world-famous architect Zaha Hadid will design the swimming pool.
3 Another example _____ the athletics stadium, which will have 80,000 seats.
4 We'll use existing world-class venues, _____ as Wembley football stadium.
5 … with many famous buildings and places: _____ example, Big Ben and Buckingham Palace.
6 They will all have modern facilities, for _____ free WiFi.
7 A good example of _____ is the new high-speed train line.

5b Answer these questions about the sentences above.

1 Look at sentences 1 and 5. What are the differences in punctuation?
2 In which sentence (1 or 5) is the example a simple noun phrase, and in which is the example a verb clause?
3 Which other phrase has the same language patterns as *for example*?
4 In the other sentences, are the examples noun phrases or verb phrases?

5c Identify the errors in these sentences.

1 In my city, there are many places to go, such as many people go to the cinema.
2 Another example the art galleries.
3 The old buildings are important: for example there is the castle and the palace.
4 My city is a better place to live now. A good example of it is the low crime rate.

PRONUNCIATION

6a 10.9 Pausing and emphatic stress When you give a talk or presentation, it is important to pause and to emphasise key words. Listen and mark the pauses like this //, and underline the words with extra stress. Why do you think those words have extra stress?

First, we want to deliver a magical experience, with an electrifying atmosphere for competitors and spectators.

Our aim, or special ambition, is to inspire young people in Britain and across the world to play sport.

6b Listen again and repeat.

6c Look at Audio script 10.7 on page 160. Mark the pauses and stress on the first sentences of each section. Practise saying those sentences.

TASK
GIVING A PRESENTATION

7a Nairobi, in Kenya, and Abu Dhabi, in UAE, would like to host the Olympic Games. Work with a partner and prepare a short presentation about one of the cities. Use the Key language and the Useful phrases on this page to help.

Pair A: Turn to page 143.
Pair B: Turn to page 147.

> ### USEFUL PHRASES
>
> We are here to represent …
> The special ambition for our city is …
> There are three main topics.
> First of all, … Secondly, … Finally, …
> Thank you for your kind attention.

7b Take turns to give your presentation to another pair and listen to their presentation. Make notes.

7c Evaluate both presentations. Did you use good language? Was your pronunciation clear? Was the communication good?

8 With the other pair, look in detail at each city's plans and discuss their strengths and weaknesses. Which city do you think should host the Olympic Games?

STUDY SKILLS
IMPROVING YOUR LISTENING

1 Make a list of different situations when *you* listen to English (e.g. watching films, listening to lectures). Which are the easiest / most difficult for you? Why?

2a The skill of listening There are two main kinds of listening: listening for the general idea and listening for detail. Look back at the listening exercises in this coursebook and find some for each kind. Which kind did you find the easiest / most difficult?

2b There are a number of things you can do before you listen which can help you to understand better and get the information you need. Which do you think will help you most?

1 Use your knowledge of the topic.
2 Guess who is going to speak.
3 Guess what the speaker will say.
4 Guess the vocabulary the speaker will use.
5 Guess specific phrases the speaker will use.

3 Activate your knowledge You are going to listen to a talk about INTERPOL, the international police organisation. What do you know about it? Describe the INTERPOL emblem. What do you think it means?

4a Predicting content Here are some questions you can ask yourself before you listen to the talk. Can you add two or three more questions?

1 Where is INTERPOL based?
2 How many people work for it?

4b Predicting vocabulary Which of these words do you think the speaker will use?

accommodation   boxer   crime   criminal
databases   entertainment   financial   fingerprints
headquarters   languages   laws   literature
member   police forces   priorities   slogan   staff

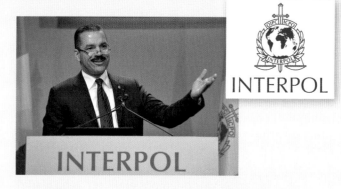

5a `10.10` Listen to the talk. Does the speaker talk about any of the things in your questions in Exercise 4a? What does she say about them?

5b Listen again. Did you hear any of the words you chose in Exercise 4b?

6a Importance markers The speaker uses a number of phrases to show that what she is saying and what she is going to say is important. Can you complete these sentences? Look at the underlined sentences in Audio script 10.10 on page 161 and check.

1 INTERPOL now has 190 member countries. And let me _____ out that it's those countries that pay for it!
2 Don't _____ that most INTERPOL officers stay in their own country.
3 But, and I must _____ your attention to this, we never break the law in any country.
4 One of our _____ is problems connected with drugs.
5 Another important _____ is trafficking in human beings.
6 Another _____ priority is financial crime.
7 The _____ important thing we do is to run a global police communication system.
8 _____ important thing we do is to provide training courses for national police forces.

6b Which type of crime that INTERPOL fights do you think is the most serious?

WRITING SKILLS
A FOR-AND-AGAINST ESSAY

7 Discuss these questions in small groups.

1   When you make a phone call, do you ever think that someone could be listening to you?
2   Do you think it is right for the police, governments or media to listen secretly to people's phone conversations?
3   Have you seen or read any news stories in your country about this kind of activity?

8a Read this student's essay about phone-tapping. Does the writer mention any of the things you discussed in Exercise 7?

8b Do you agree with the ideas in this essay?

THE ADVANTAGES AND DISADVANTAGES OF PHONE-TAPPING

When you talk on your phone, who is listening to you? Is it just the person you are talking to, or are there others who can hear what you are saying – governments, police, journalists or criminals? Listening secretly to someone's phone conversations is called 'phone-tapping' (in the UK) or 'wiretapping' (in the US). It has become a very important issue in our lives. This essay will consider whether phone-tapping is good or bad for our society.

One serious disadvantage of phone-tapping is that we cannot be sure if our conversations are private. Newspapers, for example, can use information they get from phone-tapping to write stories about celebrities. If people are listening to us in secret, we lose some of our freedom. Another problem with phone-tapping is that it is very easy for anyone to buy the equipment you need to do it.

On the other hand, a major advantage is that it helps to catch criminals, and that makes our society safer. Another advantage is that – for the police – it is possible to get information about criminals without putting police officers in dangerous situations.

To sum up, is phone-tapping good or bad? This is a difficult question to answer. Although it helps to make our society safer, people can know too much about our private lives. Therefore, we lose some of our freedom. Perhaps we need more time to understand the effects of this, but I personally think that the advantages are greater than the disadvantages.

9a Match these headings (a–d) with the paragraphs of the essay. Which form the main body of the essay?

a   Advantages   c   Introduction
b   Conclusion   d   Disadvantages

9b Where can you find these things in the essay? Write *I* for introduction, *MB* for main body and *C* for conclusion.

1   a statement of the writer's opinion
2   a statement of the importance of the subject
3   development of important ideas
4   a statement of the writer's aims
5   a summary of the main points

10a Underline the phrases that are used in the essay to talk about advantages and disadvantages.

10b Use this table to make sentences about the writer's opinions.

The main disadvantage of		the police can get information about criminals in a safe way.
One of the bad points about	phone-tapping is that	it helps to catch criminals.
The main advantage of		it is too easy to buy the necessary equipment.
One of the good points about		we cannot have private conversations.

11a Linkers **Study the use of the linkers** *although,* *on the other hand* **and** *therefore* **in the essay. Then complete these sentences.**

1   _____ phone-tapping can help to catch criminals, we can also lose our freedom.
2   There are a number of good points about this. _____, there are many more bad points.
3   There is very little data about this. _____, it is difficult to reach clear conclusions.
4   A career in the police force could be very interesting. _____, it might be dangerous.
5   _____ the crime rate is going down, people sometimes feel less safe.

11b Which other sentences and phrases in the essay can you use in a for-and-against essay on any topic?

12a Developing ideas Work with a partner. Discuss the advantages and disadvantages of these topics.

1   using CCTV cameras
2   police forces having a lot more female officers
3   sending criminals who are not dangerous to prison

12b Choose one of the topics above and write four sentences like those in Exercise 10b.

12c Write a for-and-against essay on the topic you chose above. Use your ideas from above and linkers from Exercise 11a.

11 The environment
11.1 CLIMATE CHANGE

IN THIS UNIT

GRAMMAR
- present perfect 2: *for/since*
- phrasal verbs

VOCABULARY
- noun phrases (noun + *of* + noun)
- containers and materials

SCENARIO
- checking agreement with question tags
- collaborating

STUDY SKILLS
- thinking critically about reading texts

WRITING SKILLS
- a report (on a specific situation)

'I speak for the trees, for the trees have no tongues.' In *The Lorax* by Dr Seuss, 1904–1991, US writer

SPEAKING

1 Discuss these questions in small groups.

1 What has the weather been like this week?
2 Describe the climate in your country or region. Think about the different seasons.
3 How often does your country experience these things? Which countries frequently experience them?

thunderstorms and heavy rain	droughts
temperatures above 35°C	floods	tornadoes
hurricanes and typhoons	heatwaves

READING

2a Match the internet search results on the right (A–D) with these titles (1–4).

1 The real facts about climate change
2 Heavy storms hit southern Europe
3 Extreme weather linked to global warming, Nobel prize-winning scientist says ...
4 UN warns of rising food costs after year's extreme weather

2b Which of the websites tell us these things?

1 How to solve a serious problem *C*
2 Problems that are caused by today's weather *B*
3 The connection between agriculture and weather *D*
4 Research data agrees with the claim that global warming causes extreme weather. *A*

---

extreme weather 🔍

220,000,000 results (0.3 seconds)

A *3*

New scientific analysis supports the view that record-breaking summer heat and other extreme weather events are the result of global warming.

scientific_research_weather

B *2*

The south of France and northern Italy are experiencing extremely heavy rain and 100km/h winds. Over 200mm of rain is expected to fall overnight, which will increase the risk of flooding from the River Po near Turin. Some roads have been closed as part of the emergency planning for the area.

news_weather_results

C *1*

Savetheworld provides facts on global warming, the causes of global warming, the effects of climate change – heavy storms, severe floods/droughts – and gives solutions to this global issue.

save_world_global_warming

D *4*

The warning comes as shops face a shortage of basic food due to the lack of rain in Russia and the US this year, and farmers report that wheat production is at the lowest level since the 1980s.

effects_extreme_weather

VOCABULARY
NOUN PHRASES: NOUN + *OF* + NOUN

3a Look again at the internet search results and find the examples of noun phrases with this pattern: noun + *of* + something, e.g. *the consequences of climate change*. Which noun phrase has no plural form?

3b Match the first noun in each of the noun phrases you found above with these meanings. Use some of the meanings more than once.

1 something which makes something else happen
2 a possibility that something bad may happen
3 when you do not have the quantity that you need
4 something which happens because of something else
5 a piece of something

3c Use the eight nouns from Exercise 3b to complete this paragraph.

The fact that I don't want to live in a city is the ¹ consequence of many different things. ² the part of the problem with cities is that there is a lot of air pollution. One of the ³ effect of this air pollution is that the ⁴ risk of people dying young increases. Heavy traffic is one of the ⁵ cause of air pollution, and people often use cars because there is a ⁶ lack of public transport. The ⁷ effect of air pollution on our lives are clear, but a ⁸ lack of money often means governments can't improve the urban environment.

LISTENING

4a [11.1] Listen to the opening of a radio programme about the environment. How has the presenter's opinion about global warming changed?

4b Listen again. What do the numbers 20, 1929, 96 and 50 refer to?

5a [11.2] Now listen to the scientist's answers to the presenter's questions and make notes. Use the key words and phrases in this box to help you.

globe   global warming   climate change
frequency   extreme   average temperature

5b Use your notes to complete these statements.

1 Across the globe, there has been an increase in …
2 The increase in average global temperature increases the …
3 There will be more heatwaves, but …

6 [11.3] Listen to the final part of the programme and make notes. Compare your notes with a partner. What is the main problem that the scientist discusses?

GRAMMAR
PRESENT PERFECT 2: *FOR/SINCE*

7a Complete these sentences with *for* or *since*. When do we use *for* and *since* to show the period of time? In all these sentences, is the period of time finished or unfinished?

1 I've known about global warming _for_ 20 years.
2 It has rained every day _since_ the second of June.
3 There has been no rainfall _for_ 96 days.
4 Heatwaves have become 30 times more likely _since_ 1950.

7b Find more examples of the present perfect in Audio scripts 11.1–11.3 on pages 161–162. In which examples is there a specific time period that continues up to now?

➡ Language reference and extra practice, pages 122–123

8a Put the verbs in brackets in the present perfect, then complete the sentences so that they are true for you.

1 I _have been_ (be) at this college / with my company for/ since …
2 I _have lived_ (live) in my current home for/since …
3 I _have had_ (have) my mobile phone for/since …
4 I _have known_ (know) my best friend for/since …
5 I _have studied_ (study) English for/since …

8b Compare your sentences with a partner. Who has done those things for the longest?

A: How long have you been at this college?
B: For about six months. What about you?

SPEAKING

9a Illustrating a claim Work with a partner and discuss these statements. Can you find / think of examples to justify the claims? Keep notes of your discussion.

1 Global warming has caused social and economic change.
2 My government has done a lot to reduce global warming.
3 There are still many things we haven't done which could reduce global warming.
4 The way I have lived my life is bad/good for the environment.

9b Compare your ideas with another pair of students. Use your notes to help you.

▶ MEET THE EXPERT

Watch an interview with Dr Laura Baker, a meteorologist, about tracking and analysing storms.
Turn to page 130 for video activities.

VOCABULARY
CONTAINERS AND MATERIALS

1 Work with a partner. What do you think the photos on page 89 show? Check your answer on page 136.

2a Match these containers with photos 1–8 on the right. Are these words countable or uncountable?

bottle	box	can/tin	carton
jar	packet	pot	tube

2b Match these materials with the containers above. Are the collocations countable or uncountable?

aluminium	cardboard	glass	metal
paper	plastic		

2c Which word carries the main stress in these collocations? For example, do we say a _glass_ jar or a glass _jar_?

2d What is usually found in these containers? What do you do with containers when they are empty?

READING

3a Read the interview that appeared on a newspaper website. Which of these statements best describes Kevin and Alicia?

1 Kevin is a consumer, and Alicia works for a supermarket.
2 Kevin is a journalist, and Alicia works in the packaging industry.
3 Kevin works for an organisation that protects the environment, and Alicia works for the government.

3b According to the interview, which two sentences are correct?

1 There are no arguments to support wrapping coconuts.
2 People in the UK are paying around £500 a year for food packaging.
3 Kevin thinks that the packaging industry must reduce the amount of packaging waste.
4 The packaging industry is not concerned about the amount of packaging waste that is produced in the UK.
5 The UK recycles more packaging waste than many other European countries.
6 Changes in society have little effect on how much packaging we use.

3c What do these words in the interview refer to?

1 this (line 11)
2 it (line 18)
3 we (line 31)
4 these (line 36)
5 that (line 48)
6 they (line 52)

WAR ON CRISP PACKETS

In the week that the government sets out its new environmental programme, Kevin McCabe and Alicia Stewart consider the problem of food packaging waste.

5   **KM:** On my way home from work yesterday, I stopped off at my local supermarket. Among other things, I wanted to buy a couple of coconuts. When I picked them up, I was amazed
10 that each coconut was wrapped in clear, thin plastic. Isn't this the most stupid example of packaging ever?

  AS: You've picked an unusual example of packaging, but there is a reason for
15 this. Supermarkets want to make sure that coconuts reach the consumer in the very best condition. The packaging helps to keep the product fresh; it cuts down the damage if the product gets broken; it stops coconut hairs from
20 getting into other food during transport and it allows supermarkets to put on an information label.

GRAMMAR
PHRASAL VERBS

4a A phrasal verb is formed by a verb and one or two other words (e.g. *up, down, off*). We call these other words 'particles'. The meaning of a phrasal verb is often different from the meaning of the verb without a particle. Underline the verbs in these sentences.

1 a He's going to the supermarket.
  b The amount of waste is going up.
2 a She cut her birthday cake.
  b Packaging cuts down damage.

4b Look at the verbs again. Which two are phrasal verbs? What are the differences in meaning between the phrasal and non-phrasal verbs?

5a Phrasal verbs can be transitive or intransitive. Transitive verbs need an object. Intransitive verbs do not need an object. Look at the phrasal verbs in Exercise 4a. Which one is transitive? Which is intransitive?

5b Find other phrasal verbs in the interview. Which are transitive? Which are intransitive?

↳ Language reference and extra practice, pages 122–123

6a Complete the sentences below with the particles in the box.

back   down   out (x2)   up (x2)

1 Did prices go ___UP___ or down last year?
2 What's the most interesting thing you've found _out_ recently? *discover*
3 Have you ever carried _out_ any research?
4 Has anyone in your family ever set _up_ a company or a club?
5 Have you ever borrowed anything that you haven't given _back_?
6 Why must we cut _down_ the amount of packaging waste?

6b Work with a partner. Take turns to ask and answer the questions above. If possible, develop your answers using two or three sentences.

SPEAKING

7a Problem-solving Work in small groups. Discuss what you can do to cut down waste. Think about these things: birthday cards, toys, plastic bags, fruit and vegetables, print-outs from your computer, DVDs, water.

mobile phones and clothes – recycle them

birthday presents – give cinema or concert tickets, not disposable goods

7b Turn to page 136 to check your ideas.

KM: I see. However, the fact is that here in the UK, we throw a huge amount of packaging away – 4.9 million tonnes every year. All those
25 cans, jars and boxes add about £500 a year to the average food bill. UK supermarkets give eight billion single-use plastic bags out a year. In addition, our streets are full of packaging rubbish such as water bottles, crisp packets, noodle pots and plastic bags. Isn't it
30 your responsibility to do something about this?

AS: As a matter of fact, we are doing something. A lot of thought now goes into the design of packaging, so that in many cases we use the minimum amount of material. We're
35 also using more biodegradable materials, and these end up mainly as water vapour. But people shouldn't just blame this problem on the packaging industry. Consumers and governments also need to take action.

40 **KM:** I think they are. The amount of packaging waste that's recovered and recycled in the UK has gone up for a number of years – although this country's record is poor compared with other European countries. However, even with biodegradable materials, it's not
45 enough just to put rubbish in a hole in the ground. Without sun, air and water, a rubbish bag that should break up in 15 days could still exist hundreds of years from now.

AS: Yes, that's a problem for planners. Remember too, that changes in society are
50 going on which affect the amount of packaging that's produced. For example, more and more people are living alone and they're eating more convenience food. So this issue isn't just about the packaging industry – everyone has to pull together on this.

89

PREPARATION

1 Are these sentences true for the place where you live? Compare your ideas with a partner.

In my city, …

1 there's a lot of graffiti.
2 there aren't many green spaces.
3 there are some untidy areas of wasteland.
4 my local park isn't looked after.
5 many streets feel unsafe and dangerous.

SITUATION

In New Zealand, local community groups often try to improve local environments. They apply to the government for funding for their projects.

2a Read the funding proposal below and answer these questions.

1 What is the main purpose of the project?
2 Which do you think are the three most important benefits of the project?
3 How much does it cost each year?

2b The government funding committee have some guidelines to help them assess a project proposal. Look at these guidelines and evaluate which ones the Wild City project meets.

Good projects should …

1 improve the local environment.
2 solve a problem.
3 involve local people working together.
4 need no, or little, annual financial support.
5 offer ideas for future developments.
6 make the local area 'greener'.

3a 11.4 Listen to the funding committee discuss the project. Which of the guidelines do Rick and Poppy discuss, and in what order? Do they generally agree or disagree with each other?

3b Listen again. Are these statements true or false?

1 Rick says the project is good for the environment.
2 It solves a problem because it brings local people together.
3 The project does not meet two of the guidelines.
4 The annual running costs are acceptable.
5 Projects with unpaid volunteers are often unsuccessful.

Wild City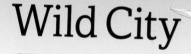

Project description: The regeneration of an area of wasteland by turning it into a small, urban wildlife park

Benefits of the project:

1 It will turn an ugly area of wasteland into an attractive nature park.
2 It will increase the number of trees and animals in this urban area.
3 It will be an educational resource for local children.
4 It might attract some visitors to the area.
5 It will bring the community together. Local people will build and look after the park.

Budget (including annual running costs):
Total cost: NZ$48,000

Cost breakdown:
Clearance of the wasteland: NZ$20,000
Purchase of 100 trees: NZ$8,000
Purchase of plants and seeds: NZ$10,000
Annual running cost. NZ$10,000

KEY LANGUAGE
CHECKING AGREEMENT

4a **11.5** **Complete these sentences from the conversation. Then listen and check.**

1 You can't get much greener than a wildlife park, _____ you?
2 The project solves a problem, _____ it?
3 They could do it unpaid, _____ they?
4 We've seen that fail before, _____ we?

4b **Use question tags when you think someone will agree with what you say or to check they have the same idea/opinion. In the sentences above, the speaker expects the listener to agree. Look at Audio script 11.4 on page 162 and find more examples of question tags.**

4c **Complete these sentences with question tags.**

1 It costs a lot of money, _____?
2 We can't pay for everything, _____?
3 They haven't answered all the questions, _____?
4 It's a good idea, _____?
5 They could make a few changes, _____?

PRONUNCIATION

5a Intonation in question tags **Listen to the sentences in Exercise 4a again. Does the intonation on the question tags go up or down?**

5b **Work with a partner. Practise saying and responding to the sentences in Exercise 4c.**

TASK
COLLABORATING

6a **You are on the funding committee considering three projects: Wild City, Super Streets and Village of Wind. Look at the information about the other two projects on page 137 and assess all three projects in order to prepare for the meeting. What are the good/bad things about all three projects? Which of the guidelines do/don't they meet?**

6b **The committee has a total of NZ$200,000 available, which can be used for one, two or all three projects. Have a meeting to decide which projects you will fund. Go through each project, checking that you agree on whether or not the project meets the guidelines. You can suggest possible changes to the projects if that means you might fund them. Use the Useful phrases below to help.**

USEFUL PHRASES

What do you think of this one?
What about the other guidelines?
What changes could they make?
Exactly. / Indeed. / Of course.
I'm not sure. / Possibly, but …

6c **Compare your decisions with other groups.**

STUDY SKILLS
THINKING CRITICALLY ABOUT READING TEXTS

1 When people think critically, they ask questions (see Lesson 6.4: Study skills). So when you read a new text, asking questions will help you to understand the text better. Add three or four questions to this list. Then check on page 138.

Where did the text appear (e.g. on a website, on a poster)?

Who wrote it, and who will read it?

2 Read the action group newsletter below and answer the questions from Exercise 1. Then compare your ideas with a partner.

Barnley Action Group
NEWSLETTER

Dear Resident

As I am sure you know, the government and British Airports Organisation (BAO) want to build a new runway at Gatsted Airport before 2022. The location they have chosen is on the north side of the airport, where our village now stands.

As local residents, we do not believe that a new runway is a good idea. Our beautiful village will not exist any more, and many families will lose their homes – families who have lived and worked in the area for a very long time. Also, the increase in air traffic will create a lot of noise and pollution.

We already know that the majority of local people are against the plans. As a result, **we are setting up an action group** in order to fight against the plans for this airport. The first meeting of our group will be in **Barnley Community Centre** on **Monday 5 July at 7.30 p.m.**

We hope you can join us then. We will decide how we can best organise our protest. Please help us to protect our homes, our way of life and our environment for yourselves and for future generations.

Roderick Chetter
President, Barnley Action Group

3a You can ask yourself other questions about the text. Read sections 1–4. Then add questions a–d below to the correct section. You may use the same section twice.

1   **Quality of information**
In the first two paragraphs, can I find examples of information that is a) fact and b) opinion?

2   **Reasons for something**
How many reasons does the writer give why it is not a good idea to build a new runway? What are they? Which do I think is the most important?

3   **What is missing**
Does the letter give arguments for and against the new runway?

4   **Language**
What do I think the phrase *a very long time* means in paragraph 2: five years? 20 years? 200 years? something else?

a   Only 4,000 people live in Barnley. Why doesn't the writer mention this fact in his letter?
b   What is the effect of the word *beautiful*, which is used to describe the village?
c   Is everything in the letter true?
d   What does the phrase *the majority of local people* mean in paragraph 3: 51%? 60%? 75%? more?

3b Now answer all the questions above.

3c Do you think the letter will have the effect that the writer wants? Why?/Why not? Imagine you live in Barnley. Will you go to the meeting?

WRITING SKILLS
A REPORT

4 Discuss these questions with a partner.

1 Have you ever read a report? If so, what kind of report was it?
2 Have you ever written a report?
3 In which situations will you need to write reports in the future, do you think?

5 Read the report below and choose the best title.

1 Plans for a new runway at Gatsted Airport
2 Reactions to plans for a new runway at Gatsted Airport
3 Opposition to plans for a new runway at Gatsted Airport

A _____

The aim of this report is to summarise the findings of a recent survey among local residents in the village of Barnley in southern Sussex on plans to build a new runway at Gatsted Airport. AEB Research was asked to carry out the survey by a local action group. The data was collected by questionnaire and interviews with 400 local residents between 6th and 17th October.

B _____

C _____

The majority of local residents (83%) said that they were against the plans for the new runway. The main reason (mentioned by 75%) was that it will destroy the village of Barnley, and many families will have to move house. These people sometimes have long connections with the area, going back hundreds of years. Another important reason (mentioned by 64%) was that the runway will cause noise and pollution.

D _____

A minority of residents (17%), on the other hand, felt that a new runway could bring benefits to the area, as it could create new jobs.

E _____

However, 96% of all residents thought that a better idea was to build a new runway at one of the other airports in the region.

F _____

To sum up, there was a great deal of opposition to the plan for the new runway. There was an almost universal feeling that the government and BAO should build an extra runway at another airport. Because of the strong local feeling, we believe that the government and BAO should consider other possible locations carefully.

6 Put these headings and sub-headings in the correct place (A–F) in the report.

1 Conclusion
2 Arguments against building the new runway at Gatsted Airport
3 Introduction
4 Alternative locations for the runway
5 Arguments for building the runway at Gatsted Airport
6 Findings

7a Asking critical questions Look at the questions in Exercise 1 again. How many of them can you answer about the report?

7b Write two or three questions you can ask yourself about the report. Use the questions in Exercise 3a to help you.

Is the information true?

8 Look back at the essay on page 85. What is the main difference between a report and an essay?

9a Match these phrases (1–6) with their functions (a–f) below.

1 The aim of this report is to …
2 The data was collected by …
3 The majority … said that …
4 The main reason … was that …
5 A minority … felt that …
6 To sum up, there was …

a the opinion of most people
b the opinion of a small number of people
c why the report was written
d a summary of the report
e how the information was obtained
f why people had particular views

9b In paragraphs C, D and E of the report, which four verbs are used to report the residents' opinions?

9c Which other phrases in the report could you use in a report on any topic?

10 You work for an independent market research company. The government wants to build a new terminal at a major airport. You have carried out a survey and found out what local people think about the idea. Write your report. Use the information on page 138 and your own ideas.

12 Sport
12.1 MINORITY SPORTS

IN THIS UNIT

GRAMMAR
- second conditional
- *too* and *enough*

VOCABULARY
- sports
- linking words

SCENARIO
- answering complex questions
- using a questionnaire

STUDY SKILLS
- time management

WRITING SKILLS
- a formal email (requesting further information)

'Sports do not build character. They reveal it.' Heywood Broun, 1888–1939, US journalist

VOCABULARY AND SPEAKING
SPORTS

1a Discuss these questions in small groups.

1 What's the most popular sport in your country to a) watch and b) play?
2 How popular are these sports in your country?

gymnastics   cycling   basketball   fencing
table tennis   dragon-boat racing   hockey   judo
polo   sailing   swimming   skiing

3 Which of the sports do you consider minority sports? What other minority sports do you know?
4 Which verbs are used to talk about these and other sports: *do, go* or *play*, e.g. *do judo, play football*?
5 Ask your partners about sports they play (or have played), and about sports they would like to do.

1b How much do you know about some of these sports? Do the quiz on page 138 with a partner.

READING

2a Read this letter that appeared in a national newspaper. What is its purpose? Tick (✓) the correct answer(s).

1 to persuade the media to report minority sports more
2 to report on Michaela's travels
3 to put pressure on the government to spend more money on minority sports

Letters&emails

Time for a change in sport

I read your story 'Not so jolly hockey' (20 October) with great interest as, for the last few weeks, I have been travelling around the country, talking to young people about minority sports. The youngsters that I met were doing a wide variety of minority sports (e.g. fencing, gymnastics, archery) and they were all enthusiastic and dedicated. However, they were also sad, disappointed and angry about the lack of media interest in their sports, and also about poor facilities and funding. All over the country, I heard the same comment: 'If we had more funding, we would do really well in international competitions.'

Let's give the young people of this country a real chance to improve their fitness, show their talents and achieve success. We need proper government investment in facilities and training. We also need a sympathetic media that tells young people about less well-known sports in order to develop their interest.

I believe it is now time for the government and the media to show the same commitment to minority sports as the young people who do them.

Michaela Scrivin
World Dragon-Boat Champion
Glasgow

94

2b Find these things in the letter.

1 a list of minority sports
2 a reason why the media should report minority sports
3 problems faced by people who do minority sports
4 young people's feelings about doing their sports
5 information about the writer's recent activities
6 a statement about what official action is required

2c Evaluating effective language Which phrases does Michaela use to show that the problems are national and general (not local), affecting many people and sports? Do you think her letter will change anything? Why?/Why not?

LISTENING

3a 12.1 **Listen to an extract from a current affairs programme and answer these questions.**

1 What time of day is this programme broadcast?
2 What are the guests' jobs?
3 How many letters/emails do they discuss?
4 Do the guests agree or disagree with the letters/emails?

3b Listen again and make notes. What is said about:

1 recent government spending on minority sports?
2 the success of British sportsmen and women in minority sports?
3 minority sports in the media?
4 children's opportunities to do minority sports at school?

3c Discuss with a partner. Do you think this programme is interesting? Why?/ Why not? What can you learn from a programme like this?

GRAMMAR
SECOND CONDITIONAL

4 Look at these sentences and answer the questions (1–3) below.

a If we had more funding, we would do really well in international competitions.
b If the media showed more interest in other sports, kids would want to try them.
c If they had more opportunities, they wouldn't be so unhealthy.

1 Do the sentences describe real or unreal situations?
2 In the *if*-clause, which tense do we use after *if*? Does this refer to past time?
3 In the main clause, which form of the verb follows *would*?

➥ Language reference and extra practice, pages 124–125

5 Correct the mistakes in these sentences.

1 If I watched more sport on TV, I'd to know the names of more sports players. *would*
2 If you had the chance to learn a new sport, what will it be?
3 They would didn't go sailing if they didn't like it. *didn't*
4 I wouldn't lend him any money for the ski trip if I don't trust him. (I'm sure he'll pay it back.) *would*
5 Would children played more minority sports if they didn't only see football on TV?

> **GRAMMAR TIP**
>
> You can use *might* instead of *would*. *Might* is less certain than *would*.

6 Work in small groups. Complete the gaps with the correct form of the verb, then ask each other the questions and discuss the unusual situations.

What would you do if …

1 you _____ (win) a million dollars?
2 you _____ (meet) your favourite film star?
3 you _____ (hear) someone moving about in your house late at night?
4 a very rich and famous, but unpleasant sports star _____ (want) to marry your best friend?

SPEAKING

7 Do you agree with these statements? Discuss in groups. Explain your answers.

1 Children play many different sports at school.
2 Top footballers would play better if they didn't get so much money.
3 We can see a wide range of sports on television.
4 My national sports teams would be more successful if they had more funding.

READING

1 **What do you know about the FIFA Football World Cup? Discuss these questions with a partner.**

1 Which countries do the fans in the photos (A–D) support?
2 Can you name any winners and hosts of the World Cup?
3 How popular is the World Cup in your country with both men and women?

2a **Read the magazine article and choose the best title.**

1 Men 1, Women 0
2 Companies spend billions on World Cup ads
3 Advertisers forget female fans
4 Record numbers of women watch World Cup

2b **According to the article, are these sentences true, false or does the article not say?**

1 The percentage of female fans has increased very quickly. _F_
2 Men are the target audience of advertisers during the World Cup. _T_
3 Sean Gabb thinks there should be more adverts aimed at women. _T_
4 During the World Cup, the costs of TV advertising are lower than usual. _F_
5 Companies did not spend a lot of money on advertising during this World Cup. _Not say_
6 An advert during a daytime TV drama costs £1,000 per second in England. _T_
7 It is not a good idea to advertise to women during daytime TV dramas. _F_
8 Dan Harper thinks the adverts were interesting for the female fans. _F_

VOCABULARY
LINKING WORDS

3a **Look at the article to find the words in the box. Then match them with categories 1–4 below.**

despite	when	since	if
however	although	so	but

1 To draw a conclusion _so_
2 To show a contrast _however, although, but_
3 To show a conditional link _if_
4 To show a time relationship _since, when_

3b **In the article, which of the words above are followed by clauses, and which are followed by noun phrases? Which one works across two sentences?**

3c **Choose a word from the box in Exercise 3a to complete each of these sentences. Sometimes more than one answer is possible.**

1 _Despite_ the heavy snow, they played a football match.
2 _When_ the World Cup took place in Japan and South Korea, the number of Asian football fans rose significantly.
3 The percentage of fans aged under eleven has increased _when/since_ football moved to prime time TV.
4 _If_ we had more money, we could advertise during the game.
5 We'd like to advertise to women. _However_, it's very expensive.
6 _Although_ we'd like to advertise to women, it's very expensive.
7 Many women watch football, _so_ we're going to aim more adverts at them.
8 She likes playing football, _but_ she doesn't watch much of it on TV.

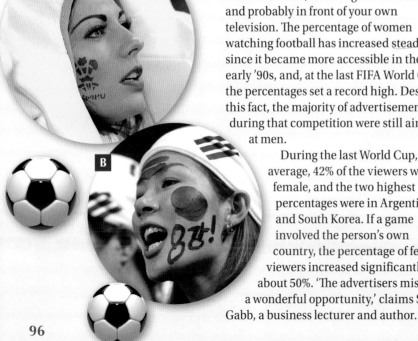

These days, female football fans are everywhere. They're in the stadiums, at the big-screen events and probably in front of your own television. The percentage of women watching football has increased steadily since it became more accessible in the early '90s, and, at the last FIFA World Cup, the percentages set a record high. Despite this fact, the majority of advertisements during that competition were still aimed at men.

During the last World Cup, on average, 42% of the viewers were female, and the two highest percentages were in Argentina and South Korea. If a game involved the person's own country, the percentage of female viewers increased significantly to about 50%. 'The advertisers missed a wonderful opportunity,' claims Sean Gabb, a business lecturer and author.

'There were too many adverts for men and there weren't enough adverts for female fans. These percentages show that more women watch important football matches than watch normal TV dramas.'

The number of women watching football games seems an opportunity that is too good to miss, but advertising companies claim that advertising on TV is too expensive during the games. In England, the TV companies charge £300,000 for 30 seconds. This is ten times more expensive than during a daytime TV drama, and this is too much money for most advertisers who focus on women.

Dan Harper, an advertiser, says that although the numbers of female fans are high, they are not high enough. It is more efficient to aim adverts at women when the audience is 80% female and the cost is much lower, during a daytime drama, for example.

SPEAKING

4 Evaluating claims Discuss these questions with a partner.

1 'The advertisers missed a wonderful opportunity,' claims Sean Gabb.

Did they? Which points in the text weaken Sean's claim? Can you think of any more arguments against this claim? What would the consequences be of more adverts for women during football games?

2 'Modern women are as interested in these things as modern men, so perhaps there were enough adverts aimed at women.'

Do you agree with Dan's claim about modern women? What differences do you see between male and female consumer habits? How do adverts show that they are aimed at men and/or women?

3 'During the last World Cup, 42% of the viewers were female.'

Who do you think watches more sport, men or women? Why? Do the TV viewing habits of your classmates support your claim?

He also claims that it is too simple to say their adverts were not aimed at women. 'We didn't just advertise shaving products during the World Cup. There were adverts for sports clothes, snacks and drinks, credit cards and fast cars. However, we think modern women are as interested in these things as modern men, so perhaps there were enough adverts aimed at women.'

GRAMMAR
TOO AND ENOUGH

5a Look at these sentences. Which three describe a problem or mistake?

a   There were too many adverts for men.
b   This is too much money.
c   There were enough adverts.
d   There weren't enough adverts for female fans.

5b Which of the phrases above mean you:

1   have the right amount of something?   c
2   need more of something?
3   need fewer things?
4   need less of something?

5c We can also use *too* and *enough* with adjectives. Find the four examples in the article.

5d Choose the correct word to complete these grammar notes.

Too comes *before/after* nouns and *before/after* adjectives.

Enough comes *before/after* nouns and *before/after* adjectives.

➥ Language reference and extra practice, pages 124–125

6a Put the words in italics in order to make sentences.

1   I *enough / free time / have* during the week.
2   I *have / too / homework / much* each week.
3   I *earn / don't / money / enough* to live a comfortable life.
4   The / *are / buses / too / and / trains / crowded* in the rush hour.
5   *There / enough / sports / aren't / facilities* in my local area.
6   My *national / good / football / team / is / enough* to win the World Cup.

6b Are the sentences true for you, your city and/or your country? Tell your partner.

SPEAKING

7a Think about some of these issues. What is the current situation in your country? Is there too much or too little of something? Do people do too much or not enough of something?

Football: money, TV, competitions, players

Sport and health: adults/children

Swimming pools and sports facilities

7b Compare your ideas with a partner and decide how things could be different.

I think young children don't play enough sport. If we had more sports facilities, the children would be healthier.

WRITING

8 Write two paragraphs about one of the issues that you discussed. Describe the situation and the solutions you suggested. Use linking words where possible.

▶ MEET THE EXPERT

Watch an interview with Rachel Pavlou, the Women's Football Development Manager for the English FA, about the rise of women's football.
Turn to page 130 for video activities.

PREPARATION

1a Make a list of the sports you have played. Put them in order of enjoyment. Compare your list with a partner and explain your order.

1b Match the different personality types in the box with the descriptions below.

social   competitive   risk-taking

1   I perform better when I challenge someone.
2   I like doing dangerous activities like rock climbing.
3   I like meeting people and being part of a team.

1c Which of the personality types above would or wouldn't suit the sports in the box? Explain your reasons.

yoga   bowling   rugby   tennis
rock climbing   snowboarding

A competitive personality wouldn't suit yoga because you don't score points in yoga.

SITUATION

Sport involves the body and the mind, and sports psychologists help professional sports people improve their performance. These psychologists can also help people find the sports that best suit their personality. Dr Sophia Mannit is a sports psychologist working in a sports centre. She uses a questionnaire to analyse customers' personalities and suggest suitable sports.

2a **12.2** Listen to her interview with Alex and make notes. Which of these situations do they discuss, and in what order?

a   going on holiday   c   doing an examination
b   playing sport with a friend   d   going on a day trip

2b Work with a partner. Can you remember any of the questions that were asked by Dr Mannit? Use your notes to help you.

2c Listen again. Check your ideas from above, and answer these questions.

1   Which personality type do you think each question relates to?
2   Which answer (A–C) does Alex choose for each question?
3   What do you think his answers show about his personality?

3a **12.3** Listen to Dr Mannit explain what Alex's answers show and make notes. What has she found out about Alex?

3b In each question, Alex's answers to the questionnaire are graded (i.e. *very*, *quite*, *not at all*) to show different degrees of agreement with the adjective. Look at Audio scripts 12.2 and 12.3 on page 163 and find examples of this language. What does each answer mean?

very competitive = really like challenging someone

quite competitive = like some challenge with someone

non-competitive = not interested in challenging someone

KEY LANGUAGE
ANSWERING COMPLEX QUESTIONS

4a `12.4` **Listen and complete these quotes from when Alex was deciding on his answers.**

1 Well, that's a _____ one.
2 I _____, I'd be happy for my friends, but I'd also want to do better than them.
3 Right. Er, let me _____ … I think I'd do A.
4 OK, _____, let me think …
5 Well, to be _____, I'd do B.
6 Hmm, that's a tricky _____.
7 I'm not sure, _____.
8 I mean, I wouldn't do A, _____ I'm not sure about B or C.

4b **Answer these questions about the quotes above.**

1 In general, why does Alex use this language?
2 Which word is similar in meaning to *difficult*?
3 In which examples does he explain his ideas?
4 Do you have similar phrases in your language?
5 How many times do you think Dr Mannit and Alex said the word *well* in Audio recordings 12.2 and 12.3? Four, eleven or sixteen times in total?

4c **Work with a partner. Ask and answer these questions. You can use the Key language when you are thinking about your answer.**

1 Do you think a sports psychologist can help you?
2 Who is your favourite sports player?
3 Which sports should every young person learn?

PRONUNCIATION

5a `12.5` Intonation in lists **Listen to this question. How are the letters at the beginning of each option a–c in the list pronounced? Choose the best intonation pattern below. Why is this pattern used?**

If you had a tennis game with a friend, would you a) train hard in order to win, b) practise a little, c) have fun and let your friend win?

1 rise, fall, rise   2 fall, fall, rise   3 rise, rise, fall

5b **Listen again and repeat.**

5c **Turn to Audio script 12.2 on page 163 and practise saying the questions.**

TASK
USING A QUESTIONNAIRE

6a **Work with a partner. Prepare a short questionnaire about personality and sports. The questionnaire will be in four sections. Sections 1–3 analyse personality; section 4 analyses sporting preferences. Turn to page 139 to see the format for the questionnaire.**

6b **Write one or two questions for each section 1, 2 and 3 (personality analysis). Make sure you grade the answers for each question (e.g. a = very competitive, b = quite competitive, c = non-competitive). You could use the situations in the box to help you prepare your questions.**

travel and holidays   making a complaint
choosing a job   buying clothes
saving money   having a party
choosing a hobby   doing an examination
playing a sport or game   giving a talk
finding some money   spending money

6c **For section 4, make a list of 12 sports, activities or games. Have a range of sports: competitive, non-competitive; risk-taking, risk-free; social and individual sports. When you interview the other students, you will ask if they have played them and if they enjoyed them.**

7 **Interview other students in the class. After each interview, tell the interviewee what you found out about their personality, and if their sporting preferences match their personality type. Can you recommend any new sports to them?**

STUDY SKILLS
TIME MANAGEMENT

1a Are you good at time management? How do you know this?

1b Look at these expressions about time. Which expressions suggest problems with time? Which describe positive feelings about time?

1 I've got all the time in the world.
2 There aren't enough hours in the day.
3 Time's running out.
4 I've got time on my hands.
5 Time's on my side.
6 It's a race against time.

1c Why will time management be important for you if you continue your English studies beyond Pre-intermediate level?

2a Work in small groups. Look at these problems some students are having with time management. What advice would you give them?

1 I'm often late for appointments, or sometimes I miss appointments completely.
2 I spend a lot of time looking for my notes. I can never find anything.
3 I sometimes study for a long time, but I don't feel I'm learning anything. I read the material, but nothing's happening – it's not going in.
4 I can't finish all the things I need to do in the day.

2b **12.6** Listen to some students and their tutor discuss the problems above. Do they mention any of your ideas?

2c Match this advice (a–h) with the problems (1–4) in Exercise 2a. Then listen again and check.

a Find out when you study best.
b Decide what's important.
c Keep a diary – and check it!
d Take regular breaks.
e Make lists of things you need to do.
f Organise your files.
g Make sure you can concentrate.
h Be nice to yourself!

2d Look at Audio script 12.6 on pages 163–164 and underline the parts of the script that tell us about the advice (a–h) above. Which two tips do you think are most useful for you?

3a Critical evaluation Look at this list of English language skills and knowledge. Which do you need to improve urgently? Which are not as urgent? Put them in order of priority (the most important first).

Listening	Grammar
Speaking	Vocabulary
Reading	Pronunciation
Writing	Confidence

3b Make sure you spend more time outside class on your priorities. What can you do to improve the top two in your own time? With a partner, compare your list from Exercise 3a and your ideas.

4 Discuss with a partner. Look at this list of activities. Which can you change to give yourself more time to work on your priorities?

- sleeping
- personal care (e.g. washing, dressing)
- eating and drinking (including preparation of meals, snacks, coffee breaks)
- travelling
- time at college
- time at work
- time with family
- housework
- socialising with friends
- sport/leisure activities
- (non-work) time on the internet

5a How can you use technology (your computer and your phone) to improve your time management?

Online calendars are good because you can switch quickly between your daily, weekly and monthly schedules so it's easy to see what's happening in your life.

If I see a useful book, I can take a photo of the cover with my phone so I don't have to write down all the details about the book there and then (author, publisher, etc.).

5b How can technology have a negative effect on our time? Think about things like social networking, long web searches, etc.

Don't waste time checking social networking sites too much. It's easy to spend more time on them than you think.

WRITING SKILLS
A FORMAL EMAIL

6 Work in small groups. Have you ever done an English course in an English-speaking country? Talk about your experiences and ideas. If you haven't done a course, would you like to? Why?/Why not?

7 You are interested in doing a summer course in the UK, which combines English with sport. You see this advert for a school in Belfast, Northern Ireland. Make a list of about six things you would like to know about the course and school. Write questions, like this:

What is the balance between English study and sport?
Is the school big or small?

8 Pepa has looked at the information on the school website. However, she still has some questions. Read her email on the right to the school. Are any of her questions the same as yours in Exercise 7?

9a Organisation Formal writing is very well organised. What is the main topic of each paragraph in the email?

9b Register Underline examples of language that show that this email is polite and/or formal, e.g. *Concerning the sports.*

9c Compare this email with the informal email in Unit 4 Lesson 4 (page 37). What differences can you find?

10 Find phrases in the email you could replace with these formal phrases that have a similar meaning or purpose.

1   With regard to …
2   Regards
3   I wish to …
4   I would like to know …
5   Dear Ms Kennedy
6   I wonder if you could …?

11 Punctuation Study the way commas are used in the email. Then put commas in suitable places in these sentences.

1   If I came earlier in the summer would the course be cheaper?
2   Concerning the evening activities will our teachers come with us?
3   As I mentioned in my last email my level of English is quite good.
4   However I still have problems understanding native speakers.

12 You are interested in going to New York to do an English course. Look at the advert on page 139 and write a formal email to the academy, asking some questions about the course, school, etc. Use your questions from Exercise 7 and the email in Exercise 8 to help you.

Emerald
SCHOOL OF ENGLISH

Study English in this friendly city where the Titanic was built!

We offer courses in:
- **General English**
- **English for Business**
- **English with Sport**

Very reasonable prices.

Visit us at:
www.emeraldenglish.com

TITANIC
BELFAST.

THE WORLD'S LARGEST TITANIC VISITOR EXPERIENCE
TITANICBELFAST.COM

Dear Sir or Madam

I would like to do your course in 'English with Sport' this summer. I am interested in visiting Northern Ireland, and your school seems ideal for me. I have found a lot of the information I need from your website, but I still have some questions. I would be very grateful if you could answer them.

First of all, if I stayed for four weeks, how many teachers would I have? Are there any exams at the end of the course? Could you tell me if I will get a certificate from the school when I leave?

Concerning the sports, I am especially interested in horse riding. I see that I can do this every afternoon, but does the cost include everything? Do I need any of my own equipment? Also, is tennis available in the evening after 7 p.m.?

As I mentioned, I am very interested in coming to Belfast, and I would like to live with a local family. However, if I am not happy with the family, can I change accommodation?

I hope you can answer my questions.

I look forward to hearing from you.

Best wishes

Pepa Martínez Unamuno (Miss)

GRAMMAR

G1 PRESENT SIMPLE

Use the present simple to talk about facts and things that are generally true: *It rains a lot in England.*

Use the present simple also to talk about regular actions and habits: *We have a beach holiday every year.*

FORMATION

With the present simple of the verb *be*, use *am*, *is* or *are* in affirmative statements, questions and negatives.
> *He is always very friendly.*
> *Are you interested in travelling?*
> *I'm not often here at the weekends.*

With the present simple of other verbs, use the verb on its own in affirmative statements.
> *They work in the same office as me.*

! Remember to add *-s* to the main verb after *he/she/it*. *Peter lives in a really big house.*

Note these spelling changes after *he/she/it*:
* Verbs ending in *-s*, *-sh*, *-ch*, *-z*, *-x* or *-o*, add *-es*. *watches*
* Verbs ending in consonant + *-y*, change *-y* to *-ies*. *carries*
* The verb *have* becomes *has* after *he/she/it*. *The city has a lot of parks.*

Use *do/does* to form the negative and questions.
> *We don't live near here.*
> *Does your country have a lot of parks?*

Present simple short answers use *do/does*.
> *Yes, it does. / No, it doesn't.*

Use *do/does* or *am/is/are* to form questions with *who*, *what*, *when*, *where*, *how*, *why*, *which*.
> *When does summer start here?*
> *What is your name?*

ADVERBS AND TIME EXPRESSIONS

You often use adverbs of frequency with the present simple, e.g. *always*, *often*, *sometimes*, *never*. The adverb comes after the verb *be*, but before other verbs.
> *It's never really hot in Greenland.*
> *It doesn't often rain in Dubai.*

You can also use time expressions with the present simple, e.g. *every day*, *once a week*, *every year*.
> *The news is on BBC1 at six every evening.*

G2 PRESENT CONTINUOUS

Use the present continuous to describe an action happening now or around now.
> *We're having an English lesson at the moment.*

Use the present continuous also to describe a changing situation.
> *The weather in the UK is definitely getting wetter.*

Form the present continuous with the auxiliary *be* + the *-ing* form of the main verb.
> *I'm trying to finish this exercise.*
> *'Is it raining?' 'Yes, it is.' / 'No, it isn't.'*

You usually just add *-ing* to the end of the main verb, but note these spelling changes.
* Verbs ending in *-e*: remove *-e* and add *-ing*: *live – living*
* Verbs ending in vowel + most consonants: double the consonant and add *-ing*: *get – getting*, *travel – travelling* (but not with vowel + *-y*: *play – playing*)

TIME EXPRESSIONS

You often use time expressions with the present continuous, e.g. *now*, *today*, *currently*.
> *We're staying at a friend's house at the moment.*

G3 PRESENT SIMPLE AND CONTINUOUS

You use both the present simple and the present continuous with verbs that describe actions (action verbs), e.g. *rain*, *work*, *play*.
> *The children play with their friends on Saturdays.*
> *The children are playing football now.*

Some verbs describe states (state verbs) such as feelings and situations, e.g. *be*, *want*, *believe*, *know*, *understand*, *like*. These verbs don't usually have a continuous form.
> *I want a drink.* ✓   ~~*I'm wanting*~~ *a drink.* ✗

Some verbs can be state or action verbs, e.g. *think*.
> *I think this city is beautiful. (= this is my opinion)*
> *I'm thinking about what to wear. (= deciding)*

KEY LANGUAGE

KL AGREEING AND DISAGREEING

I agree with you.   Mmm, you're right.
Yes, you're right.   Do you?   Don't you?   I do.   OK.
Well, I disagree with you.   I disagree.
No, neither do I.

VOCABULARY

V1 COUNTRIES AND REGIONS

Brazil, Brazilian, Canada, Canadian, China, Chinese, Ghana, Ghanaian, Poland, Polish, Saudi Arabia, Saudi (Arabian), Thailand, Thai, New Zealand, New Zealander

North America, South America, Europe, the Arab World, East Asia, South-East Asia, West Africa, Australasia

V2 WEATHER ADJECTIVES

bright, clear, cloudy, cold, dark, dry, fine, freezing, hot, humid, mild, rainy, snowy, sunny, warm, wet, windy

V3 MODIFIERS

extremely, quite, really, very

V4 ADJECTIVES TO DESCRIBE PLACES

crowded, dangerous, interesting, lively, popular, quiet, scary

V5 ACTIVITIES

scuba diving, horse riding, ice skating, mountain biking, sea kayaking, skiing, snorkelling, snowboarding, walking in a strong wind, white-water rafting, wildlife watching

G1 1 **Put the words in order to make sentences (affirmative or negative) or questions.**

1 to exhibitions / often / go / I / at weekends / .

_____

2 hot / in / very / it / is / Dubai / .

_____

3 people / do / when / in / the beach / your / go / to / country / ?

_____

4 a lot of / are / in / parks / city / your / there / ?

_____

5 taking / like / you / photos / do / ?

_____

6 your / busy / is / now / city / right / ?

_____

7 you / swimming / do / where / go / ?

_____

8 never / the / snows / it / jungle / in / .

_____

G2, 3 2 **Choose the correct form.**

1 The weather in the UK *changes / is changing* these days.
2 Summers *get / are getting* hotter all the time.
3 We sometimes *have / are having* heavy rain in summer.
4 This *causes / is causing* problems every year.

3 **Look at the answers. Then write the questions from these prompts in the present simple or present continuous.**

1 live / city / or / countryside / ?

_____

I live in the city.

2 interested in / photography / ?

_____

Yes, I'm very interested in taking photos.

3 work hard / at the moment / ?

_____

Yes, I am, but I always work hard!

4 when / usually / relax / ?

_____

I usually relax at the weekend.

5 the weather / good / summer / your country / ?

_____

Yes, it is, but it rains a lot in winter.

6 rain / at the moment / ?

_____

No, it's sunny at the moment!

4 **Write answers for you to the questions in Exercise 3.**

KL 5 **Complete the conversation with phrases a–e.**

a Do you?   d OK, fine
b Don't you?   e So do I
c No, neither do I

A: Let's look at these brochures and find something for our summer holiday.
B: ¹_____, but I don't want a beach holiday this year.
A: ²_____. I think an activity holiday would be good, for a change.
B: ³_____, but I don't like water sports.
A: ⁴_____ I do. But there are other sports we can look at. I like the idea of a horse-riding holiday.
B: Yes, that's a good idea. Where can we go horse riding?
A: Well, there are holidays here in South America, but I think that's a long way for two weeks.
B: ⁵_____ I don't agree – the flights are only about nine hours to Brazil.
A: Oh, OK then. Let's look at South America.

V1–4 6a **Complete these sentences with the correct adjective form of the nouns for countries and regions.**

1 March 6 is _____ (Ghana) Independence day.
2 Big _____ (China) cities often have a lot of traffic.
3 The _____ (Arab) language has five main regional varieties.
4 The _____ (Europe) Union's parliament is in Brussels.
5 There are three countries in the North _____ (America) Free Trade Agreement.
6 Kraków is an interesting _____ (Poland) city to visit.
7 _____ (Thailand) beaches are very crowded in summer.
8 Sometimes _____ (Canada) winters are extremely cold.

6b **Mark the stress in each noun and adjective above. Which four adjectives have a different stress from the noun?**

V5 7 **Complete these lists with the activities in V5. (You can use the activities more than once.)**

1 You do these on or in water: *diving*, _____, _____, _____, _____
2 You need animals for these activities: _____, _____
3 You do these activities on snow: _____, _____
4 You do these activities on land: _____, _____, _____, _____, _____, _____, _____

V3,5 8 **Complete each statement with a modifier in V3 and an adjective so that they are true for you.**

1 I think horse riding is *really relaxing*.
2 I think mountain biking is _____ _____.
3 I think scuba diving is _____ _____.
4 I think skiing is _____ _____.
5 I think wildlife watching is _____ _____.

GRAMMAR

G1 PAST SIMPLE: REGULAR AND IRREGULAR VERBS

Use the past simple to talk about actions and situations that are finished.

> David and I **trained** for the marathon last year.

The past form of the verb *be* is *was* or *were*.

> We **were** here last night.
> I **wasn't** at the school this morning.

With other verbs, you use just the main verb in affirmative past simple statements. Regular past simple verbs add *-ed* to the infinitive.

> train – train**ed**, watch – watch**ed**

The past simple verb does not change, i.e. it is the same after *I*, *you*, *he*, *she*, *it*, *we* and *they*.

> Note these spelling changes:
> * Verbs ending in *-e*, add *-d*: die – di**ed**, live – liv**ed**
> * Verbs ending in consonant + *-y*, change *-y* to *-ied*: study – stud**ied**, marry – marr**ied**
> * Verbs ending in vowel + consonant, double the consonant and add *-ed*: stop – stop**ped**

Many common verbs in the past simple are irregular.

↳ irregular verb list, page 165

You often say when the action happened, e.g. *in* (+ year/month), *on* (+ day) or *at* (+ time).

> The first modern Olympics were **in 1896**.
> I watched a great documentary **on Sunday**.
> We arrived **at two o'clock**.

TIME EXPRESSIONS

You often use time expressions with the past simple, e.g. *ago*, *last night (week/month/year)*, *yesterday*.

> We moved to this house two years **ago**.

G2 PAST SIMPLE: NEGATIVES, QUESTION FORMS AND SHORT ANSWERS

Use *did* to form past simple negatives and questions.

> She **didn't** give up hope.
> **Did** she paint every day?

Past simple short answers use *did*.

> Yes, she **did**. / No, she **didn't**.

QUESTION WORDS

Use *who* to ask about people.

> **Who** came to class yesterday?
> **Who** did you speak to?

Use *what* to ask about things.

> **What** did you do yesterday?

Use *when* to ask about time.

> **When** did you start English classes?

Use *where* to ask about places.

> **Where** did you go yesterday?

KEY LANGUAGE

KL1 ASKING ABOUT PEOPLE

What's he/she like?
What does he/she look like?
What does he/she like?

KL2 DESCRIBING PEOPLE

He seems (honest and shy).
She certainly isn't (chatty).
He's (hard-working).
She's got (short brown hair).
He looks like (that actor).
She wears (nice clothes).
He likes (watching sport on TV).
He has similar interests to me.

VOCABULARY

V1 PERSONALITY ADJECTIVES (1) AND NOUNS

brave: bravery
confident: confidence
creative: creativity
determined: determination
friendly: friendliness
happy: happiness
hard-working: hard work
kind: kindness
ordinary: ordinariness
sociable: sociability
nervous: nervousness

V2 TIME EXPRESSIONS AND PHRASES

last weekend, on Thursday, the day before yesterday, three days ago, yesterday, when he was a child, at the age of 16, in the early 1950s, over a period of 40 years

V3 PERSONALITY ADJECTIVES (2)

chatty, cheerful, clever, confident, horrible, lazy, miserable, nice, polite, quiet, rude, shy, stupid, unfriendly

V4 LINKERS

afterwards, at first, at the moment, then, until

G1–2 **1** **Correct the mistakes in these sentences.**

1   My mother leaved school when she was 14.
2   Did she started a new job last year?
3   When did you born?
4   Last weekend, my brother marryed his girlfriend.
5   We did not had a lot of money last year.
6   'Did they have a good holiday?' 'Yes, they had.'
7   We eated a lot of pasta last night.
8   She went to university at 2006.

2 **Complete this dialogue with the past simple of the verbs.**

A: What ¹_____(do) you think of the exhibition?
     I ²_____(think) it was pretty good.
B: Really? I ³_____(not/think) it was very good at all.
A: So you ⁴_____(not/like) the painting in the first room?
B: Oh, OK, yes I ⁵_____(like) that one – that's true.
     But I ⁶_____(lose) interest after that. But the artist
     ⁷_____(have) a really interesting life.
A: Yes, I admire her determination. She ⁸_____(be) quite a woman!

3 **Match the two parts of the sentences.**

1   Steve Ditko and Stan Lee created Spider-Man about   *b*
2   I arrived in London last
3   We had an art class every week
4   The class went to the manga exhibition on
5   We had dinner at a Mexican restaurant
6   I visited Paris

a   Wednesday. It was good.
b   ~~50 years ago. It was a big hit.~~
c   last weekend. I had tacos.
d   three years ago. I loved the city.
e   at my high school. I didn't enjoy it.
f   year. My English is a lot better now.

KL **4** **Match three answers from a–i with each question.**

1   What's your friend like?
2   What does your friend look like?
3   What does your friend like?

a   She's short and she's got black hair.
b   He loves mountain biking.
c   She seems really shy, but she isn't.
d   Just sitting around and watching TV.
e   He looks like my brother.
f   He's very kind and patient.
g   He's quite good-looking.
h   Well, she certainly isn't stupid!
i   She likes cooking and eating good food.

V1, 3 **5** **Match the parts of the words in A and B to make adjectives. (Two of the parts in B are used twice.)**

A

1 ~~creat~~	2 friend	3 hard	4 confi	5 determin
6 soci	7 talent	8 ordin	9 miser	10 cheer

B

able   dent   ful   ary   ed   ive   ly   working

1	_creative_	6	_____
2	_____	7	_____
3	_____	8	_____
4	_____	9	_____
5	_____	10	_____

6 **Use the adjectives from Exercise 5 to describe these people.**

1   She's always at work very early and leaves late.
2   He likes designing and making things.
3   She plays the guitar and she's very good at it.
4   He loves going to parties and being with people.
5   She works very hard every day because she really wants to succeed.
6   He is often happy and makes people smile.

V2 **7** **Complete these sentences with your experiences.**

1   Last weekend, I _____.
2   Three days ago, we _____.
3   At the age of 16, I _____.
4   When I was a child, we _____.

V4 **8** **Choose the correct word or phrase.**

I'm at university, in my second year, and ¹ *then /
at the moment* I'm doing film studies. I started it last year
and, ² *at first / until*, I hated it! I thought about changing
my course, but my tutor asked me to wait ³ *afterwards /
until* the end of the first year. I decided to follow his
advice, so I waited, and ⁴ *then / at the moment* in May,
I took the exams. ⁵ *At first / Afterwards*, I looked back at
the year and decided it wasn't really bad, so I decided to
continue with the course. Now I'm really enjoying it.

GRAMMAR

G1 PAST CONTINUOUS

Use the past continuous to talk about actions in progress at a time in the past.

*He **was working** at the university in the 1960s.*

Form the past continuous with the past form of *be* + the *-ing* form of the main verb.

	Subject	be (+ not)	Verb + -ing
+	I/He/She/It	was	
	You/We/They	were	working.
−	I/He/She/It	wasn't (was not)	
	You/We/They	weren't (were not)	

	be	Subject	Verb + -ing
?	Was	I/he/she/it	working?
	Were	you/we/they	

*We **were travelling** to Mexico.*
*We **weren't travelling** to the United States.*
***Were** you **travelling** by car?*
*Yes, we **were**. / No, we **weren't**.*

TIME EXPRESSIONS

You often use time expressions with the past continuous, e.g. *then, in* + year (*in 2012*), *at* + time (*at 9.00*), *at that time*.

*We were living in New York **in 2012**.*

G2 PAST SIMPLE AND PAST CONTINUOUS

Use the past simple for a finished action or series of actions in the past.

*The doorbell **rang**, so I **put down** my book and **answered** the door.*

To talk about an action in progress when another shorter action happened, use the past continuous for the action in progress. Use the past simple for the short action. This action can interrupt or stop the longer action.

*I **was reading** my book when the doorbell **rang**.*

Notice the difference between these two sentences.

*He **was speaking** when the phone rang. (= He was speaking. Then the phone rang.)*
*He **spoke** when the phone rang. (= The phone rang. Then he spoke.)*

G3 RELATIVE PRONOUNS

Use *which* and *that* to refer to things or ideas.

*It's the programme **which/that** stars Katie Holmes.*

Use *who* and *that* to refer to people.

*She's the actress **who/that** married Tom Cruise.*

Use *where* to refer to places.

*YouTube is a website **where** you can upload video clips.*

Use relative pronouns to link pieces of information about a person or thing.

Marie Curie was a scientist. She discovered radium. =
*Marie Curie was the scientist **who** discovered radium.*

The information after the relative pronoun often defines the subject.

*A search engine is a programme **that** finds information.*
*A newsreader is a person **who** presents the news on the TV or radio.*

> Do not repeat the subject after a relative pronoun. The pronoun is the subject.
> *Bill Gates is the man **who** started Microsoft.* ✓
> *Bill Gates is the man **who** he started Microsoft.* ✗

KEY LANGUAGE

KL MAKING SUGGESTIONS

Let's / Let's not (interview them about politics).
We should (have a live band on the programme).
Why don't we (invite some politicians)?
What about (interviewing rich people)?
What about (something on animals)?
What else shall we (do)?
Any ideas?
Anything else?

VOCABULARY

V1 THE MEDIA

nouns: advert, article, blog, celebrity, channel, drama, email, front page, headline, homepage, journalist, presenter, programme, social networking site, spam, video

verbs: like/respect, listen to, read, upload, use / go on, watch, write

V2 NAMES FOR PEOPLE AND FIELDS

art, artist, blogging, blogger, journalism, journalist, photographer, photography, politician, politics, psychologist, psychology, reporting, reporter, science, scientist

V3 TV PROGRAMMES

chat show, cookery programme, current affairs programme, drama, game show, lifestyle show, magazine show, news show, quiz show, talent show, wildlife documentary

G1 **1** Complete the questions in the past continuous. Then write true answers for you. Use full sentences if you can.

1 *Were* you *sending* (send) texts in the class?
Yes, I was. I was talking to my mum.
No, I wasn't. I was listening to the teacher.

2 _____ you _____(sleep) at 11 o'clock last night?
_____

3 What _____ you _____(do) at eight o'clock yesterday evening?
_____

4 _____ you _____(study) English this time last year?
_____

5 What else _____ you _____(study) then?
_____

6 Where _____ you _____(live) ten years ago?
_____

G2 **2** Complete these sentences with the past simple or past continuous of the verbs.

1 A journalist from *Russia Today* _____(stop) me for an interview while I _____(shop).
2 I _____(have) dinner last night when the phone _____(ring).
3 When we _____(walk) home from work, we _____(stop) and _____(do) some shopping .
4 Sarah _____(run) in the marathon when she _____(fall) and _____(break) her arm.
5 I _____(meet) my husband while I _____(ski) in the Pyrenees.
6 He _____(write) a book while he _____(recover) from an accident.

G3 **3** Match the two parts of the sentences. Then complete them with *who/that*, *which/that* or *where*.

1 A documentary is a programme *which/that* f
2 A producer is a person _____
3 A search engine is a computer program _____
4 A sitcom is a comedy series _____
5 A celebrity is a person _____
6 A social networking site is a website _____

a continues a story each week.
b allows you to share personal news.
c is famous for appearing on TV, e.g. a presenter.
d makes programmes.
e looks for information on the internet.
f tells you facts about the world.

4 Correct the mistakes in these sentences.

1 That's the woman which bought my car.
2 Richard Branson is the person who he started Virgin.
3 It's a word who means 'powerful'.
4 I bought a newspaper that it had the whole story.
5 It was on the programme what follows the news.

KL **5** Complete the suggestions below from the prompts.

stoke leisure centre

All facilities:
* 25m swimming pool
* gym with modern equipment
* aerobics and dance
* café
* membership half price this month

1 Why don't we _____(have / pizza)?
2 Let's _____(try / vegetarian pizza).
3 We should _____(go / Monday).
4 Why don't we _____(go / leisure centre)?
5 What about _____(go / swimming)?
6 We should _____(join / this month).
7 Let's not _____(do / aerobics).

V1 **6** Choose the correct words.

1 My sister works for a TV *programme / station*.
2 I'm interested in international affairs, so I like newspapers with serious *adverts / articles*.
3 This magazine has a lot of information about *celebrities / producers*.
4 I like a good story, so I prefer to watch *documentaries / dramas*.
5 Her last job was as a *presenter / journalist* on a reality TV show.
6 The children love animals, so they watch lots of *nature / current affairs* programmes.

V2 **7** Complete these definitions with words from V2.

1 A _____ is someone who does experiments to understand the world.
2 _____ is the study of the mind and behaviour.
3 A _____ is someone who works in parliament.
4 _____ is taking pictures with a camera.
5 An _____ is someone that paints pictures or makes sculptures.
6 _____ is finding out about the news and presenting it in newspapers or on TV.

GRAMMAR

G1 PRESENT PERFECT

You use the present perfect to talk about experiences in the past. You usually don't say when you had the experience.

They've built a new clinic.

Form the present perfect with *have* + the past participle of the main verb.

	Subject	*have* (+ *not*)	Past participle
+	I/You/We/They	've (have)	worked.
	He/She/It	's (has)	
–	I/You/We/They	haven't (have not)	
	He/She/It	hasn't (has not)	

	Have + subject	Past participle
?	Have I/we/you/they	(ever) worked?
	Has he/she/it	

Regular past participles are the same as the past simple form of the verb, i.e. add *-ed* to the infinitive.

I've visited a lot of countries.
She hasn't recovered from her illness.
Has the surgeon finished the operation?

Present perfect short answers use *have/haven't*.

Yes, I have. / No, I haven't.

You often use questions in the present perfect with *Have you ever …?* to ask about experiences.

Have you ever been to Africa?

Many common verbs are irregular.
be – was/were – been, go – went – gone, write – wrote – written, drive – drove – driven

➡ irregular verb list, page 165

G2 PRESENT PERFECT AND PAST SIMPLE

You use the present perfect when you do not give (or do not know) the exact time you did something. You use the past simple when you give (or know) the exact time you did something.

He's travelled to a lot of different countries.
In 2010, he travelled around the world.

Use the present perfect to talk about **finished** actions or situations in an **unfinished** period of time. Common adverbs with this use of the present perfect are *today, this week/month/year, so far*.

The surgeon has done four operations so far today. (= the operations are finished but the time period – today – isn't.)

When the time period is finished, you use the past simple.

The surgeon did four operations yesterday.

G3 ARTICLES

Use *a/an* with a singular noun to mention something for the first time: *He works for a medical company.*

Use *a/an* also to talk about a person's job.
He's a doctor.

Use *an*, not *a*, when the noun begins with a vowel sound (*a, e, i, o, u*): *an artist*. But note that some words that begin with the letter *h* take *an* and you do not say the *h*: *an hour*.

Use no article with plural nouns, when they refer to people or things in general.
Medical dramas are exciting.

Use *the* with a singular noun to talk about a specific person or thing, or one you already know about.
The local newspaper doesn't have much news. (= There's only one local newspaper.)
Put the flowers on the table. (= We know which table.)

Use *the* with plural nouns to refer to particular or known people or things.
I love the photos on this page. (= specific photos)
The people at the party were all very friendly. (= We know which people.)

FIRST AND SECOND MENTION

Use *a/an* (with singular nouns) and no article (with plural nouns) to talk about something for the first time.
He works for a medical company.
He creates health reports.

Use *the* when you mention the noun again.
Medical dramas are exciting.
The medical dramas are often on Channel 6.

KEY LANGUAGE

KL GIVING ADVICE AND REASONS

You should (go to the optician's).
You shouldn't (drink coffee at night).
(You should eat garlic) **because** it fights colds.
(You should do exercise) **in order to** lose weight.
(You should eat a lot of fruit) **to** stay healthy.

VOCABULARY

V1 HEALTH AND WELLBEING

clinic, dentist, depression, disease, doctor, healthcare, health insurance, heart disease, high blood pressure, hospital, illness, injury, insomnia, lack of motivation, local doctor, medicine, minor illness, nurse, operation, optician, poor concentration, poor memory, prevent, private hospital, serious illness, state hospital, surgeon, surgery, treatment, vaccination

V2 FOOD AND NUTRITION

carbohydrates, junk food, nuts, salmon, vitamins

V3 REPORTING VERBS

feel, think, recommend, reveal, say, show, state, suggest

G1 **1** **Complete the text below with the present perfect of the verbs in the box.**

be (x2)   employ   not finish   go   save   start
teach   train   not visit

Our medical organisation came to Bangladesh three years ago and I ¹_____ here since the beginning. We ²_____ about 80 men and women to become nurses, and they ³_____ to different parts of the country so that they can help people. We ⁴_____ a number of doctors and managers, too, and together they ⁵_____ smaller clinics in other parts of the country. We certainly ⁶_____ all our work here. There are a lot of small towns and villages that we ⁷_____, but I'm sure we ⁸_____ a lot of lives. It ⁹_____ a wonderful experience so far, and it ¹⁰_____ me a lot of new things!

G2 **2** **Choose the correct form.**

1 I *visited / have visited* a lot of countries in Asia.
2 Last year, I *went / have been* to China.
3 The government *built / has built* ten new hospitals in the last five years.
4 *Did you ever go / Have you ever been* to the USA?
5 My mother *phoned / has phoned* me every week when I worked in London.
6 Jake *didn't see / hasn't seen* me yesterday.
7 I *didn't finish / haven't finished* my essay last night.
8 I *wrote / have written* about 5,000 words of the essay so far.

G3 **3** **Complete the sentences with *a/an*, *the* or no article (write ø).**

1 Malaria is _____ dangerous disease in many parts of _____ world.
2 *Médecins Sans Frontières* (MSF) means '_____ Doctors Without _____ Borders'.
3 My sister's _____ nutritionist. She works at _____ hospital in _____ north of England. My brother works in _____ same hospital, but he's _____ accountant.
4 _____ children in this medical centre are all very brave.
5 _____ local hospital has lots of _____ patients.
6 There's _____ really good video on YouTube. It's about _____ Argentinian healthcare charity. Here's _____ link to it.

4 **Choose the correct meaning, a or b, for each sentence.**

1 Jason was feeling ill. He's at the doctor's now.
   a We know which doctor's.
   b We don't know which doctor's.
2 I liked that hospital. The doctors and nurses were excellent.
   a I'm talking about all doctors and nurses.
   b I'm talking about particular doctors and nurses.
3 Pam works for a clinic in Atlanta.
   a The listener knows which clinic.
   b The listener doesn't know which clinic.

KL1 **5a** **Complete the advice for these problems. Use *should/shouldn't* and a way of giving a reason.**

> 'I've had about three colds this winter – I'm getting really fed up with it!'

1 You *should* take vitamin C *to* keep your immune system healthy.
2 You _____ close all the windows _____ you need fresh air.

> 'I'm studying and I also do a part-time job in a restaurant. I get up really early to study, but I don't go to bed until about one in the morning. I always feel really tired.'

3 You _____ work so late _____ you need your sleep.
4 You _____ speak to your tutors _____ they understand your problem.

> 'I sit at my desk for hours every day. Now I find that my back hurts nearly all the time.'

5 You _____ stay in the same position at your desk _____ your body needs to move.
6 You _____ get up and stretch every 20 minutes _____ reduce the tension in your back.

5b **Can you think of another piece of advice for each person?**

_____
_____
_____
_____
_____

V1–2 **6** **Find the following people, places or health problems from V1 and V2.**

1 a person who performs operations
2 a problem with sleeping
3 the place where you usually see your doctor
4 the person who looks after your teeth
5 a physical problem, often the result of an accident
6 when you feel sad all the time
7 a medical building where you stay and pay for your treatment
8 when you don't want to do anything
9 when you can't remember things very well

GRAMMAR

G1 COMPARISONS

Comparative and superlative adjectives
Use comparative and superlative adjectives to make comparisons between people or things. Comparative adjectives compare one person/thing with another.

*The Apennine Mountains in Italy are quite **high**.*
*The Carpathians in Romania are **higher**.*

You usually make comparisons with *than*.

*The Carpathians are **higher than** the Apennines.*

Superlative adjectives compare one person/thing with several other people/things (more than two). Use *the* before the superlative adjective.

*The Alps are **the highest** mountains in Europe.*

Note the different ways of forming the comparative and superlative adjectives.

	Adjective	Comparative	Superlative
one-syllable adjectives	cheap	cheap**er**	cheap**est**
• ending in -e	strange	strang**er**	strang**est**
• ending in -y	dry	dr**ier**	dr**iest**
• ending in vowel + consonant	flat	flat**ter**	flat**test**
most two-syllable adjectives	peaceful	**more** peaceful	**most** peaceful
• ending in -y	pretty	prett**ier**	prett**iest**
• ending in -ow	narrow	narrow**er**	narrow**est**
• ending in -er	clever	clever**er**	clever**est**
adjectives of three or more syllables	popular	**more** popular	**most** popular
	mysterious	**more** mysterious	**most** mysterious
irregular adjectives	good	better	best
	bad	worse	worst
	far	farther/ further	farthest/ furthest

G2 AS ... AS

Adding *as ... as* to adjectives allows you to compare similar features; it doesn't matter how many syllables the adjective has.

*Rome is **as beautiful as** Paris. (= Rome and Paris are beautiful.)*

Adding *not as ... as* to an adjective is another way of comparing two things. Use *not as ... as* with all adjectives.

*The Atlantic Ocean **is not as calm as** the Mediterranean.*
*This lake **isn't as big as** the first lake we saw.*

G3 EXPRESSIONS OF QUANTITY

Use *a lot of*, *many* and *much* to talk about large quantities and amounts. You use *many* with countable plural nouns and *much* with uncountable nouns.

***Many animals** are in danger because there isn't **much food** for them.*

You use *a lot of* with both countable and uncountable nouns.

***A lot of animals** are in danger because there isn't **a lot of food** for them.*

❗ It is quite formal to use *many* in affirmative sentences. In informal English, you use *a lot of*.
*I have **a lot of** squirrels in my garden.*

You use *many* in affirmative and negative statements, but you only use *much* in negative statements.

***There are many** grey squirrels in the UK, but **there aren't many** red squirrels now.*
***There isn't much** damage to the environment here.*

Use *few* and *little* in affirmative statements to talk about small quantities and amounts. They mean 'not many / not much'. Use *few* with countable plural nouns and *little* with uncountable nouns.

*There are **few tigers** in the world.*
*There's **little hope** for some animals.*

You do not usually use *few* and *little* with questions and negative statements. You use *not many / not much*.

*We **haven't got many** trees in the garden.*
***Is there much** rain in the desert?*

KEY LANGUAGE

KL JUSTIFYING CHOICES

This one is (clearer/more dramatic).
In the (first) photograph, some people are watching …
In the (foreground), you can see …
There are (a lot of people) in the background.
On the (right) of the picture, (someone is walking …)
They look (very professional).
I like the way this one …
I think this is better because …
It makes you feel (sad) …
I think we should use this one because …

VOCABULARY

V1 LANDSCAPES

nouns: beach, cliff, coast, forest, hill, island, lagoon, lake, mountain, peak, river, rock, sand, sea, wave

adjectives: beautiful, calm, cheap, deep, exciting, high, impressive, interesting, long, magical, peaceful, pleasant, popular, romantic, sandy, steep, strange, tropical, warm, wild

V2 WORDS THAT ARE NOUNS AND VERBS

cause, change, control, damage, harm, hope, plant, shop, stop

V3 CONTRAST

but, in contrast, whereas

G1 **1** Complete these sentences with the comparative or superlative form of the adjectives.

1 Samira is _____(clever) girl in the class.
2 Paris is _____(romantic) Sydney.
3 The Canary Islands are _____(tropical) other places in Spain.
4 The _____(good) way to see the countryside is to go trekking.
5 The pollution in Bangkok is _____(bad) in London.
6 I think Moscow is _____(expensive) city in the world at the moment.

2 Write a) a comparative and b) a superlative sentence about each set of figures.

1 Lewis 175cm / Kevin 185cm / Jason 166cm (tall)
 a Jason / Lewis
 Lewis is taller than Jason.
 b _____
 the tallest boy.
2 Lake Erie 19m / Lake Ontario 86m /
 Lake Superior 147m (deep)
 a Lake Ontario / Lake Erie
 b _____
3 a Porsche £35,000 / a Hyundai £18,000 /
 a Smart car £7,000 (expensive)
 a a Smart car / a Hyundai
 b _____

G2 **3** Rewrite these sentences so that they mean the same. Use *(not) as … as.*

1 Nottingham is more dangerous than Oxford.
 Oxford is _____.
2 London and New York are expensive.
 New York is _____.
3 All the other lakes are more impressive than this one.
 This lake is _____.
4 Carnac is more mysterious than Stonehenge.
 Stonehenge is _____.
5 The north of France is flatter than the south.
 The south _____.
6 All the other Greek islands are more popular than this one.
 This island is _____.

G3 **4** Cross out the incorrect word in each sentence.

1 *Many / Much / A lot of* animals are in danger of extinction.
2 We *don't have much / don't have many / have little* hope for these animals.
3 There is *few / little / not much* snow in this part of the country.
4 We haven't got *much / many / a lot of* time to save the planet!
5 There's *not much / little / few* life on this island.
6 There are *not many / little / few* tigers in the world.

KL **5** Complete the conversation below with a–f.

a the way this one
b creates the wrong impression
c It looks
d this one is better because
e It makes me feel
f one is

A: Which photo do you think we should choose?
B: Well, this [1]_____ powerful, but I don't think it has the right message.
A: So do you think it [2]_____, then?
B: Yes, I think so. I think [3]_____ I think our message is clearer here.
A: Really? [4]_____ very unusual to me. [5]_____ sad.
B: Yes, but that's a good thing in this case. In fact, I like [6]_____ makes you feel unhappy. It means people will remember it for that reason.

6 Correct the mistakes in these sentences.

1 I can see mountains at the background.
2 In this photo, a man waits at a bus stop.
3 On right of the picture, there's a river.
4 The people all talk about something.
5 In second photograph, a woman is going into a shop.
6 On the left on the photo, there's a sports car.
7 It looks like very fast.

V1 **7** Circle the odd one out in each group.

1 sea / forest / river / lake
2 beach / coast / hill / sand
3 lagoon / lake / river / rock
4 mountain / hill / wave / coast

V2 **8a** Use the words in V2 to complete these questions. Change the form if necessary.

1 What problems does the world face? What are the _____ of these problems?
2 What do you _____ to do in the future?
3 Do you have any house _____? Have you got green fingers?
4 In what ways does junk food _____ your health?
5 Do you have a favourite clothes or music _____?
6 Where do you _____ for most of your food?

8b Work with a partner. Ask and answer the questions above.

V3 **9** Add commas to these sentences if necessary.

1 I like the sea but I don't like mountains.
2 My sisters all have brown eyes. In contrast my eyes are blue.
3 Red squirrels come from the UK whereas grey squirrels come from North America.
4 Madrid is very hot in summer but very cold in winter.

GRAMMAR

G1 *WILL, MIGHT* AND *MAY* FOR PREDICTIONS

Use *will* (*'ll*), *won't* (will not), *might* (not) and *may* (not) to make predictions, i.e. to say what you think about the future.

> People **will retire** later in the future.
> They **won't have** big families.
> We **might** use the internet for a lot more things.
> It **may not be** good for business.

Use contractions *'ll, won't* and *mightn't* for speaking and informal English.

> We**'ll live** longer in the future because there**'ll be** better medicine.
> There **won't be** many serious illnesses.
> But we **mightn't** find a cure for cancer.

> ! You do not use the contraction *mayn't*; you use *may not* instead.
> I ~~mayn't be~~ at work tomorrow. ✘
> I **may not be** at work tomorrow. ✔

You often use *I think / I don't think* to introduce a prediction.

> **I think there'll be** problems with pensions in the future.

You often say *I don't think + will* instead of *I think + will not.*

> **I don't think** the government **will have** the money for pensions.

You use *will* when you are more certain about the future. You use *might* or *may* when you are less certain.

> Older people **will work** for longer in the future, and young adults **might start** working later.

> ! *Might* is more common than *may* to make predictions, especially in informal English.

You usually use *will* when you ask for predictions about the future, not *might* or *may*, and you often start with *Do you think …?*

> **Do you think** we **will live** longer in the future?
> **Will** people **have** cars in the future?
> What **do you think** the future **will be** like?

ADVERBS OF CERTAINTY

You often use adverbs with *will/won't* for predictions, to say how certain you are. In affirmative sentences, you usually put the adverb after *will*; in negative sentences, you put it before *won't.*

> We **definitely won't** use petrol in the future.
> We**'ll probably use** a biological fuel.

The adverbs *definitely* and *certainly* mean you are very certain; the adverbs *probably* and *possibly* mean you are less certain.

> People **will certainly have** smaller families in the future, so they **probably won't live** in big houses.

> ! You don't use these adverbs with *might* or *may*.

G2 FIRST CONDITIONAL

Use the first conditional to talk about the result of a possible future action.

Possible future action	Result
If I get a better job,	we'll have more money.
If I don't get a better job,	we won't have a holiday.

Note the formation of the first conditional.

If-clause (condition)	Main clause (result)
If + present simple,	*will / won't* + infinitive
If you **go** to university,	you**'ll find** a good job.
If you **don't go** to university,	you **won't get** a qualification.

> ! You usually put a comma after the *if*-clause.
> You can put the main clause first; if you do this, you don't use a comma.
> You'll find a good job if you go to university.

You can also use *might* and *may* in the main clause. Then the action in the main clause is less certain than when you use *will*.

> If I get a good degree, I **might apply** to work for Microsoft. (= I'm not sure about this.)

KEY LANGUAGE

KL1 EXPRESSING OPINIONS

Personally, I think (that) …   What I think is that …
I think it's (better if …)   Why not just (turn the TV off)?

KL2 EXPRESSING AGREEMENT/DISAGREEMENT

I agree with (him/her).
I understand his/her opinion, but …
Personally, I completely disagree.
That's a good/interesting idea/point, but …

VOCABULARY

V1 FUTURE ANALYSIS

advice, analysis, consumer, improve, information, investor, needs, prediction, profit, retire

V2 AGES

adolescent, child, elderly person, middle-aged person, person in his/her mid-thirties, teenager, retired person, young adult

V3 NEGATIVE ADJECTIVES

careless, homeless, hopeless, uncomfortable, unkind, unlucky, unusual, useless

V4 POPULATION

birth rate, childcare, employer, graduate, old-fashioned, responsible, suitable

V5 LINKERS

as, because of, however, so

G1 1 Correct the mistakes in these sentences.

1 I think people might to live longer in the future.
2 May people retire later in 20 years' time?
3 Families might probably get smaller.
4 Definitely I will retire when I'm 60.
5 The number of students at university will increases.

2 Rewrite the sentences below without changing the meaning. Use the words and phrases in the box.

probably won't   might   'll definitely
won't   'll probably

1 I'm almost sure that we'll get our news only from the internet.

2 I'm not sure if couples will divorce more.

3 I don't think humans will go back to the Moon.

4 I'm 100% certain we won't have more leisure time!

G2 3 Match the two halves of these sentences.

1 If people live longer,
2 We might see the late film tonight
3 If more students go to university,
4 If parents don't earn much money,

a they won't be able to afford childcare.
b they might get more diseases when they're older.
c if the children go to bed early.
d they might not all find good jobs when they leave.

4 Complete these first conditional sentences so that they are true for you. Then compare your sentences with a partner.

1 If the class finishes a bit early today, …
2 If the weather's good at the weekend, …
3 If I get a good/better job, …
4 If I earn a lot of money in the future, …

KL1–2 5 Complete the conversation with a–f.

a I agree with   d Personally, I think
b I think it's better   e That's a good point,
c I understand her idea, f what I think is that

A: I saw Jo and Steve earlier. They're looking for some childcare for Amy so that Jo can go back to work.
B: Childcare? ¹_____ if the mother stays at home.
A: Really, Matt! Jo's got a good job. ²_____ that women need to get back to work.
B: ³_____ you – if they need the money, but Jo and Steve don't need the money.
A: Well, ⁴_____ it's better when young children can play with other children in childcare.
B: ⁵_____ but maybe for a couple of hours a day …
A: Mmm. Jo feels that if she finds childcare, she'll have the choice of working or not, anyway.
B: ⁶_____ but I think she'll go back to work.
A: Yes, so do I.

V1 6 Match the sentence halves.

1 We need to look at future
2 They'll need to get an analysis
3 Marketing companies predict
4 A financial advisor gives advice

a future trends.
b to business investors.
c consumer needs to choose what to produce in the next five years.
d of the company to decide if they make an investment.

V2 7 Find words in V2 for these people.

1 someone who is over about 60 and doesn't work any more
2 a young person between 13 and 19
3 someone between about 35 and 60
4 a person over the age of about 20
5 a very young person
6 an old person (a polite term)

V3 8 Complete these sentences with negative adjectives from V3.

1 My brother is very _____, so he makes a lot of mistakes.
2 His father was very _____ and treated him badly.
3 There are too many _____ people living on the street.
4 I never win any competitions – I'm very _____.
5 It's a very _____ film – you've never seen anything like it!
6 I can't do this homework. I'm _____ at maths!

V4–5 9 Choose the correct words.

1 Keira can't go out this evening as / because of she needs to finish her history essay.
2 I don't think Chris is suitable / responsible to be a teacher – he isn't very patient.
3 The advert says they only want employers / graduates who left university last year.
4 I hate housework, so / however I don't often do it.
5 It's difficult to find birth rate / childcare in this city.
6 Alana studied very hard, as / so she passed her exams.

GRAMMAR

G1 OBLIGATION

MUST AND MUSTN'T

Use *must* to say that it is necessary to do something.
> You **must switch** your phone **off** during the lesson.

The negative *mustn't* means that it is necessary NOT to do something.
> We **mustn't bring** food or drink into the classroom.
> You **mustn't take** anything from the crime scene.

SHOULD

Use *should* to recommend doing something or not doing it.
> You **should say** it again. I don't think he heard.
> You **shouldn't use** your phone in a restaurant.

Must and *should* are modal verbs. You use modal verbs with other verbs to talk about obligation, ability, possibility, etc. *Must* expresses obligation. *Should* expresses recommended actions.

A modal verb always comes before an infinitive without *to*.
> I **must phone** my mother this evening.

The forms *must* and *should* do not change after *he/she/it*.
> James **must visit** his family this weekend.
> She **shouldn't call** him again.

Form questions with modal verbs by putting the verb before the subject of the question.
> What time **must we get** the bus?

(DON'T) HAVE TO

You can also use *have to / has to* to say that it is necessary to do something.
> Forensic scientists **have to be** very careful in their work.

The negative *don't have to / doesn't have to* means that it is NOT necessary to do something.
> You **don't have to study** law to be a scientist.

It is possible to use *must* to ask a question, but it is often better to use *Do/Does … have to …?*
> **Must I sign** the form too?
> **Do** you **have to leave** now?
> **Does** he **have to analyse** the evidence?

MUST AND HAVE TO

Must and *have to* have very similar meanings. They both mean something is necessary.

You usually use *must* when you believe that something is important (it is your opinion).
> I **must get up** early tomorrow.

You usually use *have to* to talk about rules and laws (i.e. someone else thinks it is important).
> We **have to get** a visa to visit the United States.

Remember that the negative of *must* (*mustn't*) and *have to* (*don't/doesn't have to*) are very different.
> You **mustn't use** your mobile phone in the cinema. (= it is not allowed)
> You **don't have to use** your mobile phone – use my office phone. (= it is not necessary)

G2 HAD TO AND COULD

Must does not have a past form. To talk about something that was necessary in the past, use *had to*.
> The doctors **had to operate** to save his life.

In negative statements, to say that something was not necessary, use *didn't have to*.
> We **didn't have to pay** for the tickets – they were free.

Use *Did … have to …?* to ask if something was necessary.
> **Did you have to wear** a uniform to school?

Use the modal verb *could* to talk about ability in the past.
> I **could run** fast when I was younger.

You use *couldn't* to say that you were not able to do something or that it was not possible.
> I **couldn't finish** the book – it was really difficult.
> We **couldn't study** astronomy at our university.

Use *Could …?* to ask about ability in the past.
> **Could you understand** that lecture on physics yesterday?

KEY LANGUAGE

KL DEVELOPING AN ARGUMENT

This **caused** a revolution in knowledge.
It **meant that** ideas could spread.
It **led to** education for everyone.
It's **connected to** the production of books.
… **so** people had to learn to read.
This **means that** society is more literate.

VOCABULARY

V1 CRIME

analyse, analysis, analyst, burglary, commit, crime, discover, DNA, evidence, fingerprints, investigator, reveal, scene, solve (a crime)

V2 SUBJECTS

astronomy, biology, chemistry, economics, history, mathematics, medicine, physics

V3 NOUNS, ADJECTIVES AND VERBS WITH PREPOSITIONS

afraid of, belong to, connected to, happen to, a history of, interested in, lead to, proud of, receive from, have a (good) relationship with, separate from, spend (money) on, successful in, thanks to

G1 1 **Complete these sentences about what police officers *have to* do, *don't have to* do and *mustn't* do.**

1 They *have to* arrive on time to work every day.
2 They _____ be rude to the public.
3 They _____ wear a uniform.
4 They _____ be very careful when they're at a crime scene.
5 They _____ damage the evidence.
6 They _____ study science.

2 **Choose the correct verbs.**

1 You *mustn't / don't have to* study law to be a forensic scientist.
2 I *should / shouldn't* spend some time with my parents. I haven't seen them for ages.
3 We *mustn't / have to* commit crimes – it's against the law.
4 You *must / don't have to* turn off your mobile phone in class so that it doesn't interrupt the lesson.
5 We *mustn't / have to* have a passport to travel outside the UK.
6 I *should / don't have to* join the gym again – my membership has run out.
7 You *have to / don't have to* check your essays carefully when you've written them.
8 We *mustn't / don't have to* get up early today, as it's a public holiday.

G2 3 **Rewrite these sentences without changing the meaning. Use the correct form of *had to* or *could*.**

1 Was it necessary to tell the police everything?
   Did you have to tell the police everything?
2 He wasn't able to walk after the accident.
   _____
3 Were you able to understand that lecture?
   _____
4 They weren't able to collect all the evidence at the scene.
   _____
5 It wasn't necessary to study economics at my school.
   _____
6 I was able to speak Russian when I was a child.
   _____
7 It was necessary to study Latin at our school.
   _____
8 Was it necessary for her to spend all that money yesterday?
   _____

KL 4 **Complete the text below with the phrases in the box.**

| causes | so | This has led | This means |

We've had a lot of trouble in our town recently. A few months ago, one of the biggest supermarket companies in the country opened a huge shop in the centre of the town. [1]_____ to all kinds of problems: smaller shops have closed [2]_____ there isn't a choice of shops any more, and a lot of people come from villages around the town to shop at the supermarket. [3]_____ that there are a lot more cars on the road, which [4]_____ a lot more noise in the town.

V1 5 **Complete these sentences with words from V1.**

1 Someone _____ a crime.
2 _____ go to the crime scene.
3 They take _____ from objects at the scene.
4 They collect other _____ and take it all to the crime lab.
5 The scientists at the lab _____ the evidence …
6 … and they _____ information about the criminals.
7 The investigators _____ the crime.

V2 6 **Find words in V2 for these definitions.**

1 the study of living things
2 the study of the past
3 the study of illnesses and injuries
4 the study of the stars and planets
5 the study of natural forces, e.g. light and movement
6 the work of chemicals and how they change and combine
7 the science of numbers and shapes
8 the study of the production and use of money

V3 7 **Match the two parts of these sentences.**

1 I've always been afraid
2 He's studying the history
3 The police are interested
4 They received the report
5 The chemistry lab is separate
6 She's always been successful

a from the rest of the school.
b in talking to a man at the crime scene.
c of flying.
d of the United States.
e in solving difficult crimes.
f from the forensic lab.

GRAMMAR

G1 VERB PATTERNS

You sometimes put two verbs together. When you do this, the second verb is often in the infinitive with *to*.

> I **seemed to sleep** well last night.
> Older people **tend to need** less sleep.

The second verb can also be in the *-ing* form.

> Do you **like having** a doze after lunch?
> These days, we **keep hearing** about light pollution.

When the first verb is a verb + preposition, the second verb is in the *-ing* form (because a verb after a preposition is always in the *-ing* form).

> Have you **thought about changing** your job?

Here are some common verbs that follow these patterns.

Verb + infinitive with *to*		Verb + *-ing* form	Verb + preposition + *-ing* form
hope	decide	keep	think about
manage	need	enjoy	succeed in
tend	seem	suggest	look forward to
want		try	talk about

Some verbs can have either an infinitive with *to* or an *-ing* form after them, e.g. *like, hate, love*. When you use the *-ing* form with these verbs, you mean '(not) enjoy'.

> I **love skiing**.
> I **hate lying awake** all night.

When you use the infinitive with *to*, you say what you (don't) prefer.

> I **like to go** to bed early.
> I **hate to fall asleep** in the living room.

G2 FUTURE INTENTIONS

There are different ways of talking about your plans for the future. You use the form *be going to* when you have a definite intention to do something, i.e. you are sure that you will do it, but it is not 100% fixed.

> I**'m going to study** astronomy at university.
> When Liam finishes the night shift, he**'s going to meet** some friends for breakfast.
> I**'m not going to do** a distance-learning course.

	Subject + *be* (+ *not*)		Verb
+	I'm He's/She's/It's You're/We're/They're	going to	start …
–	I'm not He/She/It isn't You/We/They aren't		

	be + subject		Verb
?	Am I Is he/she/it Are you/we/they	going to	start …?

You can also talk about plans with *hope to* and *would like to*. These are less certain than *going to* – you use them for ambitions and desires.

> Sandra **would like to leave** the bank and find another job.
> We **hope to buy** a new house next year.

> ! Note how you form the questions and negatives of these verbs.
> **Would** you **like to travel** round the world?
> **Do** you **hope to have** children one day?
> I **wouldn't like to** work at night.
> I **hope not to be** late tomorrow. ✓
> I **don't hope to be** late tomorrow. ✗

KEY LANGUAGE

KL1 ASKING ABOUT PREFERENCES

What would you prefer to do?
What would you rather do?

KL2 EXPRESSING PREFERENCES

I'd rather (go to the concert).
I'd prefer to (see a film).
I'm more interested in (the cinema) than (the theatre).
I'd love to (see the drummers).
I don't fancy (that film / going to the opera).
I don't mind.
I'm not keen on (concerts).

VOCABULARY

V1 SLEEP

doze, dream, fall asleep, feel sleepy, good night's sleep, go to sleep, heavy sleeper, insomnia, light sleeper, nap, nightmares, sleep in, sleep through, sleepless, talk in (your) sleep

V2 JOBS

astronomer, baker, call-centre worker, cleaner, engineer, lorry driver, nurse, office worker, police officer, security guard, teacher

V3 *-ED/-ING* ADJECTIVES

amazed/amazing, bored/boring, embarrassed/embarrassing, excited/exciting, fascinated/fascinating, frightened/frightening, interested/interesting, surprised/surprising, tired/tiring

V4 SOCIAL ACTIVITIES

boat trip, café, cinema, concert, dancing, dinner, firework display, museum, play, sports event, theatre

V5 TIME EXPRESSIONS

after some time, at last, at that moment, before long, finally, in the end, soon, suddenly

G1 **1** Choose the correct form.

1 I tend *to dream / dreaming* a lot when I'm away from home.
2 Karen really enjoys *to study / studying* literature.
3 You seem *to have / having* a high temperature.
4 You should think about *to be / being* more active.
5 I keep *to fall / falling* asleep after lunch.
6 She wants *to get / getting* a job with a TV company.
7 We're really looking forward to *go / going* on the boat trip.
8 What did the doctor suggest *to do / doing*?
9 The children were at a friend's so we managed *to sleep / sleeping* in on Sunday.
10 We're talking about *to go / going* to the new exhibition. Do you want to come?

G2 **2** Complete Janine's list of hopes, desires and intentions for the next year. Look at the key, then use the correct form of *hope*, *would like* or *going to*.

✓✓✓ = intention   ✓✓ = desire   ✓ = hope

1 *I'm going to* read *A Brief History of Time*. ✓✓✓
2 _____ pass my final exams in June. ✓
3 _____ save money for a summer holiday. ✓✓✓
4 _____ spend the summer in France. ✓✓
5 _____ watch the tennis at Wimbledon in June. ✓
6 _____ find a really good job after the summer. ✓✓
7 _____ be nicer to my little brother. ✓✓✓
8 _____ move to a different city. ✓

3 Write three sentences about your hopes, desires and intentions for the future.

1 I hope _____.
2 I would like _____.
3 I'm (not) going to _____.

KL1–2 **4** Complete the conversation below at a job centre with the words in the box.

fancy   interested   mind   prefer   rather

A: So you want a job that you can do at night.
B: That's right.
A: OK, well, there's a job here as a security guard.
B: On, no, I don't ¹_____ that. It sounds dangerous.
A: Right. Something less dangerous … let's see. What about working in a call centre?
B: Mmm, no. Boring.
A: Well, what kind of job would you ²_____ to do?
B: I don't ³_____ , really, but I'm more ⁴_____ in working outside.
A: Outside? Do you drive?
B: Yes, I do.
A: OK … lorry driver?
B: Well … I think I'd ⁵_____ drive a car …

V1 **5** Complete these sentences with words and phrases from V1.

1 When you're in a deep sleep, you can _____ most noises.
2 It's very depressing if you have a completely _____ night.
3 It can be very good for you to _____ for half an hour after lunch.
4 If you can't _____ at first, it's a good idea to get up and have a hot drink.
5 I always _____ when I watch TV late at night.

V3 **6** The underlined adjectives are all in the wrong sentences. Correct them.

1 Playing tennis for three hours is really bored!   *tiring*
2 I'm always very embarrassed after a long meeting.
3 I'm sure that working in a call centre is extremely frightening.
4 Forgetting an old friend's birthday is very ~~tiring~~.
5 Being alone in a strange town at night can be embarrassing.
6 Children get frightened when they don't have anything to do.
7 I was tired and didn't want to go to sleep after the horror film.
8 I was so boring when I fell over in the street the other day.

V4 **7** Which activity in V4 would be good for:

1 a family who like doing things on water?
2 someone who likes stories and cultural events?
3 a couple who want to be active?
4 a teenager who likes pop groups?
5 someone who wants to learn about the past?
6 people who like good food?

V5 **8** Complete the text below with the time expressions in the box.

after some time   at that moment   before long
Finally   suddenly

In my last year at university, I shared a small flat with a friend. One night, I was sleeping when ¹_____ I woke up, feeling frightened. I didn't know why I was feeling frightened, but ²_____ , I heard a loud crash from the living room. I waited and waited, and ³_____ , I decided to find out what was happening. I went to the living room, but I didn't want to go in, so I stood behind the door for ages. ⁴_____ , I stepped into the room and switched the light on. My friend was on the floor, asleep. I spoke to him and shook him, and, ⁵_____ , he woke up. Then he told me that he often walked in his sleep and fell over chairs or tables without even noticing!

GRAMMAR

G1 USED TO

Use *used to* + infinitive to talk about habits and states that happened in the past, and which usually do not happen now.

> We **used to have** long lunch breaks, but now we have short breaks.
> I **used to enjoy** working here, but I don't now.

> **!** There is no present form of *used to*.
> I ~~use to~~ work late every day in this job. ✗
> I work late every day in this job. ✓

You can always use the past simple instead of *used to*, but you do not use *used to* for single past actions (i.e. that happened only once).

> I travelled to China for work once. ✓
> I ~~used to travel~~ to China for work once. ✗
> I used to travel to China for work. (= a lot of times)

Form the negative and questions with *did*.

		Subject	(not) used to	Main verb
+		I/you/he/ she/it/ we/they	used to	work.
–			didn't (did not) use to	
?	Did		use to	work?

> **!** Note the spelling *use to* in negatives and questions.
> We **didn't use to have** many employees then.
> **Did** you **use to have** a big office?

Form short answers with *did*.

> Yes, we **did**. / No, we **didn't**.

> **!** Do not confuse the past simple and past participle of the verb *use* with *used to*.
> We **used to spend** our summer holidays by the sea. (= used to)
> I **used** the phone while you were out. (= past simple of use)

G2 PRESENT SIMPLE PASSIVE

You often use the passive when you want to focus on the object of an active sentence. You do this by putting the object at the beginning of the sentence.

> A lot of jewellery is made from gold.

The subject of an active sentence becomes the agent of the passive sentence, and you use *by* to introduce it.

active

Children in India make these clothes.

passive

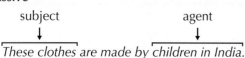

These clothes are made by children in India.

You often use the passive when the agent is unknown or when it is unnecessary (because it is obvious).

> The gold **is brought** to Europe. (= We don't know the agent.)
> Silver **is used** in jewellery a lot too. (= The agent is obvious.)

Form the passive with the auxiliary verb *be* + past participle.

(be)	Subject	be (+ not)	Past participle
+	I	am	employed.
	He/She/It	is	
	You/We/They	are	
–	I	'm not (am not)	
	He/She/It	isn't (is not)	
	You/We/They	aren't (are not)	
?	Am	I	employed?
	Is	he/she/it	
	Are	you/we/they	

KEY LANGUAGE

KL MAKING OFFERS AND PROPOSALS

That seems a bit/rather (high/low).
I'm not sure we can (pay that much / go that low).
How about ($100 each)?
If you (order 1,000), we can (offer 15%).
What about if we (order 750)?
That sounds fine.
Shall we call it ($87)?

VOCABULARY

V1 WORK

colleague, department, employee, industry, long service, lunch break, market leader, promotion, report, staff, training course, work as a team

V2 COMPOUND NOUNS

outer space, special appearance, pocket calculators, washing machines, recordable CDs, credit cards, spacecraft, space shuttle, electronic equipment, gold wires, human hair, glass makers, public buildings

V3 IMPORT–EXPORT

nouns: abroad, bargain, brand, buyer, delivery, discount, exports, imports, lower price, manufacturers, market, orders, price, quantity, the general public, retailers, sales, supply

verbs: bargain, export, import, offer, order, supply

V4 SEQUENCING PHRASES

after (five) to (six) days, following that, lastly, next, to begin with

G1 **1 Read this short text about a company. Then complete the sentences below with the correct form of *used to*.**

When I was younger, I worked for a really good company for a few weeks a year. I wanted to work for it after I left university, but it closed a few years ago. The business was importing books from the USA – only educational books. I worked there in the holidays when I was at college, so the books were very useful for me. We could take copies of any book we wanted, but I only took about three or four while I was there. The only problem was that the money wasn't very good, but it helped to get me through my studies!

1 The writer _used to_ work for an import company.
2 It _used to_ import books from Europe.
3 It _used to_ import educational books.
4 The writer _didn't used to_ take lots of books.
5 The money _didn't used to_ be very good.

2 There are mistakes in six of these sentences. Find the mistakes and correct them.

1 We used to work very late, but we don't now.
2 The company use to pay very good money.
3 I didn't used to work very hard.
4 I used to go on a long business trip to Korea last year.
5 I also went to Hong Kong several times.
6 Did you used to travel a lot on business?
7 We used have longer holidays than we do now.
8 'Did you use to work harder?' 'Yes, we used.'

G2 **3 Choose the correct form.**

1 This company *imports* / *is imported* diamonds. Most of the diamonds *import* / *are imported* from the Netherlands.
2 One of the shops in the village *sells* / *is sold* lovely chocolates. The chocolates *make* / *are made* by hand.
3 We can *book* / *is booked* hotels and flights for you. All the booking *does* / *is done* online.
4 The offices *clean* / *are cleaned* every evening. The cleaners *come* / *are come* at eight o'clock.

4 Look at these pairs of sentences. Which is better, the a) active or b) passive version?

1 a Mum makes dinner for the family every evening.
  b Dinner is made for the family every evening.
2 a Oil is very important. Dead plants and animals make it.
  b Oil is very important. It is made from dead plants and animals.
3 a The cleaners don't clean the office on Sundays.
  b The office isn't cleaned on Sundays.

KL **5 Put these words in the correct order.**

1 interested / our / of / you / which / in / are / products / ?
  Which of our products are you interested in?
2 price / is / per / what / unit / the / ?
  What is the price per unit?
3 expensive / that / quite / sounds / .
  That sounds quite expensive.
4 can / units / discount / you / 2,000 / I order / a / me / if / offer / ?
5 can't / I / for / I'm / units / afraid / 2,000 / .
  I'm afraid for 2,000 I can't.
6 about / how / if / 3,000 / units / order / you / ?
  How about if you order 3,000?
7 deal / that's / a / !
  That's a deal!

V1, V3 **6 Find words in V1 and V3 for these definitions.**

1 the person who makes the products
2 the people that you work with — colleague
3 one person who works for a company employee
4 the person who sells the products sales
5 the person who finds the products for a shop to sell buyer

V1, V2 **7 Complete this puzzle with the first part of the compound nouns below.**

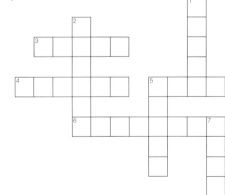

Across
3 _____ shuttle
4 _____ calculator
5 _____ service
6 _____ course

Down
1 _____ hair
2 _____ leader
5 _____ break
7 _____ wires

V4 **8 Choose the correct phrase.**

It's easy to make your own paper. [1]*To begin with / Lastly*, take some ordinary paper and tear it into small pieces. Put it in water until it is soft. [2]*Following this / To begin with*, change the water and mix the paper and water in a food processor until the mixture is thick (the pulp). [3]*Lastly / Next*, put the pulp in a bowl with more clean water and mix it well. Put the mixture on a square mould, like a shallow box, and add any 'personal' decorations to your paper, e.g. leaves. Put heavy books on top of the mould. [4]*After / Next* about 30 minutes, take the books off. [5]*Lastly / Next*, put the paper in a warm place until it is completely dry.

GRAMMAR

G1 PRESENT CONTINUOUS FOR FUTURE ARRANGEMENTS

You can use the present continuous to talk about the future.

> What **are** you **doing** on Friday evening?
> We**'re having** dinner with my husband's boss.
> We **aren't meeting** him until nine.

➥ irregular verb list, page 165

When you use the present continuous for the future, you are certain that the action will happen.

> The taxi**'s coming** at six o'clock. (= We've booked the taxi.)
> The minister **is giving** a speech tomorrow morning. (= It's organised.)

You often use the present continuous when you have made arrangements, so you usually give a time or mention other people.

> I**'m meeting** Melanie at the theatre this evening.

There is very little difference between the present continuous and *going to*.

> I**'m having** a tennis lesson tomorrow afternoon.
> We**'re going to spend** the weekend by the sea.

G2 PAST SIMPLE PASSIVE

You use the passive when you want to focus on the object of an active sentence.

➥ present simple passive, page 118

You often use the past simple passive to talk about the history of something.

> The first car **was designed** in Germany, but the first car for the general public **was made** in the USA.

The important information is what happened, not who did the action. If you want to mention the agent, you use *by*.

> The Sony Walkman **was produced** in Japan. It **was invented by** Akio Morita.

You often use the passive when the agent is not known, not important or obvious.

> The book **wasn't published** on time.
> The new James Bond film **was released** last month.
> The new Microsoft software **was launched** in May.

Form the past simple passive with *was/were* + past participle.

> 'When **was** the first Harry Potter book **published**?'
> 'It **was published** in 1997.'
> 'Was the new car a success?' 'No, it **wasn't liked** by the public at all.'

KEY LANGUAGE

KL GIVING EXAMPLES

For example/instance, …
Another example is the …
… as well as …
A good example of …
It's just a few minutes from the centre.

VOCABULARY

V1 PEOPLE AND ORGANISATIONS

ambassador, assistant, civil servant, committee, department, head of department, minister, president, representative, spokesperson, staff

V2 DIGITAL ADVANCES

adjectives: digital, easy-to-use, portable, powerful, trendsetter

nouns: competition, digital advances, fault, mobile electronic devices, online, product launches, smartphone, slogan, software, tablet

verbs: launch, improve, present, register, release, set up, store

V3 ADJECTIVES

comfortable, comprehensive, easy, electrifying, fantastic, high-speed, magical, magnificent, memorable, modern, quick, spacious, spectacular, world-class

V4 LINKERS

although, on the other hand, therefore

G1 **1** Write present continuous sentences from these prompts.

1 minister / fly / Geneva tomorrow / .
The Minister is flying to Geneva tomorrow

2 you / stay / at / Hilton Hotel / this week / ?
Are you staying at Hilton Hotel this week ?

3 I / give / talk / on education this afternoon / .
I giving a talk on education ...

4 situation / get / worse / .
The Situation is getting worse

5 they / not / build / new stadium / next year's Olympics / .
They aren't building new stadium ...

6 the president / come / to / conference / ?
Is the president coming to conference.

2 Now decide whether the sentences in Exercise 1 refer to the future (F) or the present (P).

G2 **3** Complete these sentences with the past simple active or passive of the verbs.

1 The internet company lastminute.com *was set* (set up) in 1997.
2 It *started* (start) by two business partners: Martha Lane Fox and Brent Hoberman.
3 The company *began* (begin) by finding last-minute holidays for people.
4 But it soon *moved* (move) into finding hotels, theatre tickets and even restaurants for people.
5 Martha Lane Fox *leaved* (leave) the company at the end of 2003.
6 Lastminute.com *was sold* (sell) to Travelocity, another internet travel company, in 2005.

4 Is the agent necessary in these sentences? If not, cross it out.

1 The company was started in 1999 ~~by its founders~~.
2 Microsoft Vista was launched in 2007 by Microsoft.
3 'Guernica' was painted by Picasso.
4 The name of the new Secretary General was announced yesterday by the present Secretary General.
5 The story was published by a popular newspaper.
6 The new building was finished in time for the conference by builders.

KL **5** Complete the short presentation below with the phrases in the box.

Secondly	A good example of this	such as	Finally
first of all	For instance	For example	

'We are here to represent the government and people of Singapore. The special ambition for our city is that we will be the next host for the Climate Change conference. Why Singapore? Well, ¹_____, we are in a good location. ²_____, we are only a few hours' flight from three billion people. ³_____, it is a six-hour flight from Beijing or Seoul to Singapore. ⁴_____, we have good conference centres ⁵_____ the Pan-Pacific Singapore Hotel. ⁶_____, we are a hi-tech location. ⁷_____ is our 95% wireless broadband coverage anywhere on the island.'

V1 **6** Which job has each of the new members of the government got? Match these descriptions (1–6) with the jobs below (a–f).

1 Marcus Antrim will work for the British government in Washington.
2 Geraldine Smith has the top job in economics.
3 Alistair Frank helps Geraldine Smith.
4 John Wilson has the most important job in the department that works with schools and universities.
5 Janet Laurence has a desk job, working for John Wilson.
6 Alison MacDonald gives the government's opinions to the newspapers.

a Minister of Education
b Civil Servant in Education Department
c Head of Finance Department
d Assistant to Head of Finance
e Press spokesperson
f Ambassador

V3 **7** The underlined adjectives are all in the wrong sentences. Correct them.

1 Your report was excellent. It covered everything and was really spacious.
2 The French world-class train is much faster than the British one.
3 I'm sure I'll sleep better in our new bed – it's much more fantastic than the old one.
4 A capital city needs lots of high-speed hotels these days.
5 Karen's new apartment is very comprehensive.
6 Thanks for inviting us to your party – we had a comfortable time.

V4 **8** Complete these sentences with *although*, *on the other hand* or *therefore*.

1 It was very cold yesterday, _____ it was very sunny.
2 My job is not very challenging. _____, I have decided to find something more suitable.
3 In some ways, Julian is very pleasant. _____, he is sometimes aggressive.
4 _____ my new flat has only two rooms, it's very spacious.

GRAMMAR

G1 PRESENT PERFECT WITH *FOR* AND *SINCE*

Use the present perfect to talk about experiences in your life, because 'in my life' is an unfinished period of time. Note the difference between:

*Agatha Christie **wrote** a lot of crime novels. (She is dead, so past simple)*
*PD James **has written** a lot of crime novels. (She is still alive, so present perfect)*
*Heatwaves **have become** 30 times more common.*

Use the present perfect with state verbs (e.g. *be, have, know*) and *for* or *since* to talk about situations that began in the past and are still continuing.

*My brother **has had** high blood pressure for years.*
*Jane **has known** about it since March.*
*I've **been** in a bad mood all day!*

Use *for* to give a period of time.

*We've had the same English teacher **for two years**.*
*There has been no extreme heat here **for several years**.*

Use *since* to say when the situation began.

*I've worked here **since June 2011**.*
*It hasn't rained **since April 2nd**.*

You often start asking questions about a person's experiences in the present perfect, but then use another tense to ask for more details. If the answer is positive, it is often the past simple.

Have you ever experienced a tornado?
– Yes, I have.
What was it like?
– It was very scary.

Have you ever been to the US?
– No, I haven't. I've wanted to go there for years.
Where do you want to go?
– I think the major cities like New York, Washington, San Francisco first of all.

G2 PHRASAL VERBS

Phrasal verbs are combinations of a verb and one or two other words, often prepositions. These other words are called particles. Here are some common phrasal verbs.

Verb	Particle
cut	down
find	out
give	back
throw	away

*I really must **cut down** my smoking!*
*We don't **throw** any paper **away**.*

Phrasal verbs often have a different meaning from the verb on its own.

cut down = reduce
find out = discover

Phrasal verbs can be intransitive or transitive. Intransitive verbs, e.g. *go up*, do not need an object.

*Prices **have been going up**.*

Transitive verbs, e.g. *give out, throw away*, need an object.

*The man was **giving out leaflets** in the high street.*
*Don't **throw that book away**!*

When a phrasal verb has a noun as the object, you can put the noun after the verb or after the particle.

*Supermarkets **give out** a lot of plastic bags.*
*Supermarkets **give** a lot of plastic bags **out**.*

When the object is a pronoun, it goes after the verb.

*Can you **give** these **out**?*

KEY LANGUAGE

KL CHECKING AGREEMENT (QUESTION TAGS)

That's quite normal, **isn't it?**
There are a couple of other problems, **aren't there?**
The project solves a problem, **doesn't it?**
We haven't seen that before, **have we?**
You can't get greener than that, **can you?**
They could do it unpaid, **couldn't they?**

VOCABULARY

V1 CLIMATE AND EXTREME WEATHER

air pollution, climate, climate change, drought, extreme weather, floods, global warming, heatwaves, heavy rain, hurricanes, rainfall, seasons (spring, summer, autumn, winter; wet, dry, monsoon season), temperature, temperatures above 35°C, thunderstorms, tornadoes, typhoons

V2 NOUN PHRASES

a shortage of basic food, part of the emergency planning, the causes of global warming, the effects of climate change, the lack of rain, the result of global warming, the risk of flooding

V3 CONTAINERS

bottle, box, can, carton, jar, packet, pot, tin, tube

V4 MATERIALS

aluminium, cardboard, glass, metal, paper, plastic

V5 LOCAL ENVIRONMENT

community, community projects, derelict, dump, graffiti, green electricity, green spaces, litter, regeneration, rubbish, run-down, scruffy, unsafe, untidy, urban area, ugly area, wasteland, well-kept, wind farms, wind turbines

G1 **1** **Write sentences from these prompts, using the present perfect simple and *for* or *since*.**

1 Sea levels / continue to rise / many years / .
Sea levels have continued to rise for many years.

2 Antarctica / lose / four trillion tonnes of ice / 2002 / .
_____

3 James Lovelock / write about / the environment / more than 50 years / .
_____

4 Environmental issues / be / a concern / the 1960s / .
_____

5 Freeman Dyson / argue against / global warming / many years / .
_____

6 Farming / change dramatically / the 1940s / .
_____

2a **Complete these sentences so that they are true for you.**

1 I've learnt _____ *for / since* _____ .
2 I've known _____ *for / since* _____.
3 I've studied at this school *for / since* _____.
4 I've had _____ *for / since* _____.
5 I've had this _____ *for / since* _____ .
6 I've worked _____ *for / since* _____.

2b **Compare your sentences with a partner.**

G2 **3** **Complete the sentences below with the verbs and particles in the boxes. Change the form where necessary.**

Verbs: carry   cut   find   ~~go~~   pick   set
         throw   write

Particles: away   down   down   ~~into~~   out   out
         up   up

1 A lot of thought *goes into* food packaging.
2 They _____ _____ research into global warming at the moment.
3 Supermarkets should _____ _____ the quantity of packaging that they use.
4 My friends want to _____ _____ a paper recycling business.
5 Can you _____ _____ some information about nuclear power for me?
6 We _____ _____ so much rubbish when we were younger – now we recycle more.
7 _____ that litter _____ ! We don't want rubbish on the streets here.
8 I know I _____ _____ your phone number but I can't find it anywhere.

4 **Correct the mistakes in these sentences.**

1 Are those your socks on the floor? Pick up them!
2 The price of petrol has been up going recently.
3 Can you give back me that book on recycling?
4 The founders of IBM have up set a new business.
5 Do you away throw old things?

KL **5** Match these statements (1–8) and question tags (a–h).

1 The train's going to leave on time,
2 You can't recycle glass bottles here,
3 They've rebuilt the community centre,
4 Recycled paper doesn't cost more than ordinary paper,
5 They haven't burnt the evidence,
6 This isn't the cause of the problem,
7 Your idea really solves the problem,
8 You can get a discount if you return the bottles,

a can you?
b can't you?
c does it?
d doesn't it?
e have they?
f haven't they?
g is it?
h isn't it?

V1 **6** Circle the odd one out.

1 climate / heavy rain / tornado
2 drought / extreme heat / global warming
3 spring / winter / heatwaves
4 wet / heavy rainfall / floods
5 thunderstorms / season / hurricanes
6 tornadoes / flood / typhoons

V2 **7** **Match the sentence halves.**

1 If it continues to snow,
2 The houses have been built higher
3 Air pollution is considered to be
4 The lack of rain is causing
5 As part of the emergency planning,
6 The effects of climate change mean

a to reduce the risk of flooding.
b severe droughts in north-east Africa.
c the school has an extra electricity supply.
d we will have a shortage of food later this year.
e that northern Europe will get colder and more extreme weather.
f one of the causes of global warming.

V3, 4 **8** Unjumble the anagrams to make containers and materials.

1 Soft drinks usually come in MNAIIMLUU SNAC.
2 ARJS are usually made of SLASG.
3 REPPA has a lot of uses.
4 We can buy milk in TOTLEBS or CRANOTS.
5 A lot of BEXOS are made from DRACDRABO.
6 I'd like a BUTE of toothpaste.

GRAMMAR

G1 SECOND CONDITIONAL

You use the second conditional to talk about the result of an action. The action is unreal, i.e. it can't happen or is very unlikely to happen.

If we practised more, we would be better at hockey.
(= We don't practise, so we aren't good at hockey.)
If we had more time, we would practise.
(= We don't have the time, so we don't practise.)
If I was rich, I'd buy a sailing boat.
(= I'm not rich, so I can't buy a sailing boat.)

! It is also possible to use *If I/he/she were* in the second conditional.
*If **she were** younger, she'd become a sports teacher.*
*If **I were** you, I'd start taking some exercise.*

You can also use the second conditional to talk about possible future actions, but the actions are unlikely to happen.

What would you do if you won a million dollars?
If I won a million dollars, I wouldn't go to work any more!

If-clause (condition)	Main clause (result)
If + past simple,	would / wouldn't + infinitive without to
If they **showed** more interest.	they'**d** (would) get more help.
If I **didn't** get the job,	I'**d** (would) be really unhappy.

! You usually put a comma after the *if*-clause.

You can also use *might* or *could* in the main clause.
*If they spent more money on sports, we **might win** more medals.*
*If you stayed with me in the summer, we **could visit** Athens together.*

You can also put the main clause first. If you do this, you don't use a comma.
They'd spend more money if people showed more interest.

G2 TOO AND ENOUGH

Use *too much/many* + noun to mean 'more than we need or want'.
*We've spent **too much money**.*
*There are **too many adverts** on TV.*

Use *enough* + noun to mean 'the correct amount'.
*I've had **enough chocolate cake** for now, thank you.*

Use *not enough* + noun to mean 'less/fewer than we need/want'.
*There aren't **enough opportunities** for women.*
(= fewer than we want)

Use *too much* with uncountable nouns and *too many* with countable nouns.
*I've got **too much work** at the moment.*
*This company has got **too many problems**!*

Use *(not) enough* with both countable and uncountable nouns.
*We didn't have **enough good sportspeople** at the last games.*
*Have you got **enough time**?*

You can also use *too* and *(not) … enough* with adjectives.
*Mark doesn't do any sport. He's **too lazy**.*
*James will win the race. He's **fast enough**.*
*Gill won't pass the exam. She's **not clever enough**.*

! Be careful of the word order with *too* and *enough*.
too much / too many / enough + noun: *We haven't got **enough people** for the team.*
too + adjective: *I'm **too tired**.*
adjective + *enough*: *You aren't **quick enough**.*

KEY LANGUAGE

KL ANSWERING COMPLEX QUESTIONS

Er, …, Hmm, OK, Right, Well, …
Let me see, …
Let me think, …
I think I'd …
That's a difficult one
That's a tricky question
To be honest, I'd …

VOCABULARY

V1 SPORTS

archery, badminton, basketball, cycling, dragon-boat racing, fencing, football, gymnastics, hockey, judo, polo, sailing, skiing, swimming, table tennis

V2 LINKING WORDS

although, but, despite, during, however, if, since, so

V3 PERSONALITY TYPES

careful, cautious, competitive, individualistic, non-competitive, risk-seeking, self-sufficient, sociable, unsociable

G1 1 **Match the two halves of the sentences.**

1 If I needed more money for my sport,
2 I would get a lot fitter
3 Our players might win more matches
4 If more people were interested in this sport,
5 We would host a dragon-boat festival
6 What would you do

a I'd try to get funding from a company.
b it would receive more funding.
c if they practised more seriously.
d if you won a lot of money?
e if I played more sport.
f if we thought enough boats would enter.

2 **Complete this text with the correct form of the verbs.**

What ^{1}_____ you _____(do) if you ^{2}_____(not have) enough money to continue your sports club?

I'm in that position now. I run a badminton club, and we're in danger of closing because we don't have enough members. If we ^{3}_____(have) more members, we ^{4}_____(get) enough money to pay the sports centre that we play in. They've put their prices up – if their prices ^{5}_____(not be) so high, we ^{6}_____(be) in a better position. If we ^{7}_____(not have to) spend all our money on paying for the club, we ^{8}_____(have) enough money to advertise for more members. The other problem is insurance – we have to have insurance, and that costs money, too. If we ^{9}_____(not have) insurance, we ^{10}_____(have to) pay a lot of money if someone had an accident.

One way of getting more members would be to accept any players into the club, but if we ^{11}_____(do) that, we ^{12}_____(get) people who can't play well enough. Can you give me any advice?

G2 3 **There are mistakes in four of these sentences. Find the mistakes and correct them.**

1 We can't get funding enough for our club.
2 There are too much aspects to this problem.
3 They aren't showing enough interest in our idea.
4 Most of our players aren't enough competitive to win.
5 I can't play another game. I'm too tired.
6 There are too many adverts for expensive trainers on TV.
7 It costs much too money to do this sport.
8 My sports psychologist told me I wasn't risk-seeking enough.

KL 4 **Complete the conversation below with the words and phrases in the box.**

| I'd   a tricky question   to be honest   think |
| Let me   mean |

A: OK, here's a question for you. Imagine you can have all the TV sports channels free for six months, or you can become a free member of a gym for 12 months. What would you do?
B: Hmm, OK, now that's ^{1}_____!
A: I know it is. So, TV or gym? What's it going to be?
B: Well, I'm not sure. ^{2}_____ see. I love football, especially the English Premier League, but, ^{3}_____, I think ^{4}_____ take the gym membership.
A: Really? I ^{5}_____, those TV sports channels are *very* expensive. Especially the big English games that you like.
B: I know! However, I ^{6}_____ I'd take the gym membership instead of the TV sports channels.

V1 5 **Find the sports in V1 for these descriptions.**

1 It's played by two teams of 11 people.
2 This involves a lot of people on a river.
3 This can be played with two or four people. It's very fast.
4 This is like a fight between two people, with no equipment.
5 This is usually done on the sea. You can do it alone or with other people.
6 You can do this alone or with others. You have to have bikes.

V2 6 **Complete these sentences.**

1 Some women don't like football, but _____.
2 Despite the growing number of female fans, advertisers _____.
3 The number of female football fans is increasing, so _____.
4 Although a record number of female fans watched the World Cup, _____.

V3 7 **Choose the correct adjectives 1–4 in this job advert for a tennis instructor.**

| Jobs in sports coaching |

We are looking for the right person to teach the tennis stars of the future

You will work on your own and be responsible for all the tennis instruction at the club, so you must be ^{1}*competitive / self-sufficient*.

We need a ^{2}*sociable / risk-seeking* person who will spend a lot of time with our young people, both playing tennis and socially. You will need all your skills to teach the children to be ^{3}*competitive / non-competitive* in their matches. You will need to try new ways of teaching and take risks in this job, so we can't accept candidates who are too ^{4}*risk-seeking / cautious*.

▶ MEET THE EXPERT

1 HUMAN PLANET

1 Discuss these questions.

1 What are deserts and jungles? Consider differences and similarities.

2 What are the interesting or difficult things about living in those places?

2 Match the words in bold with the explanations below.

Scientists sometimes go on **expeditions** to places such as jungles and deserts. Before the trip, there is a lot of **kit** to buy and **preparation** to do. Every expedition team includes **a medic** in case people get ill. This can happen because these new environments are **challenging**.

1 A nurse or doctor
2 Difficult, and creates problems
3 Things to do before you go on a journey
4 Equipment, the things you need to take on a journey
5 Trips to other countries to discover new things

3 ▶**1** Watch the interview with James Moore, an expedition medical consultant. Put these topics in the correct order. What images can you remember from the topic areas?

1 James's personal difficulties with life in the jungle
2 Life in the Sinai desert
3 James's work experience and background
4 Local people
5 Important advice for travellers
6 Differences between the desert and the jungle
7 What people learn from travelling to extreme environments

4 Watch the interview again and take notes for each section.

5 Discuss these questions with your partner. Use your notes to help, and add your own ideas.

1 What different types of work does James do?
2 What information does he give about life in the desert and in the jungle?
3 What can visitors learn from local people?
4 What advice about preparation does James give?
5 Would you like to go on an expedition to an extreme environment? Why?/Why not?

2 PEOPLE

1 Discuss these questions.

1 What animation films and TV programmes do you watch or know?
2 What comics or illustrated books do you remember from your childhood?

2 ▶**2** Watch the interview with Karen Rubins, a comics artist. In what order does Karen talk about these topics?

1 Her early interests in comics and art
2 Her stories and her drawing habits
3 Osamu Tezuka
4 Manga today
5 The first manga artist
6 Reasons she loves manga

3a Match the sentence halves. Which of the topics in Exercise 2 are they about?

1 He invented …
2 I've drawn comics in all kinds of different genres: …
3 You're in the story with the characters …
4 I like my stories to have something to say …
5 I really loved drawing …
6 His style is very simple and cartoony …

a … and something to think about.
b … and feeling what they feel.
c … horror, comedy, science fiction, action and adventure.
d … manga as we know it.
e … yet all his stories have a message.
f … when I was growing up.

3b Watch the interview again and check your ideas. Make more notes as you watch.

4 Discuss these questions.

1 What did you learn about these topics?
   a Karen's early years
   b Tezuka and manga
   c Karen's creative habits and work
2 Which stories do you know which 'have a message', or make you feel what 'the characters are feeling'?
3 In general, who influences you in your life, study, work and interests?

4 HEALTH

1 Before you watch the interview, discuss these questions with a partner. Keep notes of the points that you both make.

1 What do you think brain food is?
2 Why is the food below important, for both the brain and the body?
  water   oily fish   meat, fish, eggs and nuts
3 What kind of diet do you think is bad for brain health?
4 Which country do you think has the healthiest diet for the mind and body?
5 In shops, there are special food products for physical health. Are special products for brain health a good idea?

2a ▶ **4** Watch the interview with Dr John Briffa, a doctor who specialises in nutrition, and take notes.

2b What answers does he give to the questions in Exercise 1?

3 Watch the interview again. Complete the sentences with verbs.

1 … any food or drink that _____ the brain to function well is essentially a brain food.
2 … if the brain doesn't have enough water in it, it _____ not to work as well …
3 These _____ to help the day-to-day running of the brain …
4 … the omega-3 fats […] also help _____ the risk of heart disease.
5 Some of these foods, for example, _____ highs and lows of sugar levels …
6 … more traditional foods will do a lot in order to _____ our brain function …

4 To what extent do you agree with these statements? Discuss in groups.

1 It is not easy to live a healthy lifestyle in the modern world.
2 The health and nutrition stories in the media change very often, so you cannot believe any of them.
3 My government often gives public information and advice about nutrition and health.

5 NATURAL WORLD

1 Discuss these questions.

1 Do you like taking photographs?
2 When and why do you take photos?
3 Have you taken any photographs recently? Show and/or describe them.

2a ▶ **5** Watch the interview with Gareth Philips, a photographer. Which of these things does Gareth mention?

1 When he took his first photographs
2 His reasons for liking photography
3 His photographic style
4 What he does on a photo assignment
5 Money and fees
6 Choosing the images for use

2b Check your ideas with a partner. Can you remember any details for each topic?

3a Gareth talks about the work process and selecting photographs. Look at these sentences. Which ones do you think are different to what Gareth actually says?

1 I let the landscape or person inspire the images.
2 … out of 215 images, I would supply them 30.
3 I always choose images that are difficult to understand.
4 I want the images to stay with the viewer.
5 The viewer must be able to feel or even taste what's in the image.

3b Watch the interview again. When Gareth talks about the work process and selecting photographs, check the sentences in Exercise 3a. Change the incorrect sentences.

4a What images can you remember from the interview?

4b Discuss these questions.

1 Describe the images that you can remember from the interview. What is your opinion of them?
2 You know what Gareth hopes to achieve with his pictures. For you, has he done that? Why?/Why not?
3 Describe any images that have moved you or stayed with you for a long time.

7 SCIENCE

1 Discuss these questions.

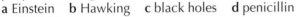

1 What basic information about the planets, the solar system and the universe do you know?

2 What do you know about these people and things?
   a Einstein   b Hawking   c black holes   d penicillin

2a ▶ 7 Watch the interview with Huw James, a scientist. Tick these words every time you hear them.

black hole(s)
universe
science/scientist/scientific

2b Compare your number of ticks with your partner. What information and images can you remember from the interview?

3 Read through these notes. Watch again and complete the notes (1–6). Compare your answers with a partner.

The universe isn't static – it's not rigid, it's [1]_____.

Black holes: nothing can escape.
Lots of mass in a very small [2]_____.

Stephen Hawking: great new ideas in [3]_____ _____ research.

BH: difficult to see – very small (20 miles) in a massive [4]_____.

Energy waves from BH travelling at the [5]_____ _____ _____ – studied as sound waves.

The discoveries of black holes and penicillin are very [6]_____.

4 Discuss these questions.

1 Which of these opinions do you think Huw has? Why?/Why not?
   a Knowledge does not need to be useful in order to be valuable.
   b Stephen Hawking will not be a famous scientist long into the future.
   c Practical science research is more important than theoretical research.
   d Scientists today are like the explorers of the past.

2 What is your opinion about statements a–d in question 1?

3 Huw wants scientists to discover 'a planet orbiting another star that we can live on'. Why do you think this would be a fascinating discovery?

4 What would you like scientists to discover?

8 THE NIGHT

1 Discuss these questions.

1 Where is Antarctica? What do you know about the place?

2 Scientists from many countries work there. What work do you think they do? What challenges do they face working in Antarctica?

2a Read these sentence beginnings and endings. They come from an interview with Karen Fowler, a scientist who works in Antarctica. Can you match the endings to the beginnings?

1 I work as a communications …
2 The polar winter in Antarctica is …
3 It is quite difficult to …
4 It is really important to …
5 During the polar winter, working in the dark can be …
6 It really is just a beautiful, serene …

a … know what time of day it is.
b … manager in Antarctica.
c … keep yourself in a normal working routine.
d … incredibly cold.
e … environment to work in.
f … extremely challenging.

2b ▶ 8 Watch the interview with Karen and check your answers.

2c Compare your answers with a partner. What else do you remember from the interview?

3 Try to answer these questions. Then watch the interview again to finalise your answers.

1 What exactly does Karen do in Antarctica?
2 How many months does the period of 24-hour darkness last?
3 What is the importance of mealtimes?
4 Is getting used to the darkness a quick or a slow process?
5 What helps workers in Antarctica to see in the dark?
6 What does she like about working in Antarctica?

4 Work with a partner and do the role-play.

Student A: You work on a scientific research facility in the Antarctic. A journalist is going to interview you about your work and life. Decide what kind of work you do and imagine life at the research facility.

Student B: You are a journalist writing an article about Antarctic workers for an international geography and society magazine. What questions can you ask to get ideas and information for your article?
Consider work duties, daily routines, social life and free time, problems and difficulties.

10 GLOBAL AFFAIRS

1 Discuss these questions.

1 Write down the names of five international brands or companies. What is the image or reputation of these brands, companies and their products?
2 What do you think of these brands and companies?
3 How do some companies become famous brands?

2 (▶10) Watch the interview with Nick Cooper, a brands specialist. In what order does Nick talk about these topics?

1 New markets, new brands
2 The importance of brands to companies
3 The financial value of a brand
4 Social media

3a Nick uses these topic sentences and introductory clauses to present his key points. Look at the words/phrases in the box and match them to the sentences/clauses (1–7) below.

emotional connection   actual value
consumer opinions   emotional part
customer loyalty   social media companies
need to learn   connect directly   rational
emotional   30% of value   create value   innovative
fastest growing market   half of revenue

1 A brand is a combination of two things: …
2 What's really important is the …
3 A brand is important to a company in a number of ways: …
4 Another reason why brands are so important is …
5 The way we measure the value of a brand comes from two things: …
6 Some of the brands coming out of the BRIC countries are really fascinating.
7 Social media is having a big effect on brands right now.

3b Watch the interview again and check your answers. Then add more information for each key point.

3c Compare your answers with your partner.

4 Discuss these questions.

1 Do you have an 'emotional' connection to any brands? Are you brand loyal at all?
2 Do you sometimes pay more money to buy a certain brand?
3 What examples of companies using social media can you think of?
4 Do you use social media to connect with any companies or brands? If so, how?

11 THE ENVIRONMENT

1 Work with a partner. What do you know about extreme weather and the environment?

2a Read the notes below from a short talk about the weather and answer these questions.

1 What is the general topic of the talk?
2 How many main sections are there?

2b (▶11) Watch the interview with Dr Laura Baker, a meteorologist. Complete the titles of the main sections (A–D).

Storms and extreme weather

Ⓐ _____ main types of storm

1 tropical storms – ¹_____ to the equator two types:
 • hurricanes (²_____ Ocean)
 • typhoons (Pacific Ocean)
2 extra-tropical storms: ³_____ and Europe

Studying **Ⓑ** _____
Observational ⁴_____ measure details of storm.
⁵_____ model produces 3D picture of storm
Specially designed plane – seats removed, specially designed ⁶_____ added
Measure (pressure, temperature, ⁷_____ _____)

Ⓒ _____ through a storm
Very strong wind – airports were closed
Flew at ⁸_____ levels to measure the strong winds – bumpy and scary

Climate **Ⓓ** _____
Causing global temperature to ⁹_____
Not sure how this affects future weather patterns
Perhaps stronger storms and more ¹⁰_____ rainfall

3 Watch the interview again and complete the notes (1–10).

4 Answer these questions with a partner.

1 Describe the images that you remember from the video. How do they connect to the notes?
2 What new things did you learn from the video?
3 Describe a time when you experienced a difficult, funny or otherwise memorable time due to the weather. Plan your narrative first.

12 SPORT

1 Discuss these questions.

1 Which sports do people usually think of as either mainly male or female?
2 Describe some differences between male and female sports and sporting culture in your country. Consider participation, watching, competitions and status.

2 ▶12 Watch the interview with Rachel Pavlou, the National Women's Football Development Manager at the English Football Association. Complete the key points from the interview by choosing the correct phrase in these sentences.

1 Rachel *didn't play / played* football with boys when she was younger.
2 The London 2012 Olympics *was / was not* very positive for women's football.
3 Women's football *has changed a lot / hasn't changed much* in the last 20 years.
4 The English Football Association *has / doesn't have* a long-term plan to develop women's and girls' football.
5 In the past, the broadcasters and sponsors *were / weren't* very interested in women's football.
6 Rachel wants women's football in England to be the *biggest / second biggest* team sport inthe world.

3a When Rachel speaks, she supports her key points with extra information, examples or a brief argument. Watch the interview again and make notes for each of the key points in Exercise 2.

3b Compare your notes with a partner.

4 Discuss these questions.

1 What are the reasons for differences between male and female sport and sporting culture?
2 Has your country held any major sporting events?
3 What are the benefits and drawbacks of hosting major sports events?
4 Which major sports event would you like to go to?

130

COMMUNICATION ACTIVITIES

LESSON 1.3 EXERCISE 7A (PAGE 11)

BELIZE

LOCATION:	On the coast	In the jungle
ACTIVITIES:	• diving • sea kayaking	• jungle trekking • white-water rafting
HOLIDAY SEASON: November to May	dry, average temperature: 30°C	

PERU

LOCATION:	On the coast	In the mountains
ACTIVITIES:	• snorkelling • sea kayaking	• white-water rafting • horse riding
HOLIDAY SEASON: November–April	sunny and hot, 26°C	cloudy and wet, 20°C
OTHER ATTRACTIONS		Machu Picchu (ancient temple)

CHILE

LOCATION:	In the desert	In the mountains
ACTIVITIES:	• horse riding • mountain biking	• skiing • snowboarding
HOLIDAY SEASON: June–October	clear skies and sunny Daytime temperature: 15°C	cold and snowy

LESSON 1.4 EXERCISE 3 (PAGE 12)

C **cloud** /klaʊd/ *noun*

a white or grey shape in the sky that is made of small drops of water: *There were no clouds in the sky.*

S **snow** /snəʊ/ *noun*

soft white pieces of frozen water that fall like rain when the weather is very cold: *The fields were covered with snow.* | *Several roads were blocked by deep snow.*

A **autumn** /ˈɔːtəm/ *noun*

the season when the leaves fall off the trees: SYNONYM **fall** *AmE*: *This shrub has orange berries in autumn.* | *His new book will be published in the autumn.*

S **sun** /sʌn/ *noun*

the thing in the sky that gives us light and heat: *The sun's gone behind a cloud.* | *She lay in the sun reading.*

S **sea** /siː/ *noun*

the salt water that covers large parts of the Earth SYNONYM **ocean** *AmE*: *We swam in the sea.* | *The ship was lost at sea.* | *The Red Sea lies between Arabia and North Africa.*

H **horse** /hɔːs/ *noun*

a large animal that people ride on or use for pulling heavy things: *I learned to ride a horse when I was four.*

From *Longman WordWise Dictionary*

LESSON 5.2 EXERCISE 8A (PAGE 41)

dangerous animals   environmental problems
unemployment   green spaces   cinemas
elderly people   computers   pictures
books and CDs   friends   pairs of shoes   free time
doing homework   playing computer games

In my country, In my city, In my college, In my workplace, In my house,	there are many / a lot of / few … there is a lot of / little … there aren't many / a lot of … there isn't a lot of / much …
I People in my family	have got many / a lot of … haven't got many / much … spend a lot of time … don't spend a lot of time …

C **cool** /kuːl/ *adjective*

1 slightly cold, especially in a nice way ANTONYM **warm**: *It was hot in the day, but pleasantly cool at night.* | *After his run, he had a shower and a long, cool drink.*

2 calm, rather than nervous or excited: *She tried to **stay cool** and not panic.*

3 (spoken informal) If you say that someone or something is cool, you like or admire them: *It was a really cool party last night.*

H **hot** /hɒt/ *adjective* (**hotter, hottest**)

1 Something that is hot has a high temperature ANTONYM **cold**: *It was a very hot day.* | *You'll feel better after a hot bath.* | *My coffee is still too hot to drink.*

2 Hot food has a burning taste because it has a lot of spice in it: *a hot curry*

D **dark** /daːk/ *adjective*

1 **it is dark** When it is dark, it is night time: *It's only five o'clock and **it's** already **dark**.* | *I want to get home before **it gets dark** (= becomes dark).* | *Come inside, **it's dark out** (= it is dark outside).*

2 A dark place is one where there is little or no light ANTONYM **light, bright**: *a dark, quiet room* | *It was very dark in the forest and we could hardly see.*

3 A dark colour is strong and closer to black than to white ANTONYM **light, pale**: *a dark blue dress* | *I'd like a carpet that's a bit darker than this one.*

4 Someone who is dark or who has dark hair or eyes has black or brown skin, hair or eyes ANTONYM **fair**: *a beautiful dark-haired woman* | *Tony's dad was dark, but his mother had blonde hair.*

W **warm** /wɔːm/ *adjective*

1 quite hot: *It's lovely and warm in this room.* | *Cover the bowl to keep the soup warm.* | *It was a warm day, so we sat outside.*

2 Warm clothes stop you from feeling cold: *I must buy a warm coat to wear this winter.*

3 friendly: *We gave the visiting students a warm welcome.*

F **fine** /faɪn/ *adjective*

1 very good: *We sell fine food from around the world.* | *The team gave a fine performance.*

2 very thin, or in very small pieces or amounts: *a shampoo for fine hair* | *a scarf made from very fine silk* | *The sand here is fine and soft.*

3 (spoken) good enough SYNONYM **OK**: *'I've only got water to drink.' 'That's fine.'*

4 (spoken) healthy and reasonably happy: *'How is your mother?' 'She's fine, thanks.'*

5 If the weather is fine, it is sunny and not raining: *I hope it stays fine for the picnic.*

C **clear** /klɪə/ *adjective*

1 easy to see, hear or understand: *His writing isn't very clear.* | *Some of the exam questions weren't very clear.*

2 If something is clear, it is certain and people cannot doubt it: *It soon became clear that John was lying to us.* | *It's not clear how many people were hurt.* | *Sarah made it clear that she wanted to come with us.*

3 If a substance or liquid is clear, you can see through it SYNONYM **transparent**: *clear glass*

4 A clear sky has no clouds.

D **dry** /draɪ/ *adjective* (**drier, driest**)

1 Something that is dry has no water in it or on it ANTONYM **wet**: *Get a dry towel out of the cupboard.*

2 If your mouth, throat or skin is dry, it does not have enough of the natural liquid that is usually in it: *My skin gets so dry in the winter.*

3 If the weather is dry, there is no rain ANTONYM **wet**: *It's been a very dry summer.*

B **bright** /braɪt/ *adjective*

1 Something that is bright shines a lot or has a lot of light: *the bright flames of the candles* | *a nice bright room*

2 Bright colours are strong and not dark: *a bunch of bright yellow flowers*

3 intelligent: *Maria is one of the brightest students in the school.*

– **brightness** *noun* (no plural)

M **mild** /maɪld/ *adjective*

1 not too severe, strong or serious: *Dean had a mild case of flu* | *a mild punishment*

2 not having a strong taste: *The sauce is very mild.*

3 Mild weather is not too cold: *It's very mild for January.*

From *Longman WordWise Dictionary*

Analysis of
questionnaire

High scores in section A

You are probably a **visual** learner. Visual learners like to see information. A lot of learning in schools, colleges and universities is visual learning because it involves reading.

TIPS Look again regularly at what you study. Use different colours to organise and highlight information. Write things down several times. Copy things you want to learn onto the computer, then read the print-outs.

High scores in section B

You are probably an **auditory** learner. Auditory learners like to hear information. They understand best when they are listening or discussing.

TIPS Get information from radio programmes or sound files on the internet. Record things you want to remember and listen to them later. Say things aloud. Sing things to music you know. Study with other students and talk about what you're learning.

High scores in section C

You are probably a **physical** learner. Physical learners remember best by moving around and touching things.

TIPS Put information on cards that you can move around or put on the walls of your home or room. When you study, walk around with your textbook or notes in your hand and read the information aloud. Spend time 'in the field' (e.g. visiting a museum or working in an office).

ALL STUDENTS
Have a look at the tips in the other sections – perhaps there is something there that can also help you.

One of the ways we like to work is by asking you to do things in pairs or small groups. Some students think this is a waste of time. They don't want to listen to and talk to other students; they want to communicate with the teacher. However, here at the York Language Centre, we believe there are many advantages to working in pairs or small groups:

- It increases the amount of time each student can talk; you can't all have long conversations with the teacher, but it is possible to have quite long conversations with your partner, and that speaking practice is important.

- It helps students become more confident, especially if they're a little shy about speaking in front of the whole class.

- It encourages students to become more independent learners – they're not always waiting for the teacher to tell them what to do.

- It provides variety in the lesson – sometimes the teacher is talking, sometimes you work in pairs or groups, and sometimes you have a big class discussion – this makes the class more interesting.

- You can learn interesting things from other students, not only from the teacher!

- It gives the teacher the chance to see how everybody is working and communicating. The teacher can go round the class and listen carefully to students and make helpful comments.

There are probably many more reasons that are not on this list. So we hope that you understand why we work in pairs and small groups, and enjoy this way of learning, even if it is new for you.

COMMUNICATION ACTIVITIES

LESSON 4.1   EXERCISE 7B (PAGE 31)

In your life

1. How many countries have you visited in your life?
2. How _____ ?
3. Have you ever ridden a motorbike?
4. Have you ever _____ ?

This year

5. How many exams have you done this year?
6. How _____ ?
7. Have you had a holiday this year?
8. Have _____ ?

This week

9. How much television have you watched this week?
10. How _____ ?
11. Have you been to the cinema this week?
12. Have _____ ?

Today

13. How many phone calls have you made today?
14. How _____ ?
15. Have you eaten any fruit today?
16. Have _____ ?

Which country did you visit first?
Did you like it?

LESSON 8.4   EXERCISE 10 (PAGE 69)

Soon, we could see it better, and we all knew what it was – the ghost of a man! We couldn't move. Before long, it was standing next to us, looking at us. Then it spoke: 'Do you know what time it is?' At that moment, we were extremely confused and scared, but then we realised that the ghost was a local shepherd* – and he didn't have a watch! He just wanted to ask us the time! Later, we laughed a lot about that ghost.

*shepherd: a person who takes care of sheep

LESSON 1.2   EXERCISE 4B (PAGE 9)

World weather average conditions

	January		July	
Bangkok	32°C	☀	32°C	☁
Beijing	1°C	☁	31°C	☁
Cairo	19°C	☀	35°C	☀
Dubai	24°C	☀	40°C	☀
London	8°C	☁	23°C	☁
Moscow	–7°C	☁	23°C	☁
New York	4°C	☁	29°C	☁
Rio de Janeiro	30°C	☁	24°C	☁
Seoul	1°C	☀	29°C	☁
Sydney	26°C	☁	16°C	☀

LESSON 5.1   EXERCISE 2B (PAGE 38)

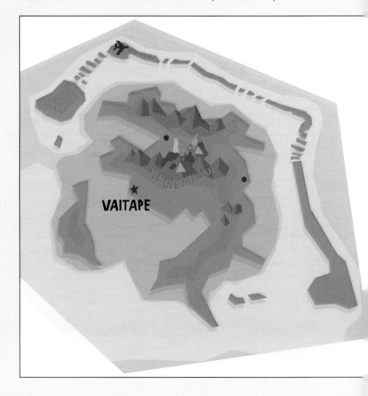

VAITAPE

LESSON 5.4   EXERCISE 4B (PAGE 44)

> *Sp*
> The wether can change very quick and it's easy lose
>   *Gr*
> your way. If you don't have much experiment, its
>   *WW*   *^P*
> better go with someone who can you guide. If you
>   *WO* *P*
> have any difficulties.

LESSON 6.2   EXERCISE 10 (PAGE 49)

Situation A

You want to borrow some money from your rich aunt to start your own business. With your partner, make two lists:

1 the problems you might face
2 the solutions to those problems.

Problems	Solutions
• Your aunt refuses to lend you any money. • No one in your family will lend you any money.	• Borrow some money from other family members. • Get a job with a company or other family organisation.

Try to think of some more problems and solutions. Then role-play the situation with your partner.

'What'll you do if your aunt refuses to lend you any money?'
'I'll borrow some money from other family members.'
'Yes, but ...'

Situation B

Your younger brother/sister is a university student. He/She spends too much time having fun and not working.

Problems	Solutions
• He/She doesn't do well in his/her exams. • He/She doesn't listen to you.	• Persuade him/her to study more. • Ask his/her friends to help.

LESSON 8.1   EXERCISE 6 (PAGE 63)

How much do you know about sleep?

1 How long should it take people to fall asleep at night?

a) 0-5 minutes   b) 5-10 minutes   c) 10-15 minutes

2 How many hours' sleep do parents lose a year when they have a new baby?

a) 50–400 hours
b) 400-750 hours
c) 750-1,100 hours

3 Why is it difficult to sleep on hot summer nights?

a) We need to cool down before we can sleep, and this is more difficult in summer.
b) We don't like listening to noises outside – and these noises seem to be louder in summer.
c) We go to bed later in summer - and keep thinking about things that happened during the day.

4 What is the record for the longest period of time someone managed to go without sleep?

a) 6 days   b) 11 days   c) 16 days

5 How many hours a night did people tend to sleep 150 years ago?

a) 7-8 hours   b) 8-9 hours   c) 9-10 hours

6 If you want to sleep, but can't, you should count sheep.

True or false?

7 If you start to feel sleepy when you're driving, it's a good idea to open the window or play loud music.

True or false?

8 Losing sleep can make you fat.

True or false?

9 Elephants sleep standing up during NREM sleep, but lie down for REM sleep.

True or false?

10 Fish close their eyes when they sleep.

True or false?

Check your answers on page 138.

LESSON 9.2   EXERCISE 5 (PAGE 73)

- Location of industry? north/south of country, etc. / near the capital / on the coast
- Age of industry? old/new / 20th/21st century
- Type of industry? mining / oil / automotive / car / shipbuilding / steel / food / electronic / entertainment, etc.
- Names of well-known companies? Sony, Ford, etc.

LESSON 10.3   EXERCISE 1B (PAGE 82)

These cities have not hosted the summer Olympics: Nairobi, New York, Abu Dhabi

These cities have hosted the summer Olympics: London (1908, 1948, 2012); Los Angeles (1932, 1984); Paris (1924); Mexico City (1968); Moscow (1980); Seoul (1988)

LESSON 11.2   EXERCISE 1 (PAGE 88)

The photo shows packaging waste being processed on a conveyor belt and waste being sorted for recycling.

LESSON 11.2   EXERCISE 7B (PAGE 89)

7 tips for cutting down waste – one for every day of the week

1 Send e-cards (for birthdays, etc.) and not paper or card ones. The thought is what's important, not the material.

2 Give old toys to other families.

3 Reuse plastic bags. To help you remember to do this, keep some in your pocket or bag – they don't take up much space.

4 Buy your fruit and vegetables from a local market.

5 Think before you print. How many times have you printed something and not looked at it again? If you do print, use both sides of a piece of paper.

6 Hire DVDs rather than buying them.

7 Save about 40 litres of water a time by having showers instead of baths.

1   Which do you already know about? Which are new to you?
2   Which do you do? Which could you do?
3   Which are good ideas? Are there any you don't like? Why?

LESSON 12.1   EXERCISE 1B (PAGE 94)

language leader

News | Sport | Comment | Business | Money | Life & Style | Travel

Sport ⟩ **Sports quiz**

Sports quiz answers

1 c)	5 Yellow
2 a)	6 Sailing
3 False (There are three higher grades: red-and-white striped, red, and white belts.)	7 Yellow
	8 b)
	9 Drums
4 True	10 b)

Super Streets

Project description: The aim of the project is to clean the streets of graffiti and litter and to reduce crime. Members of the local community will form 'Street Teams', which will be responsible for cleaning up graffiti and litter. CCTV will reduce anti-social/criminal behaviour.

Benefits of the project

1 In the local area, there is a lot of graffiti and rubbish. The street teams will clean things up regularly and create a better local environment.
2 The local community will take responsibility for the local area.
3 The street teams will bring the members of the community closer together.
4 CCTV will help reduce street crime and make the streets safer.
5 A safer and cleaner environment will attract new businesses to the area.

Budget (including annual running cost):
Total cost NZ $45,000

Cost breakdown

Cleaning equipment: NZ $20,000
Purchase of ten CCTV cameras: NZ $25,000
Management of the CCTV cameras: NZ $10,000 per year

Village of wind

Project description: The aim of the project is to create a community wind farm. It will provide electricity for local homes, and we will sell spare electricity in order to raise money for other community projects.

Benefits of the project

1 It will provide green electricity for the village (and help fight global warming).
2 It will turn an area of wasteland into a modern wind farm.
3 It will make money for the community by selling electricity to the country. This money could fund other community projects e.g. a youth club.

Budget (including annual running cost):
Total cost: NZ $32,000

Cost breakdown

Clearance of wasteland: NZ $20,000
Installation of ten wind turbines: NZ $12,000
Note: There will be no annual running costs because the wind farm will make money that will pay for maintenance and management.

COMMUNICATION ACTIVITIES

LESSON 11.4 EXERCISE 1 (PAGE 92)

Where did the text appear (e.g. on a website, on a poster)?
Who wrote it, and who will read it?
When was it written?
What is it about?
Why was it written?

LESSON 11.4 EXERCISE 10 (PAGE 93)

Plans for a new airport terminal

- 1,000 local residents interviewed (February 4–11)
- 64% against new terminal – aircraft noise, more traffic on local roads
- 25% in favour – good for local businesses
- 11% undecided – need more information about the plans
- 94% think government should pay more attention to views of local residents

LESSON 8.1 EXERCISE 6 (PAGE 63)

How much do you know about sleep?

1 c) (Less than 5 minutes means you're sleep-deprived.)

2 b)

3 a)

4 b)

5 c) (Although this can change with the seasons.)

6 F (They think it may be more distracting than relaxing. Relaxing imagery or thoughts may be better.)

7 F (You need to stop, and take a nap. That's the best and safest thing to do.)

8 T (New research shows a connection between lack of sleep and obesity.)

9 T

10 F (Fish don't have eyelids.)

LESSON 12.1 EXERCISE 1B (PAGE 94)

language**leader**

News | Sport | Comment | Business | Money | Life & Style | Travel

Sport ⟩ **Sports quiz** ⟩

Sports quiz

1 The first table-tennis match was between two university students. At which university?
a) Beijing, China
b) Bologna, Italy
c) Cambridge, UK

2 Which sport took the name of someone's house?
a) badminton
b) hockey
c) polo

3 The highest grade of judo is the black belt.
True or false?

4 In fencing, clothes must be white.
True or false?

5 In archery, what colour is the centre of the target?

6 Which sport is connected with the America's Cup?

7 In cycling, what colour shirt does the leader of the Tour de France wear?

8 In which culture did gymnastics begin?
a) Roman
b) Ancient Greek
c) Incan

9 What musical instrument is connected with dragon-boat racing?

10 Where were the first football World Cup finals in 1930?
a) Chile
b) Uruguay
c) Switzerland

Turn to page 136 for the answers.

LESSON 12.3   EXERCISE 6A (PAGE 99)

Questionnaire format

Section 1: How competitive are you?

1 If you _____, would you a) _____, b) _____, c) _____?
2 If you _____, would you a) _____, b) _____, c) _____?

Section 2: How risk-taking are you?

1 If you _____, would you a) _____, b) _____, c) _____?
2 If you _____, would you a) _____, b) _____, c) _____?

Section 3: How social are you?

1 If you _____, would you a) _____, b) _____, c) _____?
2 If you _____, would you a) _____, b) _____, c) _____?

Section 4: What are your sporting preferences?

Have you played any of these sports?
Did you enjoy them?

1 _____   5 _____   9 _____
2 _____   6 _____   10 _____
3 _____   7 _____   11 _____
4 _____   8 _____   12 _____

LESSON 12.4   EXERCISE 12 (PAGE 101)

MANHATTAN LANGUAGE ACADEMY

Learn English in the heart of the
Big Apple – the city that never sleeps.

General English classes,
all levels, all nationalities.

Small class sizes guaranteed.

Amazing modern facilities –
all you need to study.

Special afternoon options include:
Business English, film-making,
team sports, American musicals.

Full programme of social activities.

Weekend trips available.

Accommodation service available.

LESSON 9.3   EXERCISE 8A (PAGE 75)

STUDENT A

- You are selling a new digital camera, Model DC3, that costs $100.
- You want to get some big orders for this new product – up to 2,000.
- You can offer discounts – up to 20%.
- Longer delivery times are better for your company – up to eight weeks.

LESSON 3.2   EXERCISE 9 (PAGE 25)

STUDENT A

USEFUL PHRASES

What's 1 Down?   What's 1 Across?
This is someone who/that …
This is something which/that …
This is a place where …

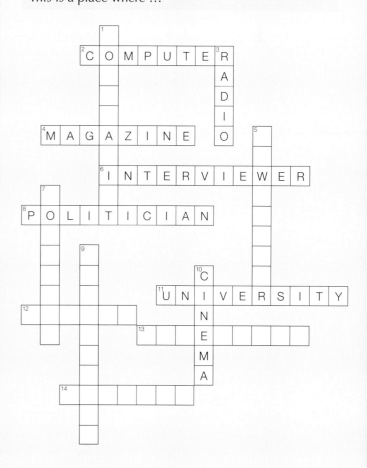

COMMUNICATION ACTIVITIES

LESSON 4.3 EXERCISE 7 (PAGE 35)
STUDENT A

Name: _____

Year of study: Second

Subject: Chemistry

Health problems:
Frequent headaches, can't concentrate, make simple mistakes, sometimes get stomach aches.

Study routines/habits:
Often study late in the laboratory, doing experiments.
Also like to work sitting on my bed using my laptop.
Never late with assignments and essays (work hard to do this).

General lifestyle:
Eat a lot of snacks, as no time to cook.
Cycle to college, but do no other exercise.
Take a lot of headache medicine.
Few friends and not much social life.

LESSON 2.3 EXERCISE 6A (PAGE 19)
STUDENT A

TOSHI

Young Japanese man.
Engineer (works for a big company).
Personality – friendly (nice smile), extremely polite and clever, not very chatty.
Likes – sport: plays football/tennis.
Going to the cinema. Rap and hip-hop music.
Dislikes – cooking (usually goes to cafés/restaurants).
Appearance – smart, fashionable clothes. Short black hair. Glasses.
Other information – smokes a little, speaks good English.

LESSON 8.3 EXERCISE 7A (PAGE 67)
STUDENT A

SYDNEY FESTIVAL

WHAT'S ON?

Daily festival listings: Friday 24th August

EVENING EVENTS (6 P.M.–8 P.M.)

THEATRE AND MUSIC
Chinese opera in the Sydney Opera House.

CINEMA
A remake of *Frankenstein*, including an interview with the director. Café open.

ART
Food for the eyes: An exhibition of art about food, and art made of food, from famous paintings by the Dutch Masters to a contemporary sculpture of Sydney made of biscuits. The evening event includes a barbecue on the terrace.

LESSON 9.3 EXERCISE 8A (PAGE 75)
STUDENT B

- Your ideal order is 500 cameras. You can increase this, but you are not sure how popular the camera will be.
- You would like to pay about $80 per item.
- Your company would like a fast delivery, so that you can soon sell the camera to the online retailers.

STUDENT A

Look at your photos and prepare to describe and discuss them. Look at each pair of photos for each link: Animal hunting (C1 and C2) and Animal captivity (E1 and E2). Compare and contrast the two pictures in each pair. What are the similarities and differences? What are the strengths and weaknesses of each photo with regard to their use on the website?

Which photo do you think is best for each link? Why? Use these words to help you.

market stall   animal skin   cage   glass   gun   hunter   lock   bars

LESSON 10.1   EXERCISE 7 (PAGE 79)

STUDENT A

What is Yo-Yo doing on Thursday?
He's meeting the ambassador at ten o'clock.

Diary appointments for: **Yo-Yo Ma**

	a.m.	p.m.
Monday	10.00 1 _____ about the trip from Turkey to China	4.00 Perform in a classical music concert at the Ataturk Cultural Centre
Tuesday	Travel to Iran	3.00 2 _____ in Tehran
Wednesday	10.30 Meet the Iranian Minister of Education	4.00 3 _____
Thursday	11.00 4 _____	3.00 Watch a traditional music performance
Friday	10.00 Appear on a local radio show	2.00 5 _____ 8.00 6 _____

Diary appointments for: **Paulo Coelho**

	a.m.	p.m.
Monday	10.00 12 _____ about the trip to Thailand	4.00 Attend the International Culture Conference in Bangkok
Tuesday	10.30 Make a speech at the International Culture Conference	4.30 13 _____
Wednesday	9.30 Meet the Thai Minister of Culture	3.30 14 _____ at the Brazilian Embassy 7.00 15 _____ the Brazilian Ambassador
Thursday	9.00 16 _____	2.30 Appear on a TV show about animal conservation
Friday	10.00 17 _____	2.00 Hold a press conference with the school headmaster 8.00 Fly to Brazil

Notes for presentation

Plans, points and claims	Examples
Opening section	
A truly green games	solar power
Successful sport in new venues	
Finance guarantee	40 billion US dollars
Sports venues	
The Olympic Park holds all the venues.	athletics stadium, swimming pool
New and modern sports venues	stadium made of golden glass
Everything will use solar power.	stadium lights, media centre
Olympic Village	
Will be next to the Olympic Park.	
Convenient for the athletes	walk to the venues, use electric golf buggies
15,000 single rooms	
Buildings will be green.	made from recycled materials
Food from many countries	India, China, Jamaica
Transport	
The Olympic Park is in the desert, outside the city.	
Will build excellent transport from the city to the Park.	high-speed railway (20 mins)
Use green public transport.	electric buses

Abu Dhabi Olympic Games Presentation

The green Games in the desert

Opening section

Hello, everyone. Abu Dhabi is a great opportunity for the Olympic Games and the environment. We will give the world a truly green games. For example, we will use solar power for all our electricity. Our games will show the world how to use clean electricity to improve our lives, and our spectacular Olympic Park will be perfect for great sporting success. This will, of course, be expensive to build, but we guarantee to have the full 40 billion US dollars.

Sports venues

Olympic Village

Transport

LESSON 7.1 EXERCISE 9 (PAGE 55)

STUDENT A

You are a second-year student. Tell a new student at your university what he/she has to / mustn't / should do in order to be successful at the university.
Think about studying, accommodation, making friends, health and well-being.

You have to …
One thing you mustn't do is …

LESSON 3.2 EXERCISE 9 (PAGE 25)

STUDENT B

USEFUL PHRASES

What's 1 Down? What's 1 Across?
This is someone who/that …
This is something which/that …
This is a place where …

LESSON 8.3 EXERCISE 7A (PAGE 67)

STUDENT B

SYDNEY FESTIVAL

WHAT'S ON?

Daily festival listings: Friday 24th August

NIGHT EVENTS (9 P.M.–11 P.M.)

FIREWORKS CONCERT
Rock and modern pop music with fireworks. At Sydney Harbour.

THEATRE FUN
Circus and mime performances. Stories without words, but stories with drama and laughs.

MUSIC AND FILM
Watch the great science-fiction film *2001: A Space Odyssey* while the Sydney Symphony Orchestra performs the film's music live.

STUDENT B

Look at your photos and prepare to describe and discuss them. Look at each pair of photos for each link: Animal hospitals (B1 and B2) and Animal sanctuaries (D1 and D2). Compare and contrast the two pictures in each pair. What are the similarities and differences? What are the strengths and weaknesses of each photo with regard to their use on the website?

Which photo do you think is best for each link? Why? Use these words to help you.

hold   stethoscope   table   eye drops   neck   bucket   lie down   animal keeper

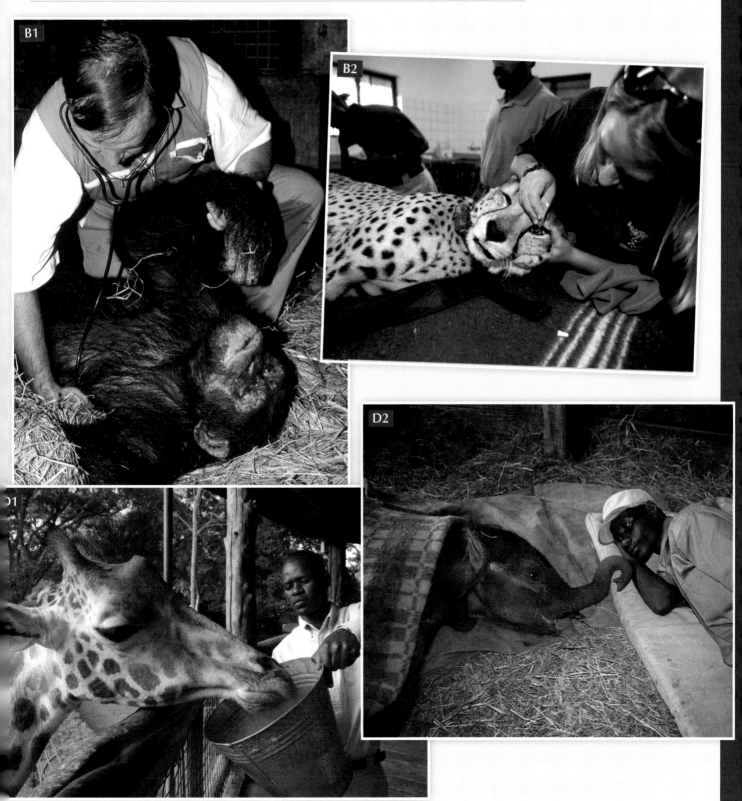

LESSON 10.1   EXERCISE 7 (PAGE 79)

STUDENT B

What is Yo-Yo doing on Thursday?
He's meeting the ambassador at ten o'clock.

Diary appointments for: **Yo-Yo Ma**

	a.m.	p.m.
Monday	10.00 Give a press conference about the trip from Turkey to China	4.00 7 _____ at the Ataturk Cultural Centre
Tuesday	8 _____	3.00 Visit a music school in Tehran
Wednesday	10.30 9 _____	4.00 Travel to Afghanistan
Thursday	11.00 Visit a children's hospital	3.00 10 _____
Friday	10.00 11 _____	2.00 Have dinner with the president of Afghanistan 8.00 Fly to China

Diary appointments for: **Paulo Coelho**

	a.m.	p.m.
Monday	10.00 Give a press conference about the trip to Thailand	4.00 18 _____ in Bangkok
Tuesday	10.30 19 _____ at the International Culture Conference	4.30 Visit a charity for homeless children
Wednesday	9.30 20 _____	3.30 Give a poetry reading at the Brazilian Embassy 7.00 Have dinner with the Brazilian Ambassador
Thursday	9.00 Go to an elephant sanctuary	2.30 21 _____ about animal conservation
Friday	10.00 Teach creative writing at a village school	2.00 22 _____ with the school headmaster 8.00 23 _____

Notes for presentation

Plans, points and claims	Examples
Opening section	
First ever Olympic Games in Africa	
City has experience.	hosted All-Africa Games
No need to build venues	
Low-cost Games	
Sports venues	
All the venues exist.	
All used before for the All-Africa Games	
Have everything the Olympic Games needs.	athletics stadium with 60,000 seats
Save a lot of money.	London spent £2 billion on new venues
Reduce costs, but keep high quality.	
Olympic Village	
Just outside the city	
Perfect location for the athletes	safe and quiet, clean air
10,000 double rooms	
Village has everything they need.	medical facilities, cinemas, global food
Transport	
Will improve the public transport system.	a city-wide tram system
Good transport for the athletes to the venues	special bus lanes

Nairobi Olympic Games Presentation

The low-cost games

Opening section

Hello, everyone. Nairobi is a great opportunity to hold the first ever Olympic Games in Africa. Nairobi is ready for the challenge. We have hosted large sporting competitions before, such as the All-Africa Games. Therefore we have the experience, and we also have the venues. This will be the low-cost Games because we do not need to build any new sports venues at all. Nairobi is already ready!

Sports venues

Olympic Village

Transport

COMMUNICATION ACTIVITIES

LESSON 4.3   EXERCISE 6A (PAGE 35)
STUDENT B

Name: _____

Year of study: First

Subject: Psychology

Health problems:
Lacking energy, lacking motivation to study and go to classes.

Study routines/habits:
Get books from the library, but don't read them.
Always work late the night before an essay deadline.
Sometimes miss classes.
Tutors are not happy with my work.

General lifestyle:
Many friends, like to meet them for coffee.
Live in a shared house, frequent parties.
Vegetarian. Eat well, as often have dinner parties at home.
Go swimming once a week.

LESSON 2.3   EXERCISE 6A (PAGE 19)
STUDENT B

ISABELLE

Young French woman.

No job (unemployed). Looking for office work. Comes from rich family.

Personality – very friendly, cheerful, chatty, confident. Not very tidy.

Likes – going out: cafés, cinema, parties. Playing classical guitar. Cooking.

Dislikes – washing up, sport.

Appearance – not professional or smart. Quite scruffy (untidy, old clothes), short blonde hair.

Other information – non-smoker, speaks very good English.

LESSON 8.3   EXERCISE 7A (PAGE 67)
STUDENT C

SYDNEY FESTIVAL

WHAT'S ON?

Daily festival listings: Friday 24th August

LATE-NIGHT EVENTS (11 P.M.–1 A.M.)

COMEDY
The Best of British Comedy: Ten top comedians from the UK will make you laugh all night long.

DANCE
Bollywood Bonanza: Incredible live performances of the dances from Indian films.

MUSIC
Up and Coming: Five of Australia's latest young rock and pop groups.

JAZZ/POETRY
Club Cool: Jazz music, poetry readings, an underground bar and restaurant – the recipe for a fun 1960s-style night out.

LESSON 7.1   EXERCISE 9 (PAGE 55)
STUDENT B

You are a new student at university. Ask Student A, a second-year student, for information and advice about university life and study. Is there anything you have to / mustn't / should do? Think about studying, accommodation, making friends, health and well-being.

Do I have to …?
Should I …?
Is there anything that I …?

LESSON 1.1   RECORDING 1.2

L = Liu Shan, M = Mo, A = André

Extract 1

L: Hello. I'm Liu Shan and I'm Chinese. In the picture, this woman is dancing to a traditional song. She's my mother and she comes to this park every week. I love this part of the park because it is so full of life. Right now, many different groups are playing different music, people are dancing and so many people are taking photographs. Like me. In this place, you can feel something special and be together with many people.

Extract 2

M: Hi. I'm Mo. I'm Australian, but I'm studying here in Dubai. My photograph doesn't show what I can see right now, but it does show exactly where I'm standing. I'm at the top of the Burj Khalifa building and I'm looking down on this great city. Right now, far below me, people are walking to work and all the cars are moving around, and they have no idea that I'm looking at them. In a city, you need a quiet place to stop and think, and I come here often for that reason. I take a lot of photographs here at different times of the day because the view is always different. What do you think of this picture from today?

Extract 3

A: Hello, I'm André. I'm Brazilian and I live in Rio. I'm a student; I'm studying science, but right now I'm playing football with my friends. This photo shows my favourite place and also my favourite way to spend time with my friends. We come to the beach twice a week and we always play football. I love the fun and energy, and it helps us relax when we aren't studying. It's easy to get here from the city centre, and when you're on the beach you forget about the crowded city and you feel free. But, currently, the beach is getting busy because the summer is coming – we try not to hit people with the ball, but you never know.

LESSON 1.3   RECORDING 1.3

S = Simon, D = Diana

S: So, Diana, any thoughts?
D: I think the Antarctic wildlife cruise is a great idea. I like that activity.
S: Mmm, so do I. It's unusual, and everyone loves penguins. It's certainly something for older customers.
D: I agree with you. I also think it's a good activity for our main customers.
S: Do you? I disagree. Our main customers like very adventurous activities. A cruise isn't very adventurous, is it?
D: Well, it's not adventurous, but it is something new. And whale watching is great.
S: Yes, you're right. So, are there any problems?
D: Well, the holiday season seems very short.
S: I see. How long is it?
D: It's only four months long. I don't like that.
S: No, neither do I. It means we can't sell a lot of holidays. OK, what about the other adventure?
D: In the mountains? Well, let's see … they can go walking and horse riding in the mountains. I don't like those activities.
S: Don't you? I do. Horse riding's always popular, and everyone can go walking.
D: Well, I disagree with you. I think they're very boring.
S: Well, I think those activities are fine, especially if we want new customers who are first-timers. Everyone can do those activities.
D: Well, everyone can read, but that doesn't mean we want to offer trips to a library, does it? Anyway, what about the weather? It says it's windy. That's not so good.
S: Mmm, you're right about the weather.
D: So, I think there are a few problems.
S: I understand, but the Antarctic cruise is very different. Perhaps this is a good place for older customers and first-timers. Let's look at the other places, then decide.
D: OK, so where are the other destinations?

LESSON 2.1   RECORDING 2.1

Extract 1

Chimokel married Benjamin when she was 16. She has two children and lives on a small farm. They wanted to send their children to school, but they needed a lot of money. A neighbour told her about the running races with money prizes, so she started running! She trained for one year, early every morning in the hills. Benjamin looked after the boys, and she did extra work on the farm. She was determined to do well. Then, amazingly, she won the Nairobi marathon. It was her first race! She was very happy when her boys went to school after that.

Extract 2

Soula is a creative person. She studied graphic design and, after working for a few companies, she started her own business five years ago. She designs and sells greetings cards and photographs. She started with nothing, and it was difficult to do everything. She is very hard-working, so she often worked through the night. She also spent a lot of time building the business through the internet, on social media like Twitter and Facebook. Last year, she won an award – 'Most Promising Young Designer' – and an important shop became a regular customer. That was a lovely reward for many years of hard work.

Extract 3

Sarah started her journey in April 2011. First, she travelled from London, across Europe and Asia to Japan by bike and kayak. Then, she left Japan in a rowing boat in order to go to North America. On her journey, she saw many wonderful places and she got great support from all the local people. They were really kind and friendly. Cycling across the Gobi desert was difficult, but she never gave up! Some of the things that she did were very dangerous, but Sarah is brave and confident, and this helped her to succeed.

LESSON 2.2   RECORDING 2.4

I'd like to invite Esperanza Spalding. She's a jazz singer and a musician from the USA. Her early life wasn't easy. She lived in a poor part of Portland, Oregon, with her mother. Her mother was an important influence, and Esperanza has a lot of respect for her. Esperanza had a long illness as a child, and didn't go to school all the time. Instead, she learnt at home. Erm … she first became interested in music at the age of four. She trained as a classical musician, but, as a teenager, she also liked blues, hip-hop and other styles of music. She discovered the bass when she was 14 … because she was bored with other instruments. Er … her first album – 'Junjo' – came out in 2005. In 2011, she won a Grammy music prize for Best New Artist. I admire her

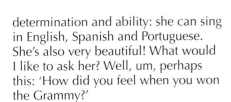

determination and ability: she can sing in English, Spanish and Portuguese. She's also very beautiful! What would I like to ask her? Well, um, perhaps this: 'How did you feel when you won the Grammy?'

LESSON 2.3   RECORDING 2.7

R = Robert, G = Gao Ying

R: Hello.

G: Hi Robert, it's Gao Ying.

R: Oh, hi. How are you? How did the interviews go?

G: Oh, I'm fine. The interviews were fine, too. Have you got ten minutes or are you busy?

R: I'm fine for time. Tell me about the people. Who did you see first?

G: Well, the first person was a guy called Martin. He's a young doctor, he's Canadian.

R: Oh, that sounds good. What's he like?

G: Well, I'm not sure. At first, he wasn't very friendly and he certainly isn't chatty. He works long hours, so he's hard-working, I guess. He seems honest.

R: I see, so, erm … what does he like? What are his interests?

G: Well, he likes watching sport on TV, but he doesn't play any. Um, what else? He doesn't smoke, in fact he hates smoking. Oh, he said he likes cooking, when he's got time.

R: OK, so perhaps he's a bit quiet. What does he look like? Does he look tidy and smart? Or does he look scruffy, like a punk or something?

G: Well, he's a doctor, so he looks professional. He wears nice clothes. He's got short brown hair. In fact, he looks like that actor who plays Mr Bean.

R: Really? I'm not sure that's a good thing! What about if he's like Mr Bean, as well as looking like him? We don't want to him to damage the flat with his stupid accidents!

G: Indeed, but I'm sure he just looks like him.

R: You never know! Anyway, what do you think? Would you like to live with him?

G: Mmm, yes, I think so. I'm happy to live with a quiet person.

R: What, like me?!

G: Yeah, exactly! And I'd like to live with a Canadian – you know, my sister lives in Toronto. Also, doctors are usually honest and responsible. What about you?

R: Well … erm … he sounds quite quiet … tell me about the others first …

LESSON 2.4   RECORDING 2.10

1   I was eighteen when I left my home town and went to live by myself. I didn't know how to cook anything! My mum prepared all my food. The first meals I cooked were really simple – pasta, things like that, very basic. But I felt very proud of myself – and also independent. I was really happy. It was fun to go to the shops and choose what to eat. I know a lot of people hate shopping for food, but at the time it was all new and quite exciting for me. I don't think anyone showed me how to cook. I just learnt by myself, little by little. There were lots of cookery books, so it was easy to learn. Later, when I was quite good at it, I invited my friends to dinner.

2   About ten years ago, I got a job in Japan – in Tokyo, actually. I wanted to learn some Japanese, and I bought a book called *Japanese for Busy People*. I clearly remember the cover of the book – it was light blue. People say Japanese is a difficult language, but some things are quite easy – like the pronunciation. It's a bit like Italian. But it was very difficult to remember the words – they were so different to my own language. For example, the Japanese word for 'train' is *densha*. How do you remember that? It isn't like anything you know. So I didn't enjoy that part of it. But the main problem was that I was very busy with my job. It was funny, because the name of the book was *Japanese for Busy People*, but I was really busy myself and didn't have time to study. So my progress was extremely slow. But, after some time, I learnt how to make full sentences, and that gave me a feeling of real power.

LESSON 3.1   RECORDING 3.1

1   In 1992, I was working for an internet service provider. It was a new company, one of the first in the country to help people get onto the internet. We had two or three thousand customers. It was funny, though, because often they didn't really know how to use the service. They phoned us and asked

questions like: 'OK, I'm connected. What do I do now?' So we said: 'Well, what do you want to do? Do you want to send an email?' And they said: 'Well, I don't know anyone with an email address.' Things became easier a year or two later when people started to find out about the world wide web.

2   The first blog probably appeared in 1994. Of course, we didn't use the word 'blog' back then, and it was very different to today's blogs. Actually, it was really a website. It belonged to an American journalist, Justin Hall. At first, Hall used it to give us a kind of guided tour of the internet. But then he started writing about his personal life – his relationships, his plans, his fears. This became his main subject. Once, while he was taking a road trip across America, he wrote about his experiences along the way, sharing everything with us. Hall was, I guess, the first blogger.

3   In 1994, I was living in a large house in west London with three friends from Australia. Together, we decided to set up an internet café – or cyber café, as we called it then. It was one of the first in the UK. We used the ground floor of a computer company in central London. It quickly became a very popular place – we had a lot of celebrities there. One day, an extremely famous pop star came in. Everyone was really surprised and stopped what they were doing. We worked very hard for about five years, but we didn't make much money. It wasn't a great business, but it was a great experience.

LESSON 3.3   RECORDING 3.4

Hello and welcome to *Fame and Fortune*, the programme that brings you the freshest news and views from the worlds of politics, business and entertainment. In today's programme, we interview the Prime Minister about her family life, we meet the hottest young film directors in Ireland, and there's music from the chart-topping band The Hoodies. Our business specialist, Tony Cotton, visits the Google offices in the States, and Lynne Miller brings you the latest celebrity gossip. First of all, over to the news studio for the headlines of the week …

LESSON 3.3   RECORDING 3.5

J = Jeff, K = Kate, B = Bill

J: OK, then, Bill, Kate, you've read the brief for the new programme. To summarise, it's a magazine-style programme with a young adult audience, and it's for the early Friday evening slot. The working title is *Fame and Fortune*. Now's the time to sort out some details. Any ideas? Kate?

K: Well, Jeff, I think we should include some politics in the programme.

J: Politics? Really?

K: Yes, I know politics is usually a turn-off for this audience, but I think we can do it in a new way.

J: Oh yes, and how do we do that?

K: Well, um, why don't we get some politicians on the programme? However, let's not interview them about politics. Instead, let's ask them about their lives – you know, interests, family, perhaps their life before politics.

J: OK, so, er, politicians without politics.

K: Exactly.

B: I like it.

J: So do I. Anything else? Bill?

B: What about music? We should have a live band on the programme.

J: I agree, but, then again, so many programmes do that.

B: That's true, but why don't we get the band to perform three or four songs, rather than just one?

J: Mm, nice idea, that way we get a much better idea about the band.

K: Fine, but what about the 'fortune' part of the programme? What about interviewing rich people?

J: No, I … I don't think that's a good idea. We don't need more interviews, and rich people are often really boring. I think we should do something about high-profile businesses, you know, er, like Google, Sony, Apple. You know, the big businesses that have all the exciting new ideas and products.

K: Great idea. So, we've got some politics, music and business, all with a fresh angle. I think these things are good for the target audience, but the programme is an hour long. What else shall we put in the programme?

B: What about something with animals?

K/J: Animals!?

J: And just how are animals connected to fame and fortune exactly?

B: Well, I thought that perhaps we could find pets that have unusual talents, you know, cats that can sing. And then we could have a competition, and, um, you know, make them famous.

K: And you really think that young adults, after a hard week at work, are interested in that?

B: Well, I don't know, um, well, perhaps not, er, perhaps that's not a good idea. Why don't we …

LESSON 4.1   RECORDING 4.2

Extract 1

Sad news from head office concerning our work in Africa. Unfortunately, we've closed our mobile clinics in Ethiopia because of severe financial problems. Last year, we ran ten health centres in Africa, but this year, we've received very little money and we can't continue to offer healthcare across the continent. We've decided to close the two Ethiopian centres and we hope to raise more money by …

Extract 2

Working here is the best thing I've ever done. When I worked in the UK, I got bored with the daily routine, but out here, I find every day interesting and demanding. I'm working in a small clinic in the middle of the jungle and I've never done such important work before. The villagers in this region can't get to government hospitals because there are no good roads, so this clinic is the only hope they have. I usually do about two operations a day and, so far, in my time here, I've probably saved about a hundred lives. When your work is very important, you don't …

Extract 3

E = Employee, V = Vera

E: The lack of food in this region causes many health problems for the local people. We wanted to reduce their need for doctors like us, so, on the first of January 2012, we started to plan a training course for local people so that they can help with some of the minor health problems. Finally, after many years of planning and raising money, in June of this year, we started a training programme. So far, we've trained 500 people. By the end of the year, that number will be 1,000. Vera is doing the course at the moment.

V: This course has given me many new skills. Before, I didn't know how to help people in my village. Now, I'm sure I can make a difference.

E: Vera finishes the course next week and then she'll return to her village …

Extract 4

I often work for IMA and I've worked in Kenya, Nepal and Peru. However, my current position, here in Sri Lanka, is perhaps the most difficult job I've had so far. Last year, an earthquake hit this area, and this caused a massive amount of damage. I've never seen so much destruction before. I help the doctors in a couple of clinics   one here and another in a smaller village about ten kilometres away. I see people with serious illnesses and injuries. Today, I've seen 40 patients, and I don't finish work for another four hours. These are busy days indeed. I started work at seven …

LESSON 4.3   RECORDING 4.3

M = Mavis Much, A = Abigail Parker, D = Dane King

Interview 1

M: Hello, I'm Mavis. What's your name?

A: Hi, I'm Abi. Abigail Parker.

M: Nice to meet you, Abigail. What year are you in?

A: This is my final year, I'm studying History.

M: I see, so you've got your exams soon. So, how can I help you?

A: Well, it's about my exams, really. I get very nervous before exams, and already I'm not sleeping very well.

M: I see. Well, of course everyone gets nervous before exams.

A: I know, but I'm, like, really nervous. And not sleeping is a real problem.

M: Yes, I understand. Tell me about your study routine. How hard are you working?

A: Well, I'm studying all day every day. I usually go to bed at about one, and get up at six, but I don't sleep much in that time.

M: I see, and are you eating well? Drinking much coffee?

A: I have three meals a day, and yes, I drink loads of coffee – it keeps me going, really.

M: OK, and, er, what about exercise?

A: Exercise? That's not a word I like! I've never played sports in my life.

M: I see, well, what I think …

Interview 2

M: Hello, I'm Mavis. What's your name?

D: Hi, I'm Dane. Dane King.

M: Nice to meet you, Dane. Are you in the first year here?

D: Yes, I am.

M: And what are you studying?

D: I'm doing Biology.

M: Right, and how can I help you?

D: Well, it's a bit embarrassing, really.

M: Go on.

D: Well, I really miss home. I'm from the US.

M: Yes, I guessed from your accent. So you feel homesick?

D: That's right. Really badly. I didn't make many friends here yet, and I miss my mom, you know, her home cooking and everything.

M: Well, there's no need to be embarrassed about that.

D: I know, but it feels like the only time I'm happy is when I go to a McDonald's restaurant, and I do that nearly every day now. And I'm losing interest in my studies. I just want to go home.

M: OK, well, I think …

LESSON 4.3   RECORDING 4.4

M = Mavis Much, A = Abigail Parker, D = Dane King

Interview 1

M: I see, well, I think I can help with your sleeping problem. I think you should take more breaks during the day in order to relax a little. The problem is that you are too stressed all day. Also, you shouldn't drink a lot of coffee because it stops you from relaxing.

A: But I need it. I have to keep going during the day, and because I'm not sleeping at night, I need it to keep me awake in the daytime.

M: I know, but it causes you problems as well. Try drinking just two or three cups a day. And you certainly shouldn't drink coffee in the evening, because that definitely keeps you awake.

A: OK, but can't you just give me some medicine, like a sleeping pill or something?

M: Sleeping pills? No, I don't think you should take them. If you make a few changes to your lifestyle, you will be OK.

A: But my friend who's studying medicine said sleeping pills can work.

M: Yes, but your friend is still studying, so I think you should listen to my advice, honestly.

Interview 2

M: OK, well, I think you should join a sports club.

D: A sports club? Why?

M: To make friends, and also to stop you thinking about home all the time. If you play sport, your mind will stop thinking about home.

D: I guess so. But I only play baseball, and they don't play that in this country.

M: But you're from America, and you're pretty tall, so I'm sure you've played basketball before.

D: Sure, when I was at school, but I'm not that good at it.

M: I'm sure you're better than most of the British students who play it. And anyway, you need to meet other people in order to make some friends.

D: I guess I can try joining the university basketball club.

M: Good. And you ought to change your eating habits. You know, you shouldn't go to McDonald's every day, because you need variety in your diet.

D: I know, but I have to eat, and I can't cook. My mom always cooked for me.

M: Well, perhaps you should join a cookery society as well, to learn how to cook.

D: Is that the only advice you have? Joining clubs and societies?

M: There's no need to be rude.

D: Heck, I'm sorry. It's just very difficult living in a different culture. I get stressed very easily.

M: That's OK. Let's talk a little more …

LESSON 5.1   RECORDING 5.1

1 Islands have their own kind of magic, and Greenland is one of the most magical of them all. Greenland lies off the coast of North America. It's the biggest island in the world; 2,655 kilometres from north to south, and 1,290 kilometres from east to west. So there's a lot of land, but it's not very green. That's because an ice cap – a thick layer of ice – covers 85 per cent of Greenland. Snow falls on Greenland in every month of the year. The snow gets deeper and deeper and turns to ice. As a result, Greenland has the second largest ice cap in the world. On average, the ice is one and a half kilometres thick, but in some places it's thicker than that – more than three kilometres thick, in fact. In large parts of the island, there are no people at all. About 55,000 people live around the coast, where the climate isn't as cold as in the centre. Their main work is fishing.

2 Yes, it probably looks familiar … and of course it is. I'm in Trafalgar Square, in the heart of London. Sometimes it's easy to forget that Great Britain is an island, too. In fact, Great Britain is the eighth largest island in the world, and the largest in Europe. It's interesting, too, because it's actually three countries: England, Scotland and Wales. It's rich in history, and people come from all over the world to visit famous churches, museums and castles. Great Britain is more crowded than many of its European neighbours, and has a population of more than 60 million. But in parts, it's as beautiful as Italy or Switzerland. Mountains cover a lot of Scotland, where there are many long, deep lakes. Wales and the north of England are hilly, while the south and east of England are flatter. The area around London isn't as impressive as other parts of the island.

3 Madagascar is a world apart. It's the fourth largest island in the world. It lies off the coast of Africa, and split away from the rest of Africa about 100 million years ago. It's a land of contrasts and surprises. There's rainforest on the east coast of Madagascar. In the south, it's hot and dry, but the climate is cooler in the middle of the island, where there are mountains. So some parts are not as tropical as others. The population is about 18 million, and most of the people are farmers. But what makes Madagascar special is that there are unusual types of animals and plants that you can't find anywhere else in the world. The island's most famous animals are the lemurs – they look a little like monkeys and they've got long tails. But they're in danger now, because people have destroyed the forests where they live. In all, about 50 kinds of wildlife are at risk on Madagascar.

LESSON 5.3   RECORDING 5.2

N = Neil, K = Katie

N: OK, Katie, well, I've brought a couple of pictures which both show whale rescues. Here's my first one.

K: OK.

N: So, in this one, in the foreground, you can see three whales that are close to the beach. Obviously, they're having some problems, and there are some people who are trying to help them. And you can see here, in the background, loads of people are watching.

K: Yeah, it's not bad. I like the way it shows a team of people who are working together.

N: Yes, they seem very professional, don't they?

K: Sure. And what about your second picture?

N: Well, it's very different. I think this one looks very unusual. Have a look.

K: Oh yes, I see. So, these two people are throwing water over a whale.

N: Exactly, and I like the way we can only see the whale's head. I think that's pretty eye-catching. I think it's more unusual than the first one.

K: Um, I agree. But the people in this picture look less professional than in the first one. Remember, these pictures are for our website, and we need to create the right image for our charity.

N: Sure, that was my worry, too. In the first picture, the message is clear. You know that this is a team of experienced people helping the animals.

K: Exactly, so I think that one is the best of your two photos. Shall I show you mine now?

N: Sure. What have you found?

K: Well, I've got two pictures of people who are saving sea birds from oil pollution. This is the first one. It shows some people cleaning a bird. I like the colours in this picture. I think having some colour in the photos is a good idea for the website, especially as the pictures will be small.

N: Yeah, the blue and the yellow are good colours. But I think the picture is a little boring.

K: I know what you mean, but again they seem very professional.

N: That's true. What about your second picture?

K: I think this one is more dramatic. Here it is.

N: Oh yes, that's a very strong image, it's definitely stronger than the first one. I like the way the picture captures the moment when they're actually returning the bird to the wild. It's a very positive image.

K: Yes, and although it's less colourful than the first one, it's more powerful.

N: So, I think we agree that this second one is the best of yours. The first one is more boring, so I don't think we can use that one.

K: Indeed. So which one of our two choices is the best overall? Which one shall we choose as the final one for the website?

LESSON 5.3   RECORDING 5.3

N = Neil, K = Katie

K: Indeed. So which one of our two choices is the best overall? Which one shall we choose as the final one for the website?

N: Well, the bird rescue one is more dramatic, but I think we also need to show that people who work for us are professional.

K: So you think we should choose the whale-rescue picture.

N: Yes, I do. What about you?

K: Well, I do like the power of the bird rescue, but does it give the right message? How about if this time we show the professional side of Animal Aid, but in other pictures we choose something more emotional, or more unusual and eye-catching?

N: OK. We need five pictures in total, so we should be able to create a good balance for the home page.

K: Fine, so our first choice is the professional whale rescue. What's next?

LESSON 6.1   RECORDING 6.1

P = Patrick, S = Susan, B = Bob

P: Hello, Susan. Good to see you again.

S: Hi, Patrick. How are you?

P: I'm fine. Can I get you a drink? Coffee? Tea?

S: Oh, a coffee would be lovely, thanks.

P: Sure, I'll just ask Bob to do that. Bob, could you make us two coffees, please? So, what does the future hold for me?

S: Well, hopefully, good business opportunities. I've got the full report here, but I'll go through the main points first.

P: Fine. Go ahead.

S: Well, I think the two most important trends for you are about technology and age.

P: Age?

S: Yes, basically Britain is getting older. In 15 years' time, more than a third of the UK's population will be over 55 years old. And these older people will live for much longer – we know that from the statistics. They might live until they're 95, or even 100.

P: Oh. But that definitely won't be good for business. They won't have jobs, so I'm sure they won't have much money.

S: Oh, it'll definitely be good for business. First of all, they'll retire a bit later than now, so they will have some money. But the main point is that these people will definitely need things to do with this extra time, for sure, *and* they'll need things that improve the quality of their lives.

P: OK. Any examples?

S: Well, we predict that older people will travel more, so there'll be more companies that specialise in holidays for them. At the moment, holiday companies focus on families or young adults. But, in 2030, there'll be more elderly people, the over-65s, than under-25s. So, for example, holidays on cruise ships will increase. They may also want activity holidays, but that'll depend on their health and on how demanding the activities are – they probably won't go bungee-jumping, but they might go hiking and sailing.

P: OK. Er, what about daily life?

S: Well, this connects to the other trend I mentioned, technology.

P: Technology.

S: Yes, and, in particular, robots.

P: Robots?

S: Yes. Older people need things to make life easier. In the future, they might have a robot that cleans the house, they may have a robot that drives the car, they might have a robot that does the gardening.

P: You say 'might' and 'may', rather than 'will'. Why's that?

S: Well, we can't be definite about this because it all depends on the technology. At the moment, robots are very basic.

P: Yes, I think there's a robot vacuum cleaner and that's about it. Oh, and robot pets.

S: Exactly, so the technology needs to improve. Perhaps it will, perhaps it

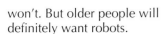

won't. But older people will definitely want robots.

P: Well, that's all very interesting. Now, where are those coffees? Perhaps I need a coffee robot! Bob, how's that coffee-making going?

B: Oh. Hi, sorry. I think the machine's broken. I'll go to the café. OK? Just got to clean up this mess the machine's made.

P: OK. Sorry about that. Now, where were we? Oh yes, technology. I guess the internet will be important.

S: Of course, in several different ways.

P: Any specific examples?

S: Well, for a start …

LESSON 6.2   RECORDING 6.4

S = Sam, E = Ellie

S: You know, Ellie, I'm thinking about getting my own place.

E: What? You want to leave home?

S: Yeah, I think it'll be good for me. I'll be more independent.

E: That's true, but what'll you do if your parents don't like the idea?

S: Oh, I think they'll be pleased to see me go. If not, I'll persuade them.

E: Really? I don't think your mum will be happy.

S: Oh, she'll be OK about it. You wait and see.

E: I hope you're right. But … what'll you do if you lose your job? You won't have any money to pay your bills.

S: Well, if that happens, I'll get some help from Mum and Dad until I get a new job.

E: Well, that's not so easy these days. You seem very confident. Sam, I don't think this is a good idea, you know. What'll you do if you feel lonely?

S: Really, Ellie. I'm not thinking of going very far away. I'll still have my family and friends just around the corner.

LESSON 6.3   RECORDING 6.5

**R = Robert, S = Sarah, G = Grace,
B = Ben, H = Henry, C = Carla**

R: OK, so that's the expert's view – let's see what you, the public, think. Now, what's your name?

S: Sarah.

R: OK, Sarah, are you a mother?

S: Yes, I am. I've got two young girls.

R: Great, so what do you think?

S: Personally, I think mothers should stay at home. I look after my kids and I think that's best for them and for me.

R: In what way?

S: Well, you know, kids should be with their mother, they need my love and, well, I know what they like and don't like. You know, it's natural.

R: OK, so does anyone disagree? Yes, you – what's your opinion?

G: Well, I understand her opinion, but sometimes mothers have no choice. They have to work. Surely it's better for the family to, to have money to buy food and stuff. I mean, what's the point of staying at home with your kids if you can't put food on the table? We're not all in happy families with two parents, are we?

R: Indeed. What do you say to that, Sarah?

S: Well, that's a good point, but I think some mothers work because they want to, not because they need to. They prefer to work rather than look after their children, and I think that's wrong, I really do.

R: OK. Does anyone else have anything to say on this?

B: Er, I do, Robert.

R: Yes?

B: I agree with Sarah. I know loads of mothers who work just because they like to have a job, not because they need to. And that's a real pity, because they're missing out on the best time in their children's lives. You can work any time, but your children are only young once.

R: OK, well, while we're on the subject of children, let's look at another question. Basically, should we limit the amount of TV young kids watch? Are they watching too much TV these days? What's your name and what's your opinion?

H: Hi, I'm Henry and I'm a dad.

R: OK then, Henry, what's your view?

H: Well, what I think is that they shouldn't watch any TV.

R: What, none at all?

H: None at all. I never watched TV when I was a kid, and I don't think my kids need to watch it now, especially when they're young.

R: Right, well, I'm sure many people will disagree with you. Let's see. Um, yes, madam, yes, you in the red dress.

C: Well, personally, I completely disagree. TV is part of the modern world, like computers and phones. We can't hide TV from our kids. I think it's better if they know that TV is a normal thing, as normal as having dinner or whatever.

R: Henry?

H: Well, that's an interesting idea, but TV is different to phones and having dinner. The kids just sit there, like vegetables. It's not good for them, not good at all.

C: But why not just control how much they watch? You know, have a maximum of two hours a day or something.

H: Well, I know we won't agree, but the best control is to sell your TV. If you do that, they'll do something else.

S: That's just silly.

H: You're the one that's silly.

R: OK, OK, calm down everyone. Let's take a break now, and after the ads we'll look at the role of the father in the family.

LESSON 7.1   RECORDING 7.1

R = Researcher, I = Iris Battle

R: Well, first of all, thank you for meeting me.

I: Not at all. I hope I can help.

R: Well, as you know, we're doing some research for a documentary series about forensic science – we want to call it 'Crime-scene scientists – the reality'. We think we should show the truth about your work, because we think the TV dramas don't give a true picture of what happens in a crime lab.

I: Yes, that's a good point. There are many differences between those crime dramas and our actual work. For example, we work in two separate teams, the crime-scene analysts and the scientists. The analysts search for and collect the evidence, and then the scientists do the tests in the lab. However, in the TV dramas, the analyst often does both things – that is, the collection and the testing.

R: So, when the crime-scene analysts are at the crime scene, what do they have to do?

I: Well, I'm a scientist, not an analyst, so you shouldn't ask me. You should ask an analyst to get the full picture.

R: That's a good idea, but can you give me an overview now?

I: Sure. Well, the photographer takes pictures of the crime scene, and at the same time someone interviews any witnesses. Then they collect any evidence, and this is when they have to be very careful. They have to wear rubber gloves because they mustn't damage any of the evidence. Basically, they look for fingerprints, hairs, perhaps blood. It all depends on the crime, really. Also, they have to take very careful notes. This is important because we, the scientists in the lab, must know where the evidence has come from.

R: Right. Now, on TV, most of the crimes are murders. Is that true for you?

I: Oh, no, not at all. Ninety percent of our work is with burglaries or stolen cars, you know the kind of thing. You should make that clear in your documentary.

R: Yes, indeed. We should get that correct. OK, so what about the lab work?

LESSON 7.1   RECORDING 7.2

R = Researcher, I = Iris Battle

R: Yes, indeed. We should get that correct. OK, so what about the lab work?

I: Well, first of all, we always tell the police that they must be patient, because our work in the lab takes time. On TV, a police officer doesn't have to wait very long to get test results, perhaps just a few hours. In reality, an officer has to wait 20 days to get a DNA test result. Secondly, we work in a lab, so there are certain lab rules. We have to turn our mobile phones off, and we mustn't eat or drink in the lab, that kind of thing.

R: Now that we have these TV dramas about forensic scientists, have there been any changes in your work?

I: Well, there's been a positive change in our image. Now, science is an interesting or glamorous profession. It's incredible really, so many young people are now applying to work in crime labs. And the thing is, we're scientists not police officers, so you don't have to study law. Instead you have to study chemistry or biology.

R: Interesting. So, um, can I have a look around your lab?

I: Well, I'm not sure. My boss says all visits must only be for work reasons.

R: Well, this is kind of for work. I mean, we must get the documentary right.

I: I suppose so. Well, OK, but you must turn your phone off and you must be quiet, or my boss will kill me!

R: Hmm … murder in the crime lab. Could be a good story for the TV show …

LESSON 7.3   RECORDING 7.4

P = Presenter, J = Julian Blake

P: So, Julian, could you tell us about one of your choices, please, and just give a few reasons for your choice? Unfortunately our time is limited …

J: Right, well, one of my choices is the printing press. Now, Gutenberg invented the modern printing press in 1457, and I think this caused a revolution in knowledge, society … and, well, in everything really.

P: In what way?

J: Well, the main reason I think it's important is that the printing press meant we could produce books and newspapers in large numbers and very quickly. Before then, writing was a slow process, and each copy of each book took weeks to make. Suddenly, we could make a hundred copies of a book in a day. This meant that ideas could spread much more quickly than before. This caused great changes in society, too many changes to talk about now. Another reason the printing press is important is that it led to education for everyone. This is connected to the fast production of books because if you have books, you can have a school. As well as that, the idea of education for all is also connected to the need for reading skills. The written word became important at work, and so people had to read, and so they needed education.

P: OK then. A key reason for choosing the printing press is that it meant that ideas could spread quickly and this caused many changes in society. Secondly, you claim that it led to education for all. Anything else?

J: Well, yes. The other thing is that the printing press means that writers can make money, which, as I'm a writer, is something I'm rather pleased about. But seriously,

without the printing press, you can't make thousands of copies and therefore you can't make any money. The printing press meant that people could become professional writers and journalists, which I think has been very good for society, don't you?

P: Well, yes, I do, I suppose. However, I disagree with your point about education. After all, we didn't have general schools until about 400 years after the invention of the printing press. Is there really a connection?

J: Well, er, that's a fair point, but I still say that the mass production of books caused changes in the way people worked, and this led to wider education.

P: Mmm. OK, we'll leave that discussion there for the moment and let's move on. Sandra, what have you chosen?

LESSON 7.4   RECORDING 7.8

The next thing I'm going to talk about is some of the problems that women in science face in the UK.

The first problem is what happens in schools. In the UK, schools are not doing enough to encourage girls to study science. Most school science is about learning facts, and boys are happier about facts. Boys want to know if something is right or wrong. Women are more interested in evaluating things, deciding if something is good or bad. So schools have to show girls what you can do with facts. Then girls will be more interested in science.

The next problem is male attitudes, what men think about women in science. Early in my career, I was often the only woman working in my lab in Oxford. One male colleague called me simply 'the girl'. Over the years, men have made comments to me such as 'You don't look like a scientist.' I realised there was a problem in the UK when I went to France. In the lab where I worked in Paris, the atmosphere was different. This was because about 50% of the people working there were women.

Another problem for women in science is the issue of children. This is very important for female scientists in their late 20s and early 30s. In the lab in Paris, having children was not such a big problem for a woman's career. It didn't have a negative effect on the careers of those French women.

But in Britain, if a woman takes time out to have a child, things can be very hard for her later. If she wants to return to work after having children, it's difficult to compete with men. While she was having her children, male scientists were doing their research – and publishing it!

The last problem I'm going to mention today is confidence. I believe that, at some point in their careers, someone needs to give women scientists some confidence. They have to have more confidence in their abilities. They also have to have more confidence to apply for jobs, and to do good interviews.

In the end, if you're not a woman, and if you're not a scientist, talking about women in science might not seem very important. But if you're both of those things, you might feel uncertain … about where your career or life is going.

LESSON 8.1   RECORDING 8.1

W = Dr Wilson, A = Abolaji,
S1 = Student 1, S2 = Student 2,
S3 = Student 3, S4 = Student 4

W: All right, Abolaji, you're next. Are you ready?

A: Yes.

W: OK, then, start when you like.

A: Good morning, everybody. Let me start with a question: Do you like sleeping? … Yes, I thought that was the answer. Well, today I'm going to talk to you about sleep. I hope to show you that sleep is a very important and interesting subject. But please stay awake – don't fall asleep during my presentation!
Scientists are starting to understand sleep much better than before, and I'll mention some new research in my talk. Because of the limited time, I'll cover three areas:
1 how much sleep we need
2 the types and stages of sleep, and
3 some problems with sleep in today's society.
So, let's look first at how much sleep people need. Most people spend around a third of their lives asleep, although the need for sleep decreases with age.
Let me ask you some other questions. How much sleep do you think a one-year-old baby needs?

S1: Um, twelve hours?

S2: Twenty?

S3: Eight?

A: Well, a one-year old baby needs about fourteen hours of sleep a day. How about a child of five?

S4: Twelve hours?

A: That's right. Good guess. A five-year-old needs about twelve hours. And an adult? How much does an adult need?

S3: Er, eight?

A: Exactly. An adult needs about seven to eight hours. However, different people need different amounts of sleep. Some adults need to sleep for ten hours or more a day, while others only need half that amount – or less. Elderly people tend to sleep less than younger adults at night, but they doze more during the day.
Let's turn now to the different types of sleep, and I apologise for using some rather technical language here. There are two types of sleep, known as REM sleep and NREM sleep. Does anyone know what these are? Er, well, REM means 'rapid eye movement'. And NREM stands for 'non-rapid eye movement'. You can see it on my slide here: REM – rapid eye movement; NREM – non-rapid eye movement. During NREM sleep, our brains are not very active. However, in REM sleep, the brain suddenly becomes more active – like the brain of a person who's awake. Our eyes move rapidly, and we have dreams … or nightmares.
OK, have a guess. How much of our sleep do you think is REM sleep – when our brain is alive, and we have those dreams and nightmares?

S2: How about 50:50?

A: That's an interesting guess. Because actually, in babies, REM sleep is about one half of sleep. But what about adults?

S1: A third?

A: Nearly. Nearly. In adults, REM sleep is only about one-fifth of our sleeping time … so about 20% … so that means most of our sleep … about 80% … is NREM sleep, when the brain isn't very active.

LESSON 8.1   RECORDING 8.2

A = Abolaji, S1 = Student 1,
S2 = Student 2, S3 = Student 3

A: OK. Turning to the stages of sleep, we can identify five stages in a night's sleep, as you can see on the slide. In different stages of sleep, our brains put together thoughts and experiences, and then store them in an organised way. This gives us clearer memories. Recent experiments suggest that the final stage of sleep, REM sleep, is very important for organising our memories and helps to improve our learning. NREM sleep is important for making our memories stronger. Experiments have also shown that the brain works in a different way after we've had a good night's sleep. The final area I want to talk about are things that can stop us sleeping well. Can you tell me some things that might stop you sleeping?

S1: Noisy neighbours?

S2: Um, lots of traffic.

S3: Uh, you're worrying about things.

A: Yes, these are all true. Another thing is too much light. Street lights and security lights mean that even when we're asleep, it's never completely dark. And the evidence suggests that the quantity and quality of darkness in our lives affects our health – 24-hour shopping, global travel, etc. Because of this, our days are becoming longer and the nights shorter – and this could also damage our health, as we're not getting enough sleep.
To sum up, I hope I've succeeded in showing you that sleep is a very important and interesting subject. We sleep less as we get older, but everybody's different – some people need more sleep, others less. There are two types of sleep – NREM and REM; most sleep is NREM, but REM is when dreaming happens. During the five different stages of sleep, our brains organise our memories and make them stronger. But too much light and our modern way of life can have a negative impact on our sleeping patterns and, as a result, on our brains and our health. Thank you for listening. Are there any questions? Is anyone still awake?

LESSON 8.3   RECORDING 8.5

C = Christine, E = Emma, P = Paul

C: OK then, so what shall we do tonight? Emma? What's on at about six o'clock?

E: OK, Christine, let me see. OK, well, there are two things to choose from. Both start at six.

P: Uh-huh.

E: There's a classical-music concert and an open-air movie.

P: Tell us more about them.

E: Sure, Paul. So, first, the classical music concert is Beethoven's symphony number nine, which includes some singing, you know, in a choir. Then, the open-air movie is an Indian film; it's a Bollywood film, you know, with loads of songs and dancing.

P: Sounds fun.

E: Yes, it does … and that's the lot. What would you prefer to do, Christine?

C: Hmm, I don't fancy the movie. I'd prefer to go to the classical concert. What about you, Paul?

P: I think I'd rather see the movie. I'm not that keen on the concert. I don't really like classical music. What about you, Emma, what would you rather do?

E: Well, to be honest, I don't mind. The movie sounds good because I've never seen a Bollywood film before, but the concert sounds good because it's in the opera house.

P: It's in the opera house?

E: Yes, didn't I say? Are you more interested now?

P: Yes, I am. I haven't been there yet, and I'd like to see it at night. They have lots of colourful lights on the outside, don't they?

E: Yes, they do. It looks fantastic at night.

C: Great! Let's go to the concert, then. What shall we do after that?

E: After that?

C: Oh yes, we have to see as much as we can. Paul's not here for long. Let me tell you what's on later, at about nine. Give me the listings page, Emma.

E: OK, fair enough.

C: OK, so there are two choices. There's a music performance, called World Beats, and a one-man theatre show.

P: Go on.

C: Right. The music tonight is by some Japanese drummers. There are 45 of them. It says here that it's powerful and unique. It's called Taiko Drumming.

E: Sounds great.

C: Uh-huh, and the second one is the one-man theatre show. In this show, there's only one actor, but he plays many different characters. It's all about the life story of Shakespeare. Apparently, 'you will laugh out loud'.

E: I never laughed when we studied Shakespeare at school.

C: Well, this show could be good.

E: Well, I'm more interested in the Japanese drummers than the one-man theatre show.

C: I thought so, but perhaps we shouldn't go to a second music event.

E: Hmm, maybe. Paul, which would you prefer to go to?

P: Oh, I'd love to see the drummers. They sound amazing. And it's a great chance to see something different and unusual. I'd rather see that than a play about Shakespeare.

C: But it says that the play's really funny. And how interesting is two hours of drumming going to be?

E: Oh Christine, I'm sure the Taiko drumming will be really interesting. I've seen some of it on TV, and I'd love to see it live.

C: OK, then, let's go and see the drummers. But tomorrow, no music, OK?

E: Well, maybe. Let's see how we feel tomorrow.

LESSON 8.3   RECORDING 8.6

C = Christine, E = Emma, P = Paul

C: OK then, so what shall we do tonight? Emma? What's on at about six o'clock?

E: OK, Christine, let me see. OK, well, there are two things to choose from. Both start at six.

P: Uh-huh.

E: There's a classical-music concert and an open-air movie.

P: Tell us more about them.

E: Sure, Paul. So, first, the classical music concert is Beethoven's symphony number nine, which includes some singing, you know, in a choir. Then, the open-air movie is an Indian film; it's a Bollywood film, you know, with loads of songs and dancing.

P: Sounds fun …

E: Yes, it does, and that's the lot. What would you prefer to do, Christine?

C: Hmm, I don't fancy the movie. I'd prefer to go to the classical concert. What about you, Paul?

P: I think I'd rather see the movie. I'm not that keen on the concert. I don't really like classical music. What about you, Emma, what would you rather do?

E: Well, to be honest, I don't mind. The movie sounds good because I've never seen a Bollywood film

before, but the concert sounds good because it's in the opera house.

P: It's in the opera house?

E: Yes, didn't I say? Are you more interested now?

P: Yes, I am. I haven't been there yet, and I'd like to see it at night. They have lots of colourful lights on the outside, don't they?

E: Yes, they do. It looks fantastic at night.

C: Great! Let's go to the concert, then. What shall we do after that?

E: After that?

LESSON 8.3   RECORDING 8.7

C = Christine, E = Emma, P = Paul

C: Great! Let's go to the concert, then. What shall we do after that?

E: After that?

C: Oh yes, we have to see as much as we can. Paul's not here for long. Let me tell you what's on later, at about nine. Give me the listings page, Emma.

E: OK, fair enough.

C: OK, so there are two choices. There's a music performance, called World Beats, and a one-man theatre show.

P: Go on.

C: Right. The music tonight is by some Japanese drummers. There are 45 of them. It says here that it's powerful and unique. It's called Taiko Drumming.

E: Sounds great.

C: Uh-huh, and the second one is the one-man theatre show. In this show, there's only one actor, but he plays many different characters. It's all about the life story of Shakespeare. Apparently, 'you will laugh out loud'.

E: I never laughed when we studied Shakespeare at school.

C: Well, this show could be good.

E: Well, I'm more interested in the Japanese drummers than the one-man theatre show.

C: I thought so, but perhaps we shouldn't go to a second music event.

E: Hmm, maybe. Paul, which would you prefer to go to?

P: Oh, I'd love to see the drummers. They sound amazing. And it's a great chance to see something different and unusual. I'd rather see that than a play about Shakespeare.

C: But it says that the play's really funny. And how interesting is

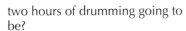

two hours of drumming going to be?

E: Oh Christine, I'm sure the Taiko drumming will be really interesting. I've seen some of it on TV, and I'd love to see it live.

C: OK, then, let's go and see the drummers. But tomorrow, no music, OK?

E: Well, maybe. Let's see how we feel tomorrow.

LESSON 8.4   RECORDING 8.11

Soon, we could see it better, and we all knew what it was – the ghost of a man! We couldn't move. Before long, it was standing next to us, looking at us. Then it spoke: 'Do you know what time it is?' At that moment, we were extremely confused and scared, but then we realised that the ghost was a local shepherd – and he didn't have a watch! He just wanted to ask us the time! Later, we laughed a lot about that ghost.

LESSON 9.1   RECORDING 9.1

C = Consultant, A = Anita, T = Tom

C: Come in. Hello. It's Anita, isn't it?

A: That's right.

C: OK, let me just have a look at the information here ... you work in the Marketing Department?

A: Yeah.

C: And you've been with the company for ... six years.

A: That's right.

C: All right, first of all let's talk about your general feelings about your job. Do you feel the same way now as you did six years ago?

A: Well, no, not really. I mean, I think I used to be more enthusiastic. Maybe it's because I'm older now.

C: Well, you're still only 28. That's not exactly old!

A: No, I suppose not.

C: What else has changed?

A: I work longer hours now. When I started, I didn't use to finish work so late. Now, I go home after seven nearly every day, but I don't think I really achieve any more.

C: I see. What about the company? Is it helping you to develop new skills?

A: Yes, up to a point. I've done one or two management training courses in the last couple of years. I think I'm ready for promotion now.

C: What about other aspects of the job? Do you get the opportunity to travel much?

A: No, not much. But I don't really mind that. You see, I have to look after my mother and ...

***

T: Good morning! I'm Tom Carroll.

C: Hello, Tom. Have a seat. Well, you seem to have the longest service record – 17 years!

T: That's right.

C: Well, you're obviously happy here!

T: I am, yes, although it used to be more fun.

C: Why's that?

T: Well, it was more sociable. I used to go out more with my colleagues, after work and for lunch. When I first started here, we had very long lunch breaks, sometimes for two hours. Now it's more like 30 minutes. And we all used the gym together. That doesn't happen much now.

C: Did you use to work more as a team?

T: Yes, I suppose we did. It's interesting you mention that. We're more on our own now. I also used to travel a lot more, too. They've cut down on that.

C: Has anything changed for the better?

T: Yes, there are more opportunities to learn new skills and develop your career. It's more professional now. Also, they didn't use to pay you properly. The money's much better now! That's probably why I'm still here!

C: What about yourself? Have you changed at the same time as the company?

T: No, I don't think so. I think I'm pretty much the same person I was all those years ago.

LESSON 9.1   RECORDING 9.2

1 She used to work late.
2 Did you use to go out more with colleagues?
3 He didn't use to listen to me.
4 She didn't use the gym every day.
5 They used their opportunities well.
6 Did the company use the results of the survey?

LESSON 9.3   RECORDING 9.3

L = Lu Han, R = Richard

L: So, which of our products are you interested in?

R: OK, well, we're interested in buying some digital music players, the IP4 model. How much are they per item?

L: Mm, let's see ... Yes, they're $100 each.

R: A hundred dollars? That seems quite high.

L: Really? I see. How much would you like to pay?

R: About $85.

L: I see. Well, I'm not sure that we can go that low, but we can offer you a discount. It depends on the quantity that you order. How many would you like to order?

R: We'd like 550. What discount can you offer?

L: Well, we can offer a 5% discount on 550, but if you order 1,000, we can offer 18%.

R: I see. I'm not sure that we can sell 1,000. What about if we order 750?

L: Well, then we can give you a 10% discount.

R: Hmm, that's still a bit low. How about 13%?

L: 13%? I'm afraid we can't offer that on 750. However, if you order 850, we can give you a 13% discount.

R: Hmm, 850, well ...

L: It's not very many more, and the discount is good.

R: Well, yes, OK then. We'll order 850.

L: Fine, and we'll give a discount. So, the final price is $87 per item.

R: Great. Now, what's your normal delivery time?

L: It's usually 30 days after your order.

R: OK, the standard time. Actually, we need delivery in two weeks. Can you do that?

L: Two weeks? No, I'm afraid we can't do that.

R: Really?

L: Really. I'm afraid they won't be ready for delivery by then. Thirty days is the best we can do.

R: OK, that'll be fine. Perhaps we can change things next time.

L: OK, then. So, you order 850 IP4 music players at $87 per item, and we deliver in 30 days. Is that a deal?

R: That's a deal.

L: Excellent. Is there anything else you're interested in? We're offering a great deal on digital cameras at the moment.

R: Really? Oh! What's the deal? If it's a good bargain, I might be interested. Which model ...?

LESSON 9.4 VIDEO RECORDING 9

L = Louise, T1 = Tourist 1,
T2 = Tourist 2

L: Good morning everyone. Welcome to the *Wonderful World of Chocolate*! My name's Louise and I am your guide this morning. There's a good number of you so please come in further, there are still a couple of seats at the front … Now, has anyone been here before? No? OK, so it's everybody's first time. All right, so let me tell you about this morning's tour. It will last about an hour and a half. First of all, I'm going to tell you a few key things about the history of chocolate, then I'll say a little bit about the company and after that I'll say a few words about how chocolate is made. All that will take about ten minutes. Then we'll go round the factory. How does that sound?

T1: Great. Will we taste any chocolate?

L: Oh, yes. Don't worry about that. There'll be a chance to taste some of our delicious products at the end!
OK. So, let's look at the history of chocolate. To start with, does anybody know where chocolate first came from?

T2: From Latin America, I think.

L: Yes, that's right. It was the Mayans (who lived in what's now Central America and Mexico) who first discovered the delights of chocolate in about 600AD. They found that they could make a delicious drink from roasted cocoa beans. Hmm. For those of you who aren't sure of the meaning of roasted… it's just another way of saying cooked in an oven.

T1: OK …

L: Good. So, the Mayans had their chocolate drink which they decided to call 'chocolatl'. It was a real luxury because cocoa beans were very valuable. In fact, people sometimes used to give them as presents, or even used them as money. Soon, chocolate spread to the Aztec civilisation around modern Mexico City.
In 1517, the Spaniard, Hernán Cortés arrived in Mexico. He travelled to meet the Aztec emperor, Moctezuma, who introduced Cortés to his favourite drink – chocolatl. They served the drink to Cortés in a cup made of gold. If you look at the slide, you can see them drinking together. When Cortés returned to Spain in 1528, he loaded his ships with cocoa beans and equipment for making the chocolate drink. Soon chocolate became a popular drink with rich people in Spain. But it took nearly 100 years for the news of cocoa and chocolate to spread across Europe, as the Spanish kept it a secret.
In the 17th century, chocolate houses – like coffee shops today – became popular in London and other European cities. But it wasn't until the 19th century that chocolate became cheaper and available to a large percentage of the population. Also in the 19th century, they found a way to make chocolate hard, solid – to make the eating chocolate we love today! So, that was a very brief history of chocolate. To sum up, it started as a drink in Central America, it came to Europe with the Spanish, it spread slowly across the continent and finally became something a lot of people could afford to eat.
Now, I know you're all very keen to start the tour, but let's now turn to the company for just a minute …

LESSON 10.1 RECORDING 10.1

Fifty countries founded the United Nations after the Second World War, on the 24th of October 1945, to be exact. After such a terrible war, they founded the UN in order to maintain world peace and security, to develop friendly relations between countries and to improve living conditions and human rights across the world. There are now 191 countries in the UN – that's nearly every country in the world – and representatives from these countries meet at the UN headquarters in New York.

For most people, the Secretary General of the UN is the face of this massive organisation. The Secretary General is the person that we usually see on the television news when the UN does something important. Over the years, the Secretary General has come from many different countries, such as Egypt, Peru and Sweden, and the Secretary General usually changes every five or ten years.

The UN works in a wide range of areas, with a general aim to improve the lives of ordinary people and to keep peace in the world. For example, the UN helps refugees, helps the economic development of poorer countries and runs the court of International Justice. Two areas that the UN is not involved in are entertainment and religious education.

LESSON 10.1 RECORDING 10.3

G = Geoff, L = Liz

G: Hi, I'm Geoff.

L: Hello, Geoff. Liz. Nice to meet you.

G: Likewise.

L: Thank you for meeting to discuss your schedule for your first trip, which is next month, to Ghana.

G: Good to be here. I'm excited about this – I hope you're not planning to make my trip too busy, as it's my first one.

L: It'll be fine, I'm sure. OK, so look at the first slide and it gives the plan for the first week. Obviously, we'll send this to you by email after we confirm it at this meeting.

G: OK.

L: So, on Saturday, you're flying to Accra, and Sunday is a rest day. On Monday, you're going to a charity theatre school for children.

G: Sounds interesting. What am I doing there?

L: Yes, so, um, at ten, you're meeting the drama teachers, then after lunch, there's a performance by the children. Then, at four, you're giving a press conference with Sandra Ominga, your assistant on this trip.

G: And the press conference is about the theatre school?

L: Yeah, and about the work that our UN department does in the region, in particular about our new youth projects. I'll give you more information about that later.

G: OK, so, back to the schedule. What am I doing on Tuesday?

L: Um, hold on, I haven't finished telling you about Monday yet.

G: But the press conference is in the late afternoon, isn't it?

L: Yes, it is, and after that, at six, you're meeting the Ghanaian Minister for Children, just for 30 minutes.

G: OK, fine. Then I'm going back to the hotel, right?

L: Um, not exactly. At eight, you're giving a lecture at the National University.

G: A lecture? No one told me about that before. I'm an actor, not a professor.

L: Um …

G: Look, this schedule looks pretty heavy for the first day, don't you agree?

L: Well, it's quite normal really. Other Messengers of Peace often do more. For example, I know that next Friday, Midori Goto is doing six different events.

G: Well, good for her. Let's move on. At least Sunday was a rest day. What's happening on Tuesday?

L: OK. Well, first of all, at 11, a local TV crew is coming to your hotel.

G: Not to my room, I hope? I'll probably be in bed at that time.

L: No, no. The interview will be in the terrace café. And I meant 11 in the morning.

G: I know, I'm normally still in bed at that time.

L: Oh, I see.

G: Well, I guess that's a fairly easy morning. What am I doing in the afternoon? I bet you've got a lot planned.

L: Mmm, yes, the afternoon and evening are a little busier.

G: Come on then, tell me the bad news …

LESSON 10.2   RECORDING 10.5

I = Interviewer, S= Speaker

I: Why was the name Apple chosen for the new company?

S: Well, it seems that Steve Jobs had some good memories of working one summer on an apple farm in Oregon. Also, at the time – 1976 – the most important technology company was Atari. The founders of Apple wanted their company to appear before Atari in the phone book, which was organised alphabetically. This was important for a business back then. So the name Apple was good because it came before Atari in the phone book. So those are the reasons Apple got its interesting name.

I: How many Apple I computers were built?

S: Only about 200. They were made by Steve Wozniak – by hand. But the sale of 50 of those computers to a local computer store really started Apple on the road to success. Of course, the following year, the Apple II was launched, and millions of them were sold.

I: Who was the Apple logo created by?

S: It was done by a guy called Rob Janoff. The whole process only took about two weeks. Rob only prepared one design, and Steve Jobs immediately approved it. The apple has a bite in it so you can get a sense of its scale, or size. Without the bite, you might think it was a cherry! The idea of the rainbow colours was to make the products more human, more friendly. You see, Steve Jobs wanted the computers to be attractive to schoolchildren. Also, the company wanted a colourful new logo because the new Apple II computer could show images in colour.

I: Why was the advert for the Macintosh liked by many people?

S: It was a very creative ad. It was based on the novel *1984* by George Orwell and, of course, the year was 1984. In the novel, Orwell gives us a vision of a future society that's controlled by a powerful leader called Big Brother. It's really a nightmare vision. Ordinary people have no freedom in this society. In the ad, you see this young woman, fighting back against the system. She destroys a TV image of Big Brother. She's wearing a white vest with an Apple Macintosh computer on it. But many people believed that the advert was an attack on another company that was competing with Apple – the computer giant IBM.

I: When was the first Apple store opened outside the USA?

S: Er … late 2003 … November 2003, I think. It was in Japan, in a smart part of Tokyo called Ginza. The next year, the first Apple store in Europe was opened, in London.

I: Which other companies were admired in 2012?

S: Well, there were a lot of American companies in the list! After Apple, there was Google, Amazon, Coca-Cola and – yes – IBM! In the top 20, nearly all the companies were American. Now, that might be because the people who make these lists are often Americans themselves! But in the list of the 40 most admired companies, there were one or two European companies, like Volkswagen and Nestlé, and a couple of Asian companies – Toyota and Samsung.

LESSON 10.3   RECORDING 10.6

Hello, everyone. First, we want to deliver a magical experience, with an electrifying atmosphere for competitors and spectators. Our aim, or special ambition, is to inspire young people across the world to play sport, and to include them in the Olympics at all times. For example, children will be the main performers in the opening ceremony. We will do whatever we can to inspire children to choose sport, wherever they live, whatever they do. These will be a truly memorable Games. A Games that will inspire young people to believe in the Olympic ideal.

I will now tell you about the incredible sports venues, the fantastic athletes' accommodation and the excellent transport system, which are all key aspects of a successful Olympic Games.

LESSON 10.3   RECORDING 10.7

Firstly, we'll build an Olympic Park in the east of London and, in this park, there will be spectacular new sports venues. For instance, world-famous architect Zaha Hadid will design the swimming pool. Another example is the athletics stadium, which will have 80,000 seats.

As well as the Olympic Park, we'll use existing world-class venues such as Wembley football stadium and Wimbledon tennis centre. In addition, the marathon running race will be on the historic streets of London with many famous buildings and places: for example, Big Ben and Buckingham Palace. The Games will look wonderful on TV screens around the world.

Secondly, next to the Olympic Park, we will build the Olympic Village for the athletes' accommodation, which will be comfortable and spacious. They will have all modern facilities, for instance free WiFi and personal shower rooms. The athletes will live just a short walk from the swimming pool and athletics stadium. They'll be right at the centre of the Olympic experience.

Turning now to transport, there are already nine train lines and 25 bus routes in the Olympic Park area, and we will continue to improve this transport service. A good example of this is the new high-speed train line which we are building. This train will take only seven minutes to travel from central London to the Olympic Park, which is incredibly quick. During the Olympics, all public transport in the city will be free for people who are part of the Games, for example the athletes, the volunteers and the spectators.

LESSON 10.4   RECORDING 10.10

S = Speaker,
A1 = Audience member 1,
A2 = Audience member 2

S: Good evening. Thank you for inviting me here this evening to talk about INTERPOL, the world's largest police organisation. Now, what do you think of when you think of INTERPOL? A lot of people get their image of INTERPOL from books or films. Perhaps they think of a French policeman from the 1960s, wearing a long pale coat. Or perhaps they think of something like a James Bond film, or *Mission Impossible*, with beautiful secret agents. Actually, INTERPOL is rather different to this, and tonight I'm going to give you an idea about the real INTERPOL. First of all, I'll say a little about INTERPOL's history. Then I'll talk about INTERPOL today; I'll tell you how it's organised and, finally, what it does. There'll be some time at the end for questions.
Although the idea for INTERPOL was born in 1914 at a conference in Monaco, the First World War interrupted its development. It was eventually created in 1923, in Vienna, Austria, although it had a different name at that time. In the beginning, there were fourteen member countries. The work of the organisation was interrupted by the Second World War. In 1946, INTERPOL reappeared with a new headquarters in Paris, and it has remained in France since then. In 1989, the headquarters was moved to Lyon, where it is today.
A1: Sorry, could you speak up a little, please? We can't hear very well at the back.
S: OK, sorry about that. I'll do my best. Now let's look at the modern INTERPOL. First of all, how is it organised? INTERPOL now has 190 member countries. And let me point out that it's those countries that pay for it! A hundred and ninety countries – that makes it the second biggest international organisation after the United Nations. The headquarters in Lyon operates twenty-four hours a day, 365 days a year. Staff from more than eighty countries work side by side, using the organisation's four official languages: Arabic, English, French and Spanish. There are also seven regional offices around the world. In all, we have about 650 staff. Yes, that's right – perhaps 650 doesn't sound a lot to you. But that figure is just for the staff in Lyon and the regional offices. Each member country also has its own INTERPOL office. The staff there come from the national police force. Don't forget that most INTERPOL officers stay in their own country, and don't spend their time travelling the world fighting crime, as they do in the books and films!
A1: Speak up, please!
S: Fine. Fine, I don't want to shout, though. Well, er, where was I? Yes, in the final part of my talk, I'm going to say something about what INTERPOL does. Basically, we help police forces catch criminals. But, and I must draw your attention to this, we never break the law in any country. One of our priorities is problems connected with drugs. Another important area is trafficking in human beings – people trafficking – especially women and children from developing countries. We also take a great interest in public safety and terrorism. Another key priority is financial crime. Why? Because criminals are using new technology to get information such as passwords or credit-card details through the internet.
A1: Why don't they give her a microphone?
S: So, how can we catch these criminals? Well, the most important thing we do is to run a global police communication system, so police around the world can share information about crime and criminals. The system allows police in one country to check the databases of police in another country. INTERPOL itself manages several databases, including names and photos of criminals, fingerprints, etc. Another important thing we do is to provide training courses for national police forces, and organise international conferences on crime.
So there we are. To conclude, we can say that INTERPOL is about 90 years old and has grown a lot from the organisation that was set up in Vienna in 1923. Today, our headquarters is in Lyon, France, and 190 countries are members. We fight international crime using modern technology. We do everything we can to make the world a safer place for you and your families. Thank you for listening. I hope those of you at the back could hear me. Are there any questions?
A2: Yes, do you think organisations like INTERPOL have too much information about us – the public? For example, everywhere we go, there are cameras taking photographs of us. And people are listening to our phone conversations without our permission. There's no private space any more. What's your opinion about this?
S: Hmm, now that's a very interesting and important question. Let me see if I can give you a short answer …

LESSON 11.1   RECORDING 11.1

P = Presenter, N1 = Newscaster 1,
N2 = Newscaster 2,
N3 = Newscaster 3

P: I've known about global warming for at least 20 years, and to be honest, I haven't been very worried about it. I understood the claims about man-made global warming, but I didn't think it was a big problem. They talked about a temperature change of a few degrees. That didn't seem a problem to me – in fact, I thought it might make the UK a nicer place to live. Maybe you did too. However, also like me, I'm sure you've noticed a significant increase in news stories like these.
N1: It's official. According to government statistics, this summer has been the wettest one since 1929. It has rained every day since the second of June.
N2: The drought in the middle of the US continues. There has been no rainfall for 96 days, and temperatures during the heatwave have been ten per cent higher than usual.
N3: South-East Asia has experienced the worst floods for 50 years, with record-breaking rainfall in the monsoon season. Today, the United Nations said the situation …
P: In the past, I think I was ignoring climate change. Now, I think I'm seeing the effects of the change in global temperature … but am I? Is global warming causing an increase in extreme weather? And how will this affect our lives? I went to meet a few scientists to get some answers.

LESSON 11.1   RECORDING 11.2

S = Scientist, P= Presenter

S: Well, across the globe, there has certainly been an increase in the frequency of heatwaves and of periods of heavy rain. I think this is a result of global warming. Basically, the increase in average global temperature increases the risk of extreme weather events occurring. For example, since 1950, heatwaves have become much more common – 30 times more likely, in fact. Remember, though, I'm talking about the frequency of these events, not their size or strength. We will have more heatwaves, but they won't all be hotter than before.

P: That was Professor Spratt of Imperial College explaining that there has been an increase in extreme weather; we're not imagining it. Floods and droughts have become more common because heatwaves and rainstorms have become more frequent. Basically, the risk, or chance, of extreme rainfall or drought is increasing.
So, what about hurricanes and tornadoes? The research data also shows an increase in the frequency of hurricanes and tornadoes over the last 30 years. Some scientists question this data. One of them is Dr Baxter of …

LESSON 11.1   RECORDING 11.3

S = Scientist, P= Presenter

P: And so how will this increase in heatwaves and heavy rainfall affect our lives? Here's Professor Spratt again.

S: Different countries in different parts of the world will experience different consequences. For instance, some countries will have serious shortages of water. There is one problem that will affect the whole globe, and that is a global increase in the cost of basic food. For example, the global price of wheat has risen by 30% since last year. This is because the droughts and floods have a negative effect on food production. In the US this summer, the worst drought for 50 years has destroyed almost half of the corn crop.
Overall, there will be significant social, technological and economic change. However, there are still many things we can do in order to reduce global warming, such as using solar power. If we reduce global warming, then we'll stop extreme weather becoming normal weather.

LESSON 11.3   RECORDING 11.4

P = Poppy, R = Rick

P: Right then, so, the next project is Wild City. What do you think of this one?

R: Well, the best thing is that it's definitely a green project. I mean, you can't get much greener than a wildlife park, can you?

P: Indeed, you can't. And it certainly makes the local area a better place to live, doesn't it?

R: Mm-hm. Urban wasteland areas really ruin any local area – they make the whole place feel unloved and dirty.

P: Exactly. So, what about the other points on the guidelines? The project solves a problem, doesn't it? Getting rid of the wasteland. And of course, it involves local people working together.

R: Sure. But there are a couple of points that it doesn't meet, aren't there?

P: Well, yes, but that's quite normal, isn't it?

R: Sure, but this project needs 10,000 dollars a year. And we can't really give them that much money.

P: No, that's true. What do you think they need that money for?

R: Well, I reckon it's to pay for the local people who'll look after the park.

P: Hmm. I guess so. Well, they could do it unpaid, couldn't they?

R: Hmm, perhaps, but we've seen that fail before, haven't we? If no one gets any money at all, then things like parks soon look bad. You know, there's more litter, you start getting graffiti, that kind of thing.

P: Mmm, yes, that's all true. Why don't we offer 4,000 dollars per year, for five years?

R: Yes, that's fine. Right, well, there's one more point that the project doesn't meet.

P: Is there? Which one?

LESSON 12.1   RECORDING 12.1

**D = Darren, N = Nikki, L = Lesley,
P = Peter, K = Keri**

D: Welcome back. I'm Darren Bright, and as usual at this time, we're looking at today's papers. Remember – this show is interactive, so if you want to comment on anything, or ask a question, just send your emails to brightinthemorning – that's all one word – @fivethirtytv.com. The address is on your screen now, and Nikki over there will receive all your emails. Morning, Nikki.

N: Hi, Darren.

D: Our first topic this morning is sport and in particular minority sports. With me in the studio are Lesley Diggot-Blake, the Minister for Sport, the journalist and commentator Peter Jones, and the actress Keri Miller. Welcome to you all.

GUESTS: Morning/Good morning.

D: There's a letter in the papers this morning from Michaela Scrivin, the World Dragon-Boat Champion. Michaela wants more investment in minority sports and more stories about them in the media. Then, she says, we would be more successful in international competitions. Lesley Diggot-Blake, what do you think? Would we be better at minority sports if we spent more money on them?

L: To be honest, I was a little surprised when I saw Michaela's comments, because this government has actually invested a lot of money in minority sports over the last few years – last year, for example, £60 million was spent on new facilities around the country. Also, people doing these minority sports are using a lot of excellent facilities that were built for the London 2012 Olympics. There was something else that surprised me. Michaela suggests that our sportsmen and women haven't been very successful in minority sports in recent years. But think about London 2012. Most Olympic sports are in fact minority sports, and our results were fantastic. Can I say, though, that success isn't just about government money …

D: All right, sorry to interrupt, we'll come back to you later, but we've got our first email. It's from Rod, in Brighton. Rod says: 'What can you read about judo in the newspapers? Almost nothing. Can you see badminton on TV? Fat chance! The media is only interested in football. If the media showed more interest in other sports, kids would want to try them.' Peter Jones, you're a journalist, what's your view?

P: Well, I couldn't agree more. I think it's a great pity some sports, like football, get so much media attention, while others, like badminton or table tennis, are often ignored. And this problem isn't going away any time soon, either.

A few years ago, the BBC decided to stop *Grandstand* – its famous sports programme. I used to watch *Grandstand* on Saturday afternoons when I was a kid, and it introduced me to all kinds of different sports. Without that kind of programme, kids won't have the chance to watch those minority sports. However, there's no doubt that during the London 2012 Olympics, people in this country watched a lot of different sports on their TVs. We have to make sure that they can continue to do so in the future.

D: All right, we've got another email here. It's from Heather in Plymouth. Heather says: 'I think kids should do a lot more sport at school. I've heard that in Sweden, kids have ten hours of sport a week. If I was the Minister for Sport, I'd give every schoolchild the opportunity to do a much wider range of sports. What about hockey or judo for all? If they had more opportunities, they wouldn't be so unhealthy.' Keri, hockey and judo at every school?

K: Absolutely. It's really important that kids get the chance to experience different sports from an early age.

I was really lucky because I went to a school where we did hockey and fencing and archery, but nowadays, most kids aren't so lucky. Most schools just concentrate on the same one or two, you know, football, basketball …

D: OK, here's another email from Gareth in Cardiff. He says: 'In Britain, we think …'

LESSON 12.3   RECORDING 12.2

M = Dr Sophia Mannit, A = Alex

M: Well, Alex, the interview starts with a short questionnaire looking at your personality, and then we'll talk more about your personal experience of sport.

A: OK.

M: Right, well, here's the first question: If you took an exam next week, would you: A) feel annoyed if your friends got higher marks than you, B) care a little if your friends' marks are higher, or C) have no interest in your friends' scores?

A: Well … that's a difficult one … I mean, I'd be happy for my friends, but I'd also want to do better than them. I'd definitely be interested in my friends' scores.

M: So, which would you do? A, B or C?

A: Right. Er, let me see … I think I'd do A. I would feel annoyed, but annoyed with myself, not with my friends.

M: OK, and the next question: If you wanted to go on a day trip, would you: A) ask many friends to go with you, B) ask a friend to go with you, or C) go on your own?

A: Well, I'm afraid I don't really go on day trips. I'm too busy.

M: I understand, but if you did, what would you do? A) go with many friends, B) go with one friend, or C) go on your own.

A: OK, well, let me think … well, to be honest, I'd do B – I don't like to do things on my own, but also big groups can be annoying. You know, no one can decide what to do, or you can't do what you want to do.

M: Fine. And finally: If you went on a weekend trip to a foreign city, would you: A) book nothing in advance and just go, B) book accommodation in advance, but not plan your sightseeing, or C) book accommodation in advance and plan your visit in detail.

A: Hmm, that's a tricky question … I'm not sure, really. I mean, I wouldn't do A, but, I'm not sure about B or C.

M: OK, well, can you remember your last holiday or trip?

A: Uh-huh. Let me think … um, I'd do B, more or less. I would make some plans, but perhaps not in detail.

M: Right, well, that's great. Thank you for that. Would you like to know what your answers mean?

A: Yes, I would. Can you tell me now?

LESSON 12.3   RECORDING 12.3

SM = Dr Sophia Mannit, A = Alex

M: Right, well, that's great. Thank you for that. Would you like to know what your answers mean?

A: Yes, I would. Can you tell me now?

M: Sure, let's see. You chose A for the first question, which shows you're very competitive. Let me check … yes, you chose B for the second one, you would ask a friend to go with you, which shows you're quite social. As you said, you don't like to do things on your own. Finally, you chose B for the third question, the one about holiday planning, which means you like a little risk, but not too much.

A: I guess that's quite true about me, although I'm not too competitive, I hope. I mean, I always like to have fun when playing sport, although team sports can be annoying.

M: I'm sure, and from these answers, I think you'd like sports such as badminton or squash, because competition is very important for you. But sports which are more individual, like swimming, would not be so good for you.

A: Really? Well, the only sport I play is tennis, and I love that.

M: Well, that's a competitive sport, isn't it?

A: Indeed.

M: And have you ever tried adventure sports?

A: No, I haven't. Why do you ask?

M: Well, the results of the questionnaire also suggest you'd like a little risk. So, you might enjoy white-water rafting, or rock climbing.

A: Rock climbing?! No way. I suffer from vertigo; I'm scared of heights.

M: Really?

A: Really.

M: I see, and have you seen a psychologist about this? I've always wanted to do some experiments about …

LESSON 12.4   RECORDING 12.6

T = Tutor, S1 = Student 1,
S2 = Student 2, S3 = Student 3,
S4 = Student 4, S5 = Student 5

T: Yes, that's a very good point, Nicole. OK, now, let's have a look at the next problem. OK, it says here: 'I'm often late for appointments, or sometimes I miss appointments completely.' Would anyone like to say something about this?

S1: Yes, keep a diary which clearly shows all your appointments … and classes.

S2: That's right, but it's not enough just to have a diary. We need to make sure we look at it. Check your diary last thing at night and first thing in the morning.

T: Absolutely. You should also write all the homework you have to do in the diary – not on pieces of paper that you can lose easily. Good. Now, next problem: 'I spend a lot of time looking for my notes. I can never find anything.'

S1: Yeah, I was like that last year. The best thing is to organise your files, using colour codes and labels – so you can find things easily. I don't have any trouble any more.

T: Thanks, Riz. So … these things show how important it is to be well-organised. OK, let's take another problem. This one says: 'I sometimes study for a long time, but I don't feel I'm learning anything. I read the material, but nothing's happening – it's not going in.' Right. Has anyone got any suggestions? Yes, Tim.

S3: Basically, it isn't a good idea to study for long periods at a time without a break. It's better to do a little at a time.

T: That's right. Be nice to yourselves! When you finish something – an essay, for example – give yourselves a break, do something for fun: go for a walk, or watch a film. This can make you work better before and after the break. And another thing – it's important that you can concentrate on your studies. You can't work well when the phone's ringing every five minutes. Don't forget, too, it's important to know when you study best. Do you study best in the morning, in the afternoon, in the evening or late at night? Everybody's different. We need to study at a time that suits us.

S4: Oh, that's interesting. I have never thought of that.

S5: Yeah, maybe some people study at the wrong time of day for their body clock.

T: OK, let's take another one … 'I can't finish all the things I need to do in the day.'

S1&4: Prioritise!

S4: Yes, decide what you need to do now, or later today, and what you can leave until tomorrow, or even next week.

T: Yes, good. Remember too: maybe there are some things that aren't important at all. It's a bad idea to waste time on them. And it's important to allow time for things you don't expect, and for emergencies. Perhaps this is the moment to say something about making lists. You probably make shopping lists of things you need to buy. Make a list of things you need to do as well. When you reduce all the things to one piece of paper, it doesn't seem so difficult. When you've done the things on your list, cross them off. It's a nice feeling! However, be realistic! Don't put a lot of big things on your list when you know you can't do them all. So, read one chapter of your textbook instead of three chapters. Putting smaller things on your list means that you can achieve them, and this makes you feel good. All right, what's the next question?

IRREGULAR VERB LIST

Infinitive	2nd form (past simple)	3rd form (past participle)
be	was/were	been
become	became	become
begin	began	begun
break	broke	broken
bring	brought	brought
build	built	built
buy	bought	bought
can	could	been able
catch	caught	caught
choose	chose	chosen
come	came	come
cost	cost	cost
dig	dug	dug
do	did	done
draw	drew	drawn
drink	drank	drunk
drive	drove	driven
eat	ate	eaten
fall	fell	fallen
feed	fed	fed
feel	felt	felt
find	found	found
fly	flew	flown
forget	forgot	forgotten
get	got	got
give	gave	given
go	went	gone/been
grow	grew	grown
have	had	had
hear	heard	heard
hold	held	held
hurt	hurt	hurt
keep	kept	kept
know	knew	known
learn	learned/learnt	learned/learnt

Infinitive	2nd form (past simple)	3rd form (past participle)
leave	left	left
let	let	let
lose	lost	lost
make	made	made
mean	meant	meant
meet	met	met
pay	paid	paid
put	put	put
read /ri:d/	read /red/	read /red/
ride	rode	ridden
ring	rang	rung
run	ran	run
say	said	said
see	saw	seen
sell	sold	sold
send	sent	sent
shine	shone	shone
show	showed	shown
sing	sang	sung
sit	sat	sat
sleep	slept	slept
speak	spoke	spoken
spend	spent	spent
stand	stood	stood
steal	stole	stolen
swim	swam	swum
take	took	taken
teach	taught	taught
tell	told	told
think	thought	thought
throw	threw	thrown
understand	understood	understood
wear	wore	worn
win	won	won
write	wrote	written

SOUND–SPELLING CORRESPONDENCES

In English, we can spell the same sound in different ways, for example, the sound /i:/ can be 'ee', as in *green*, 'ea' as in *read* or 'ey' as in *key*. Students of English sometimes find English spelling difficult, but there are rules, and knowing the rules can help you. The chart below gives you the more common spellings of the English sounds you have studied in this book.

ENGLISH PHONEMES

CONSONANTS

Symbol	Example	Symbol	Example
p	park	s	sell
b	bath	z	zoo
t	tie	ʃ	fresh
d	die	ʒ	measure
k	cat	h	hot
g	give	m	mine
tʃ	church	n	not
dʒ	judge	ŋ	sing
f	few	l	lot
v	view	r	road
θ	throw	j	yellow
ð	they	w	warm

VOWELS

Symbol	Example	Symbol	Example
i:	feet	əʊ	gold
ɪ	fit	aɪ	by
e	bed	aʊ	brown
æ	bad	ɔɪ	boy
ɑ:	bath	ɪə	here
ɒ	bottle	eə	hair
ɔ:	bought	ʊə	sure
ʊ	book	eɪə	player
u:	boot	əʊə	lower
ʌ	but	aɪə	tired
ɜ:	bird	aʊə	flower
ə	brother	ɔɪə	employer
eɪ	grey	i	happy

Sound	Spelling	Examples			
/ɪ/	i	this	listen		
	y	gym	typical		
	ui	build	guitar		
	e	pretty			
/i:/	ee	green	sleep		
	ie	niece	believe		
	ea	read	teacher		
	e	these	complete		
	ey	key	money		
	ei	receipt	receive		
	i	police			
/æ/	a	can	man	pasta	land
/ɑ:/	a	can't	dance*		
	ar	scarf	bargain		
	al	half			
	au	aunt	laugh		
	ea	heart			
/ʌ/	u	fun	sunny	husband	
	o	some	mother	month	
	ou	cousin	double	young	
/ɒ/	o	hot	pocket	top	
	a	watch	what	want	
/ɔ:/	or	short	sport	store	
	ou	your	course	bought	
	au	daughter	taught		
	al	bald	small	always	
	aw	draw	jigsaw		
	ar	warden	warm		
	oo	floor	indoor		
/aɪ/	i	like	time	island	
	y	dry	shy	cycle	
	ie	fries	die	tie	
	igh	light	high	right	
	ei	height			
	ey	eyes			
	uy	buy			
/eɪ/	a	lake	hate	shave	
	ai	wait	train	straight	
	ay	play	say	stay	
	ey	they	grey	obey	
	ei	eight	weight		
	ea	break			
/əʊ/	o	home	cold	open	
	ow	show	throw	own	
	oa	coat	road	coast	

* In American English the sound in words like *can't* and *dance* is the /æ/ sound, like *can* and *man*.

Elementary, Pre-intermediate and Advanced levels

Gareth Rees studied Natural Sciences at the University of Cambridge. Having taught in Spain and China, he currently teaches at the University of the Arts, London. As well as teaching English, he is an academic English course leader, and unit leader on courses in cross-cultural communication for the London College of Fashion. He has also developed English language materials for the BBC World Service Learning English section, and he makes films which appear in festivals and on British television.

Ian Lebeau studied Modern Languages at the University of Cambridge and did his MA in Applied Linguistics at the University of Reading. He has thirty-five years' experience in ELT – mainly in higher education – and has taught in Spain, Italy and Japan. He is currently Senior Lecturer in English as a Foreign Language at London Metropolitan University.

Intermediate, Upper Intermediate and Advanced levels

David Cotton studied Economics at the University of Reading and did an MA in French Language and Literature at the University of Toronto. He has over forty-four years teaching and training experience, and is co-author of the successful *Market Leader* and *Business Class* course books. He has taught in Canada, France and England, and has been visiting lecturer in many universities overseas. Previously, he was Senior Lecturer at London Metropolitan University. He frequently gives talks at EFL conferences.

David Falvey studied Politics, Philosophy and Economics at the University of Oxford and did his MA in TEFL at the University of Birmingham. He has lived in Africa and the Middle East and has teaching, training and managerial experience in the UK and Asia, including working as a teacher trainer at the British Council in Tokyo. He was previously Head of the English Language Centre at London Metropolitan University. David is co-author of the successful business English course *Market Leader*.

Simon Kent studied History at the University of Sheffield, and also has an M.A in History and Cultural Studies. He has over twenty-five years' teaching experience including three years in Berlin at the time of German reunification. Simon is co-author of the successful business English course *Market Leader*. He is currently Senior Lecturer in English as a Foreign Language at London Metropolitan University.

Far left: Simon Kent
Centre left: David Falvey
Centre: Gareth Rees
Centre right: Ian Lebeau
Far right: David Cotton